D0680496

Controversies & Commanders

Books by Stephen W. Sears

The Century Collection of Civil War Art

Hometown U.S.A.

The Automobile in America

Landscape Turned Red: The Battle of Antietam

George B. McClellan: The Young Napoleon

The Civil War Papers of George B. McClellan:
Selected Correspondence, 1860–1865

To the Gates of Richmond:
The Peninsula Campaign

For Country, Cause & Leader:
The Civil War Journal of Charles B. Haydon

Chancellorsville

Mr. Dunn Browne's Experiences in the Army:
The Civil War Letters of Samuel W. Fiske

Controversies & Commanders:
Dispatches from the Army of the Potomac

Controversies & Commanders

DISPATCHES FROM THE ARMY OF THE POTOMAC

Stephen W. Sears

Houghton Mifflin Company
BOSTON · NEW YORK
1999

For information about permission to reproduce selections
from this book, write to Permissions, Houghton Mifflin Company,
215 Park Avenue South, New York, New York 10003.

Library of Congress Cataloging-in-Publication Data
Sears, Stephen W.
Controversies and commanders : dispatches from the Army of
the Potomac / Stephen W. Sears.
p. cm.
Includes index.
ISBN 0-395-86760-6
1. United States — History — Civil War, 1861–1865 — Anecdotes.
2. United States. Army of the Potomac — Anecdotes. 3. United
States — History — Civil War, 1861–1865 — Biography. 4. United
States. Army of the Potomac — Biography. I. United States.
Army of the Potomac. II. Title.
E468.9.S43 1999
973.7'3 — dc21 98-37736 CIP

Printed in the United States of America

Book design by Robert Overholtzer

QUM 10 9 8 7 6 5 4 3 2 1

The Stone, Porter, and Lost Order essays originally
appeared, in somewhat different form, in *MHQ:
The Quarterly Journal of Military History.*

PICTURE CREDITS

National Archives: Stone, Porter, Stanton, Hooker,
Dahlgren, Kilpatrick. *Library of Congress:* General and
Mrs. McClellan, Lincoln and McClellan, Sickles,
Warren. *U.S. Army Military History Institute:*
Smith and Franklin.

For Sally, as always

Contents

Preface

THE HIGH COMMAND of the Army of the Potomac was a changeable and frequently disjointed collection of men. It was a rare moment indeed when the generals of the Union's principal army marched in step, or even in the same direction. A number of them all too often appeared to be fighting against rather than for the administration in Washington that employed them. Every Civil War army had its share of controversies, to be sure, but the Potomac army's controversies were unique. This book examines ten incidents of war as waged by the Army of the Potomac in which "controversy" and "commanders" were spoken in the same breath.

Three of these essays were originally written for *MHQ: The Quarterly Journal of Military History;* they have been recast here as necessary to fit my present purposes. The remaining seven were written especially for this book. The selection of subject matter is of course subjective. These incidents, and these commanders, seemed to me worthy of more investigation than they have had previously. My findings, it will be noted, do not always align with conventional wisdom.

It is entirely fitting to begin a Civil War work titled *Controversies & Commanders* with something on General McClellan. Certainly no Northern commander in that war was regarded, in his own time, as more controversial. Because of my close connection with McClellan — as his biographer, as editor of his papers, as a chronicler of his two major campaigns — I have as a matter of course evaluated what historians have written about the general over the last century or so. This opening essay offers the fruits of that evaluation.

For much of this century, it seems that in appraising McClellan his biographers took one path while general historians of the war took another. Never the twain did meet. General McClellan was, to the former, simply "the shield of the Union." To the latter he was simply (as Kenneth P. Williams famously put it) "an attractive but vain and unstable man, with considerable military knowledge, who sat a horse well and wanted to be President." Surely there is a truth to be found somewhere between these extremes. I suggest here that whatever misunderstandings may still exist regarding the general and his place in Civil War history, they may be resolved by studying individually the varied roles he played. The primary need for today's historian, I would argue, is to understand that when he stepped on a battlefield George McClellan became a totally different person — not a real warrior general after all (and therefore probably like most of the rest of us).

In sharp contrast to General McClellan, there has never been any debate over what Civil War historians without exception agree was the "ordeal" of General Stone. The military establishment's treatment of Charles P. Stone was by any measure a disgrace. A divisional commander under McClellan in the Army of the Potomac, Stone became, according to T. Harry Williams, "the innocent principal of the American Dreyfus case." Accused of disloyalty and treason, General Stone was confined in military prison (without any actual charge) for more than six months. Considering the fact that this was a full-fledged civil war, in a nation riven by divided loyalties, it is in fact surprising that the Stone case was the only one of its kind. But in a land of liberty one such case was enough.

That Charles Stone was the victim of an out-of-control congressional investigative committee, a cynically vindictive secretary of war, and a faint-hearted army command is well known. But it has not previously been known that the trigger that sent General Stone to grim Fort Lafayette was pulled by a conspiratorial band of plotters from his own command. The whole business, said a wartime editor, formed the worst blot of its kind on the Union cause.

The Stone case is followed here by an accounting of an even more famous instance of military justice (or injustice), the court-martial of Major General Fitz John Porter. Like Stone, Porter was the victim of a secret agenda concocted by his accusers. In his court-martial that opened in December 1862, Porter was charged with eight counts of disobedience of orders and misbehavior before the enemy during the Battle of Second Bull Run. From deep in the shadows, however, came the hidden accusation that Fitz John Porter was the visible representation of what was then being called McClellanism, a disease defined by detractors of that deposed general as "bad blood and paralysis" infecting much of the Army of the Potomac's officer corps. How this accusation influenced the selection of the officers sitting in judgment of Porter, and how it influenced their decision in the case, is examined here in detail. Also traced is the tortuous postwar path of the Porter case. While General Porter's cashiering may have been an injustice, at the time it may be said that a certain rough justice was also rendered, to the ultimate benefit of the Army of the Potomac.

"September Crisis" presents a cautionary tale: How General McClellan got his army back when no one — absolutely no one — in the War Department or in the administration wanted that to happen. It marks the strangest episode in the command history of the Army of the Potomac. Secretary of War Edwin M. Stanton had vowed McClellan must go, and he was willing to break up the administration over the issue. Just how far Stanton and his Cabinet allies managed to go with their "remonstrance," and the searing effect of their efforts on Mr. Lincoln, receives a new telling here.

With his genius for getting to the nub of the issue, Lincoln recognized that after the Second Bull Run debacle the army might very well not fight again for anyone other than McClellan. Thus the president, very much against his better judgment, returned the army to General McClellan. What ensued was Little Mac's finest hour. Here was not McClellan the deeply flawed warrior general but McClellan the highly expert executive general; this was what he did best. He pulled together and patched together a single army out of a rabble of separate armies and independent commands, rebuilt its command system, and reinvigorated its morale. Then he set it on the road that led to Antietam Creek.

The next essay, when it appeared in *MHQ*, bore the overly optimistic title "The Last Word on the Lost Order." Here it is retitled "Last Words on the Lost Order," and I limit the implied finality to merely *my* last words on the subject. If history is any guide, no doubt there are others with last words yet to be written on this subject.

The losing — and the finding — of General Lee's operational orders for the Maryland campaign in September 1862 represented for the Union the intelligence coup of the war. It also generated, and continues to generate, all manner of controversies. Many of these deal with matters of detail, which I hope this detailed accounting will settle. The paramount question, involving as it does the very conduct of the Battle of Antietam, is: When did General Lee learn of the loss of his operational orders? The conclusive answer, as I argue here, was not before the battle but only months afterward.

It may surprise to be told that in fact General Lee *could* have learned of the Lost Order within just forty-eight hours of its finding. In one of the strangest twists in this twisted story (kindly passed on to me by Edwin C. Fishel, the expert on Civil War intelligence), the Federals' finding of the Lost Order was promptly reported on the front page of the *New York Herald* for September 15, two days before the Antietam battle. How, we may ask, could that particular issue of the *Herald,* containing the greatest press leak of the war, have escaped the eye of General Lee, who regularly read Northern newspapers for all the military leaks they contained? An answer to that would perhaps resolve one of the final mysteries of the Lost Order.

"The Revolt of the Generals" is the first in-depth look at an especially unsavory chapter in the history of the Army of the Potomac's high command. This revolt was a shadowy conspiracy within the army's officer corps that commenced in the aftermath of the Peninsula campaign and disbanded just before Gettysburg with the appointment of General Meade to head the Potomac army. The early months were marked mostly by unfocused discontent. It was the dismissal of General McClellan, ordered by the president on November 5, 1862, that energized the dissidents. Burnside's defeat at Fredericksburg in December then furnished a specific target: General Burnside. Undermining Burnside relentlessly until he could no longer command effectively, the generals' revolt claimed its first victim. Elation was short-lived, however, when instead of the much-anticipated return of McClellan the dissidents saw Joe Hooker get the command.

Hooker pressed overdue reforms on the Army of the Potomac, but he gained the allegiance of few of his lieutenants. A veteran intriguer himself, Hooker was probably not surprised when his corps commanders turned on him after the Chancellorsville defeat. This time the dissidents saw General Meade, their own candidate, gain the command in Hooker's place, and the generals' revolt withered away.

The case of "Fighting Joe" Hooker is a good example of the need to double-check the conventional wisdom on any subject, particularly (in this instance) when it comes to historians' footnotes. Thus we discover that Joe Hooker, general commanding, did not lose his nerve in battle as we had been led to believe. Nor was he a drunkard. To be sure, Joe Hooker did not rate high as a gentleman (as gentlemen of that day defined the term), and he talked far too much and too bluntly. But he could fight, and in the Union's Civil War armies that was a much-needed skill. Mr. Lincoln, speaking of Hooker after Chancellorsville, remarked that he did not like to throw away a gun just because it misfired once, yet in the end Hooker's potential for battlefield command was never fully tapped. "In Defense of Fighting Joe" is intended to at least salvage the general's military reputation.

And then there is Dan Sickles — Sickles the Incredible, as his biographer labels him with perfect accuracy. Sickles's reputation *was* terrible. He was a political general who always knew precisely which political strings to pull, and he rocketed from raising a regiment to command of a corps in the Army of the Potomac with exactly one afternoon's worth of battle-leading — which he did badly. At Chancellorsville he floundered about far beyond his depth, but was anointed a hero in the newspapers — a hero "literally made by scribblers," growled fellow general Alpheus Williams. At Gettysburg Sickles lost a leg and his corps was wrecked, and controversy over his role on that battlefield persists to this day. Dan Sickles, political general, personified the Peter Principle before it was invented.

The Kilpatrick-Dahlgren raid on Richmond, before the opening of the spring campaign of 1864, was on the face of it just one more dismal failure by the Army of the Potomac's cavalry arm. Fatefully, however, the young and inexperienced Colonel Ulric Dahlgren carelessly took his notes and planning papers for the raid along with him, and they fell into the Confederates' hands. The chilling message of murder and pillage contained in these papers created a sensation and a lasting controversy. Today the authenticity of the Dahlgren papers can be confirmed; furthermore, grim evidence points to a link between the Kilpatrick-Dahlgren plot against President Davis and the plot, a year later, against President Lincoln. I have had the benefit of historian James O. Hall's wisdom concerning this complex incident, although I alone am responsible for the conclusions stated here regarding the roles of Judson Kilpatrick and Secretary of War Stanton in the raid.

The concluding essay offers a fresh look at what would appear to be the most inexplicable high-command decision in the history of the Army of the Potomac — the sacking of corps commander Gouverneur Warren at, almost literally, the moment of the war's final victory. Five Forks, west of Petersburg, on April 1, 1865, was an overwhelming Union triumph. Phil Sheridan commanded, but it was Warren's corps that gained the day, at which point Sheridan sent Warren to the rear in disgrace. This was in fact an event waiting to happen, and it reveals much about the inner workings of the Potomac army during the Grant-Meade era. Historian Chris Calkins's insight into this period is gratefully acknowledged.

The upheaval caused by the Warren case, like the Fitz John Porter case, would reverberate through the army for some two decades. Gouverneur Warren (again like Porter) was a prideful disciple of General McClellan — or, to some, a lasting symbol of the disease of McClellanism — and with this accounting of his fate these dispatches from the Army of the Potomac come full circle. McClellan's connection with so many of the figures mentioned here forms an almost continuous thread through these pages. George McClellan, as it were, fathered the Army of the Potomac, and while his command of it ceased before the war reached its halfway point, his influence on its high command, for good or ill, lasted through to Appomattox.

[1]

Little Mac and the Historians

Major General and Mrs. George B. McClellan

IN THE WORST OF TIMES — especially in the worst of times — General George B. McClellan had never a doubt that vindication would be his in the eyes of the Muse Clio. As he wrote his wife, on an occasion when he was feeling particularly scorned by the administration in Washington, "Well — one of these days history will I trust do me justice in deciding that it was not my fault that the campaign of the Peninsula was not successful." After he was relieved of command of the Army of the Potomac, in November 1862, the *Springfield Republican* reported, "The McClellan excitement has wholly died out. He seems willing to await the decision of history as to his brief military career."

Since that time historians in some numbers have taken up McClellan's challenge. Being a latter-day biographer of the general, and the editor of his papers, I regard their findings as worthy of analysis. It seems that over the last century and a third, historians have come down on every side of the McClellan question concerning not only his Peninsula campaign but the rest of his remarkably varied wartime career as well.

To be sure, not all the McClellan biographers (including this one) and not all the more general commentators on his career have been professional historians. Yet at least some of the volunteers in the trade (including this one) have conscientiously applied accepted standards of historical analysis to their efforts and are entitled to seats alongside the regulars on what historian Joseph L. Harsh has labeled "the McClellan-Go-Round."[1]

One way to attract biographers is to run for president. History is seldom served by these campaign biographies, however, and that is certainly true in McClellan's case. Of the half-dozen potboilers that appeared during the 1864 campaign, one only may be regarded as "authorized" — a *Life and Campaigns of . . .* effort by G. S. Hillard that was optimistically scheduled for publication one day before the Democratic convention would name its nominee. Hillard had been granted an interview by the prospective candidate, which provides the latter-day biographer with details of McClellan's early life not available elsewhere; otherwise Hillard slides back into the ruck of campaign-biography mediocrity.[2]

During the 1864 campaign much of what was written about General McClellan (both for him and against him) in books, pamphlets, and newspapers drew inspiration from the general's *Report on the Organization of the Army of the Potomac, and of Its Campaigns in Virginia and Maryland,* the 242-page official account of his time as army commander. McClellan designed the *Report* with some care to be his final draft for history. It is better described as a very rough first draft. The *New York Times* waxed sarcastic, calling it "nothing less than the *Military Memoirs of George B. McClellan,* printed at the expense of the government."

Buttressed with numerous, carefully selected documents, the *Report* leaves no doubt that everything untoward that happened during these months could not be blamed on the general commanding. As James Russell Lowell observed in the *North American Review,* General McClellan "makes affidavit in one volume octavo that he is a great military genius, after all." The Peninsula campaign, for one prime example, was lost to an enemy wielding vastly greater numbers — vastly greater because the radical Republican administration in Washington adamantly scorned to support or to reinforce the Army of the Potomac and its commander. A New York publisher made the *Report* available to voters in a low-cost edition, and McClellan autographed a special oversized deluxe edition for friends and supporters. The still-lingering legend of George McClellan as savior of the Union has its origin in his *Report*.[3]

During his time of command, the general had gone to some effort to preserve for his own use the raw materials of the history he was making. He sent copies of important documents to his wife, Ellen, which (as he told her) "I wish you to keep as my record." He explained why: "They will show, with the others you have, that I was true to my country, that I understood the state of affairs long ago, & that had my advice been followed we should not have been in our present difficulties. . . ." When relieved of command, he took away with him the entire headquarters archives of the Army of the Potomac for the period August 1861 to November 1862. The manuscript of his *Report* went to the War Department in August 1863 accompanied by the official reports of his subordinates — and that was all. He retained everything else of the Potomac army's archives, numbering in the thousands of pieces, as his personal property. As he saw it, only reports written officially for the government, by him or by his lieutenants, belonged to the government. With the exception of a few papers relating to the western Virginia campaign of 1861 that he made available, and a few dispatch books loaned to the *Official Records* project after his death, the McClellan papers remained unseen in family hands until presented to the Library of Congress in 1911 and 1916.[4]

Following his defeat in the presidential election, McClellan resigned his commission and sailed for Europe. The Young Napoleon, said observers, was accepting exile as his fate. By the time he returned to America in 1868, wartime passions had cooled. He made a comfortable living as an engineering consultant and served as elder statesman of the Democratic party. But his determination to seek the vindication of history remained as strong as ever. During his European exile he had begun a memoir — "the secret history," he called it, "of my connection with Lincoln, Stanton, Chase etc.; it may be valuable for history one of these days." By 1881 he had finished his memoir, but during a six-month stay in

Europe the single copy, left in New York for safekeeping, was destroyed by fire. Undaunted, he began work anew on what would be published posthumously, in 1887, as *McClellan's Own Story.*

This book, which contrary to McClellan's intentions put a blight on his military reputation, would remain something of a puzzle to historians and biographers for more than a century. Here was a memoir presented as McClellan's considered and final testament on the Civil War and his role in it, yet it appeared that the general had simply ignored everything factual learned from the records of the war in the two decades between 1865 and his death in 1885. "Never was there a controversial work in which the other side was more calmly ignored," wrote John C. Ropes in a review of *McClellan's Own Story.* ". . . It is impossible to get up much sympathy for General McClellan. And we do not think that this book of his will raise him in the opinion of his countrymen." It was an accurate prophecy. Seventy years later, historian Allan Nevins would remark, "Students of history must always be grateful that McClellan so frankly exposed his own weaknesses in this posthumous book."[5]

It is known now that in fact poor McClellan was betrayed by his literary executor, William C. Prime. Wartime editor of the rabidly pro-McClellan New York *Journal of Commerce,* Prime let his partisanship and his devotion to the general run away with him in seeing into print McClellan's side of the story. The general had left not even half a manuscript, with much of that only in early draft form and undergoing revision at the time of his sudden death. Prime took this as it was, undid some of the revisions, and patched together the balance of the book from McClellan writings that went back twenty years and more, much of it from the 1864 *Report.* Not content with this hodgepodge, he then added excerpts from some 250 of McClellan's wartime letters to his wife. In these letters to Ellen it had been the general's habit to pour out his innermost feelings and opinions in unbridled fashion; at their publication McClellan surely turned over in his grave. Although Prime deleted or censored the most inflammatory of McClellan's views, enough remained, writes Joseph Harsh, that historians, "finding the letters offensive, . . . read them as candid glimpses of the character flaws which foredoomed the General's military career."[6]

The general's death, and the subsequent publication of *McClellan's Own Story*, inspired several of McClellan's contemporaries to prepare articles of reminiscence and analysis. For *The Century* General James B. Fry wrote "McClellan and His 'Mission,'" a commentary on the general's messianic vision of saving the Union, a vision mentioned frequently in the letters to Ellen printed in *Story*. Former staff officer William F. Biddle furnished more admiring "Recollections of McClellan" for the professional military journal *United Service Magazine*. George Ticknor Curtis, a staunch friend and political adviser of McClellan's, wrote uncritically of his generalship in *McClellan's Last Service to the Republic* (1886), appropriately subtitled "A Tribute to His Memory."[7]

The first true biography of the general was not published until 1901 — Peter S. Michie's *General McClellan*, in Appleton's "Great Commanders" series. Michie had been a respected engineering officer during the war, and his is the only in-depth appraisal of McClellan the soldier written by a fellow soldier. It is especially valuable on that score. Michie coolly evaluated the claims in the *Report* and *McClellan's Own Story* against the realities in the *Official Records*. While finding enough of value in McClellan's overall war record to fit him in among the Great Commanders, Michie could be unsparing as well. He delivered a stinging soldier's verdict, for example, on General McClellan's conduct at Glendale and Malvern Hill during the Seven Days. On June 30 and July 1, 1862, the general commanding literally fled these two Peninsula battlefields, boarding the gunboat *Galena* for useless excursions on the James and each day leaving his army to get out of its scrape (to use a favorite expression of his) as best it could. The term Michie used for the general's actions in these battles was "astounding." Michie concluded his account of Glendale and Malvern Hill with words of caution for future McClellan biographers: "every explanation . . . put forward by his defenders must ever be in the nature of an unsatisfactory apology."[8]

An oddity among McClellan biographies is James Havelock Campbell's bravely titled *McClellan: A Vindication of the Military Career of General George B. McClellan* (1916). Campbell, a law school dean, described his work as a lawyer's brief, and it is all of that — a defense lawyer's brief. If General McClellan turned over in his grave after what William Prime inflicted on his memoir, then probably he again rested peacefully when Campbell's book appeared. Turning to Campbell's account of Glendale and Malvern Hill, we find that General McClellan on these battlefields was "wise, prudent, brave, skilful, with a mind which grasped everything down to the minutest detail and with an energy which governed all."[9]

William Starr Myers, a Princeton historian, was the first to mount a scholarly biographical effort to capture the general's life between covers and the first to utilize the McClellan papers deposited in the Library of Congress. Myers titled his 1934 work *General George Brinton McClellan: A Study in Personality.* In his preface he confessed to slighting the military side of McClellan's story (Myers identified himself as a professor of politics), "for I am fully aware of my own limitations in technical knowledge in this field." This indeed proved a handicap in writing the biography of a general. Nevertheless, Myers found the McClellan papers a rich source for exploring the personality of his subject. The figure that emerges from this effort is morally upright, stainlessly honorable, and politically naive. Surprisingly for a professor of politics, Myers exhibited a naiveté of his own in his depiction of George McClellan, presidential candidate, as a feckless innocent.[10]

Two biographies published on the eve of World War II contributed nothing in particular to a clearer understanding of the general. Clarence E. Macartney's *Little Mac* (1940), thinly researched, is wholly unexceptional. H. J. Eckenrode and Bryan Conrad, authors of the forthrightly titled *George B. McClellan: The Man Who Saved the Union* (1941), set out to prove, they write in their foreword, that their subject "was a great general and that he has been underestimated by historians." Their technique was in all cases to take McClellan's word for it: Nothing that happened was his fault; it was all a plot against him directed by his enemies in Washington.[11]

Starting around 1950, as Civil War scholarship was stimulated by the approaching centennial, most authors of general histories of the war or of the campaigns diverged sharply from the McClellan biographers in their handling of the general's role in the conflict. This was hardly a new trend — James Ford Rhodes, in his *History of the Civil War* (1917), was one of those historians targeted as underappreciating the general by biographers Eckenrode and Conrad — but it now accelerated. In his *Lincoln Finds a General,* for example, Kenneth P. Williams apparently decided not to take McClellan's word on anything. "McClellan was not a real general," came his final accounting. ". . . McClellan was merely an attractive but vain and unstable man, with considerable military knowledge, who sat a horse well and wanted to be President." T. Harry Williams reached a similar if less colorful conclusion: "McClellan was not a fighting man," he wrote in *Lincoln and His Generals.* "In Lincoln's mind, McClellan stood for strategy, preparation, delay, and at the best, barren victories." In Bruce Catton's *Mr. Lincoln's Army,* the first volume of a trilogy on the Army of the Potomac, the story told of McClellan is a self-induced tragedy of one missed opportunity after another until, finally, "his part was finished." Catton, in his subsequent *Centennial History of the Civil War,* and Allan Nevins, in *The War for the Union,* both of them major multivolume works employing extensive original-source research, made affirmation of these negative findings concerning General McClellan.[12]

In 1957, in the midst of this trend and apparently in reaction to it, Penn State historian Warren W. Hassler, Jr., published a new military biography, *General George B. McClellan: Shield of the Union.* Attended by full scholarly apparatus, with the imprint of a university press, it purported to be a balanced and objective accounting — by inference, the first such. In reality, the work falls squarely within the friendly and forgiving tradition of McClellan biography. The general's word is taken on all controverted issues and occasions; fault lies wholly with his subordinates, with his intelligence service, with his radical Republican opponents in Washington who delude Mr. Lincoln and undermine the president's faith in the general. George McClellan is revealed, in summary, as "a soldier of superior strategic and tactical ability. . . . Political enmity toward him was largely his undoing."

Hassler achieved this effect by careful and very selective use of sources and documents, especially the McClellan papers, in apparent emulation of the writings by the general himself. Nothing untoward is disclosed from the contents of McClellan's letters to his wife, for example; William Prime's sanitized versions are quoted instead. Nothing is found amiss in the general's flight from the Glendale and Malvern Hill battlefields, as if this were conduct expected of an army commander. The depths of all the major controversies — at which level in truth General McClellan is invariably to be found as one of the perpetrators — are never plumbed. Instead, the causes and the blame remain just where McClellan long ago assigned them. James Russell Lowell could as easily have said of this work, as he said of McClellan's 1864 *Report*, that its author "makes affidavit in one volume octavo" that General McClellan "is a great military genius, after all."[13]

This widening gap in interpretation between McClellan's biographers and the historians writing general accounts and studies of the war was investigated in Joseph Harsh's 1973 article "On the McClellan-Go-Round." Harsh argued that there must be a middle ground between the two camps, a pathway that would lead to a better and truer understanding of the general, if only historians would pay "serious attention to McClellan's ideas, beliefs and expressed intentions" and then recognize "the fact that these do help explain his behavior."[14] Taking up this challenge, and following where the original sources and their investigations led, the present writer published *George B. McClellan: The Young Napoleon* in 1988 and soon thereafter a companion volume of documents, *The Civil War Papers of George B. McClellan.* This new depiction of the general differs substantially from that offered at least by previous biographers, and the contents of the *Papers* in particular seem to have inspired historians to fresh efforts to decipher Little Mac's military character.

Ironically, the McClellan papers, which the general assiduously preserved so as to assure himself the rewards of history, have brought him precious few of these. His own words have betrayed him. If the "Great Commanders" series of the turn of the century were revived today, General McClellan would no longer make the list. These papers — the documents from the Army of the Potomac archives, his correspondence with colleagues and supporters, and most particularly his revealing (and uncensored) letters to his wife — offer an opportunity for analysis of a Civil War general that is unique. One of the historian's tasks, once the facts and the sequences are established, is to ask "why." In McClellan's case, with this mass of material from his own pen, there has been a temptation among some historians to couch the answers in the language of psychology.

Ever since they first appeared (in censored form) in *McClellan's Own Story*, the wartime letters to Mrs. McClellan have been scrutinized to explain both his thinking and his actions. The historian J. G. Randall, perhaps the strongest of McClellan apologists outside the ranks of the general's earlier biographers, dismissed these letters as "a kind of unstudied release, not to be taken too seriously." Yet in writing that, Randall had looked no deeper than the letters as printed in *Story*. The fact of the matter is that McClellan expressed the same views and opinions that he wrote to Ellen, sometimes even more forcefully, in his letters to leaders of the Democratic opposition, and he most certainly meant them to be taken seriously. There can be no doubting that what George McClellan told his wife in his daily letters was the whole truth and nothing but the truth as he saw it; he was, as it were, testifying under a personal oath. "In talking or writing to you," he once explained to Ellen, "it is exactly as if I were communing with myself — you *are* my *alter ego*. . . ."[15]

Early observers of McClellan's generalship, lacking the terminology of modern psychotherapy, had delivered judgments (such as Peter Michie's) that there was an "unaccountable weakness in McClellan's mental equipment" that went far toward explaining his battlefield lapses. Later, as a consequence of deeper research, especially after McClellan's papers became available, historians began to propose such terms as "messianic complex" and "paranoia" and "persecution complex" in explanation of the general's wartime actions. Finally, and perhaps inevitably, University of Houston historian Joseph T. Glatthaar, in a study of Civil War military leadership, assigned a label to McClellan's "tragic flaws in the light of modern psychology" — "paranoid personality disorder."

To be sure, it is easy to cull (as Glatthaar does) innumerable examples from McClellan's actions and from his own words that plausibly fit the textbook definition of paranoid personality disorder, in this instance the American Psychiatric Association's textbook *Diagnostic and Statistical Manual of Mental Disorders*. The risk in this approach is that it is *too* easy. Suggesting that General McClellan suffered from what we are now able to define and specifically identify as a mental illness implies that he was therefore helpless to affect his decisions and his actions. A twentieth-century definition of mental illness is applied to nineteenth-century symptoms; and, in brief, he was not to blame. This crystallizes the ultimate irony in the McClellan story. In a letter to Ellen, written on November 7, 1862, moments after he was told he was relieved of command of the Army of the Potomac, the general was consoled by this thought: "We have tried to do what was right — if we have failed it was not our fault. . . ."[16]

The further risk in this course is that it invites such a recent McClellan apologist as Thomas J. Rowland, in an article subtitled "George B. McClellan Revisited," to cull contrary evidence to show that the general was in no sense "plagued by crippling mental instability." Rowland scoffs at the very idea. He contends that with all the psychological failings attributed to him, we seem to have no choice but to picture General McClellan as "a lurking, brooding, out-of-control manic waiting to uncork on the Virginia Peninsula."[17]

The answer to this dilemma of comprehension, I think, is for historians and biographers alike to seek to understand and explain not one General McClellan but four General McClellans. Or, alternatively, to view the general and his actions (and reactions) within the framework and progression of time. He played four major roles in the Civil War, more or less in succession although of course with some overlap. The forces acting on him, forces both internal and external, were different in each sequence; therefore his responses were not the same in each. There was indeed, for a time, contrary to what Thomas Rowland believes, an out-of-control manic on the Virginia Peninsula. There was, for a time, a rational, intelligent, far-thinking strategist. There was an executive officer of considerable ability who knew how to inspire soldiers. And, finally, there most assuredly was a general who would be king.

First in chronology was the McClellan brought to Washington to pick up the pieces after the Bull Run debacle in 1861. He instantly became the premier executive officer in the Union. If it seemed that he had jumped from cavalry captain (and having never served in the cavalry) to major general with indecent speed, he was at least in a job he had trained for. He had been the best student of military history in his class at West Point. He had been sent abroad to study the administration of the leading armies of Europe. Upon resigning from the army, he oversaw the day-to-day logistics of operations on two important railroads. Now, in Washington, he was assigned the job of organizing and training the North's principal force, the Army of the Potomac. He did this exceedingly well, and in the bargain revealed a genuine talent for morale-building. His men loved him, and he in turn loved them. If there was a bad seed in this, it was perhaps that he loved his men too much to make war with them.

To the historian weighing McClellan the executive officer, a second bad seed — that he was demonstrably unable to get along with any of his Washington superiors — should come as no real surprise. There was a pattern to it, as there was a pattern to so many of his responses. Thomas Rowland regards it as specious reasoning, supporting foregone conclusions, to bring up "selected details from McClellan's past" to understand and explain his wartime actions.[18] Yet surely what historian would not find it significant that from West Point onward, McClellan had never gotten on with *anyone* in authority. He disputed those who assigned class rankings at the Academy. He scorned his superiors in the Mexican War. Back at West Point, he endlessly debated the superintendent on the pettiest of issues. During his army assignments he battled authority on the Pacific railroad survey, and suffered his fellow observers sent to the Crimea as fools. In civilian life, he repeatedly tangled with fellow executives of the railroads that employed him. McClellan the major general would have been changing his spots had he not regarded Generals Scott and Halleck, Secretary of War Stanton, and President Lincoln as fools, and worse.

Still, he trained his army to efficiency and high morale. After Second Bull Run he picked up the pieces a second time, somehow pasting the army back together on the march toward the Antietam battlefield. His harshest critics, in his day and ours, have little to say against McClellan the military administrator. However egocentric his conduct, it was of little consequence in this role.

His second role, that of grand strategist, overlapped the first and included the period, during the winter of 1861–62, that he served as general-in-chief. In historians' long-running explications of the divergence of war aims between McClellan and Lincoln, it is too often overlooked that this divergence came only late in their command partnership. Furthermore, the divergence of views when it did come was rendered largely irrelevant as it applied to the actual conduct of the war. By that time, General McClellan, as field commander, had lost the military initiative to General Lee and lost thereby his former major influence on grand strategy.

From McClellan's first days in military command, in western Virginia, to the end of the Peninsula campaign, he and Lincoln were, in today's figure of speech, on the same page. Restoration of the Union was paramount. Slavery and abolition were not issues in the war. When McClellan assured the people of western Virginia by proclamation that he would not disturb their peculiar institution, Washington raised no objection. When, upon his arrival in Washington, he spelled out his grand strategy for prosecuting the war and included in it "a rigidly protective policy as to private property" in the seceded states, it generated no debate within the administration. George McClellan was not, and never had been, an apologist for slavery. He saw it ending, as did Lincoln in this period, by some means of compensated emancipation.[19]

To be sure, McClellan the strategist made little effort to hide his innate hostility toward authority, and in the matter of his plans of campaign, for example, he managed to alienate almost every supporter he had ever had in the Cabinet. With deliberate scorn, when he sailed for the Peninsula, he tossed off a jumbled, directionless plan for the defense of Washington that left Mr. Lincoln, his sole important supporter in the administration, "justly indignant."[20]

McClellan's conviction that he had been called by God to save the Union — his messianic vision — may have been (as Thomas Rowland argues) not all that uncommon, a reflection of "religious fervor resonant with similar expressions of his time," yet that only begs the essential question. McClellan went one crucial — and unique — step further. It was harmless enough for him to believe that God guided his hand as he shaped his plans to save the Union. Under the fierce pressures of the battlefield, however, his messianic vision became his crutch, his ultimate escape from responsibility — it was beyond his power to shape an outcome that God had ordained. Thus he could tell Ellen, after the defeat of the Seven Days, that he recognized God's "wise purpose in all this. . . . If I had succeeded in taking Richmond now the fanatics of the North might have been too powerful & reunion impossible."[21]

A third characteristic of his military personality proved even more relevant here, and it had an enormous impact on McClellan's strategic vision. This was his delusion — there is no other word for it — concerning the enemy. While it is true, as Rowland among other McClellan apologists has pointed out, that McClellan was not the only general in this war to overestimate the enemy's numbers, it is equally true that no other general exaggerated in such monumental proportions or for so long a period. On the last day of his command McClellan was as ignorant of his opponent as on the first day. Most important, no other general was in a comparable position for his delusion to so profoundly influence his strategy — and, on the field of battle, his tactics.

It must be understood that McClellan did not invent these overmatches in order to gain the reinforcements he was constantly calling for. His frequent reiteration of the enemy's numbers in letters to his wife demonstrates their genuineness in his mind. Nor, as was long believed, was he victimized by the blunderings of his intelligence chief, Allan Pinkerton. Latter-day research into the operations of detective Pinkerton and his intelligence gatherers reveals that it was the general commanding, not the detective, who initiated the wildly inflated counting of Confederate forces. And once started on this course, McClellan would not, could not, look back. Pinkerton was indeed a blunderer, but he was hard-pressed trying to keep up with his chief. He was reduced finally to reporting purely speculative "general estimates," and even these did not always come up to the figures McClellan was reporting to Washington.[22]

It is only after one accepts McClellan's figures (for the sake of the argument) that his decisions and his actions assume a certain logic. He could not turn the flank of Joe Johnston's army entrenched at Manassas early in the war because he dared not divide his forces in the face of a greatly superior foe. On the Peninsula it became necessary for him to ignore every possible line of advance but the one he chose because only that one had the Richmond & York River Railroad that he needed to bring up the great guns with which to besiege Richmond. Those siege pieces were his equalizer against a veritable enemy host.

Most of his missed opportunities on individual battlefields can be traced back to this same first principle: his respect for a phantom Confederate army against which he must not unduly risk the Union's guardian army. At Antietam, the prime example of this, his advantage in numbers over Lee was better than two to one. Yet in his mind's eye he multiplied each of Lee's soldiers by three, and held back a third of his army to meet the phantom threat of a massive counterattack. Viewed from that perspective, it is not any wonder that he would tell his wife afterward that he had saved his army after a terrible struggle, and that those of good judgment had told him "that I fought the battle splendidly and that it was a masterpiece of art."[23]

It is McClellan in the role of field commander, on the battlegrounds of the Peninsula and in Maryland, that defines the true center of his wartime service. Here was the ultimate test of his generalship. The battlefield was what he had trained and administered his army to expect, what his strategic vision had led him to seek. Surprisingly — certainly surprisingly at the time — he failed the test. The military historian who evaluates the facts dispassionately (if that is possible in McClellan's case) must say that he failed the test dismally. Indeed, when he deserted his army on the Glendale and Malvern Hill battlefields during the Seven Days, he was guilty of dereliction of duty. Had the Army of the Potomac been wrecked on either of these fields (at Glendale the possibility had been real), that charge under the Articles of War would likely have been brought against him. At Antietam his failure was a virtual paralysis of decision-making, and a battle that by any measure should have been an overwhelming Union victory — should even have been that Civil War rarity, a battle of annihilation — was instead at best a tactical draw. Lee's subsequent return to Virginia gave the Union a strategic victory, which at that stage was all to the good for the Union. Still, the Antietam might-have-been — an end to the war in 1862 — marks this battle as the greatest missed opportunity of the war.

McClellan constructed an elaborate defense of his conduct on the Peninsula, in his *Report* and in *McClellan's Own Story*, that would be quoted chapter and verse by his admirers then and afterward. Reinforcements were withheld from him at a critical moment, said the general, and overall he did not receive the men he needed. The administration in Washington tied his hands strategically and tactically, deliberately hoping he would be defeated so that Stanton and his cohorts might be free to carry out their radical designs. That this is an entirely mythical construction is easily documented. The general's defenders, however, have never been silenced on the subject. Taking the most charitable view, their explanations, as Peter Michie said of them almost a century ago, "must ever be in the nature of an unsatisfactory apology."[24]

In more general terms, it has been said in McClellan's defense, of both his campaigns, that he was challenging the Army of Northern Virginia when it was young and strong and most vigorous, and that at least at Antietam he fought it to a standstill. It is true enough that at the beginning of the Seven Days Lee had the largest force, 92,000 by the best count, that he would ever have and was the closest he ever came to achieving parity with his Union opponents. McClellan credited Lee with 200,000 men, and was haunted every moment of every day of the Seven Days by that specter. "They had more than two to one against me," he wrote a home-front supporter afterward. "I could *not* have gone into Richmond with my left."[25]

Certainly Lee had the best numbers he would ever have, but just then the Army of Northern Virginia was far from what it would become in its days of glory. Lee's command system functioned miserably when it functioned at all. Lieutenants such as Magruder and Huger were liabilities; even the renowned Stonewall Jackson stumbled. The Seven Days' Battles were a bloody learning experience for Lee himself. When he insisted afterward, "Under ordinary circumstances the Federal Army should have been destroyed," he was expressing his frustration at how badly his staff and his lieutenants (and perhaps he himself) had performed.[26] The fact that nevertheless he drove McClellan headlong in retreat from the gates of Richmond is less a consequence of the vitality of his army than it is a measure of McClellan's incapacity as battle commander. At Antietam, the thesis of Confederate youthful force has no relevance at all. Lee fought the battle with the fewest men he would ever have until Appomattox. His men fought courageously, of course, and he commanded brilliantly, yet the day ended as it did because (once again) of General McClellan's incapacity on the battlefield.

The distinguished military historian Russell F. Weigley, pondering McClellan's failings as a battle leader, has suggested that the man is perhaps not the enigma historians have tried to paint; the answer, perhaps, is simpler than historians want to admit. In reviewing the *McClellan Papers,* Weigley observed that "the successful warrior chieftain . . . needs a particular kind of moral courage, an ability to confront all sorts of horrors and terrors and emotional strains and crushing responsibilities for life and death, to meet them head-on and revel in their challenges. The McClellan of the wartime letters almost never confronts anything head-on. He was never a warrior. He was a cautious, timorous man — probably not so different from most of the rest of us, but most of us lack the stuff of great generals. . . . Reading between the lines, we see in the *Papers* a McClellan who was simply and continually frightened by war, which is not so mysterious a condition."[27]

This condition, it must be said, was not a matter of lack of personal courage — McClellan had often enough demonstrated his bravery under fire in the Mexican War — but there is indeed ample evidence that the terrible stresses of commanding men in battle, especially the beloved men of his beloved Army of the Potomac, left his moral courage in tatters.[28] Under the pressure of this ultimate soldier's responsibility, the will to command deserted him. Glendale and Malvern Hill found him at the peak of his anguish during the Seven Days, and he fled those fields to escape the responsibility. At Antietam, where there was nowhere for him to flee to, he fell into a paralysis of indecision. Seen from a longer perspective, General McClellan could be both comfortable and successful performing as executive officer, and also, if somewhat less successfully, as grand strategist; as battlefield commander, however, he was simply in the wrong profession.

Mr. Lincoln grasped this failing of his general, and McClellan's stubborn, prolonged refusal to take the offensive after Antietam tried the president's patience once too often. Close study of McClellan's private letters in the period leading to his dismissal suggests that he was not overly eager to renew battle against General Lee. Furthermore, his effort to make the dismissal of Stanton and Halleck a condition of his remaining in command of the Potomac army has the look of a bluff he expected to be called. "I have the satisfaction of knowing that God has in his mercy a second time made me the instrument for saving the nation . . . ," he explained to Ellen. "I feel that the short campaign just terminated will vindicate my professional honor & I have seen enough of public life. No motive of ambition can now retain me in the service. . . ."[29]

There is some evidence that the president would later give thought to bringing McClellan back into the war in the role he had earlier shown aptitude for, that of general-in-chief. The idea, however fleeting it may have been, foundered on McClellan's growing involvement with the Democratic opposition. This initiated the general's fourth, and last, wartime role.

Recent studies of the 1864 presidential contest have included ventures into counterfactual history — that is, the "what-ifs" of this wartime election. Assuming a suspension of disbelief, then, the question becomes: What if General McClellan had defeated Lincoln for the presidency on November 8, 1864?

In view of their diverse interpretations of McClellan's other wartime roles, it is no surprise to find a lack of consensus among historians in regard to "President McClellan." (Lincoln's margin of victory — 212 to 21 in the electoral vote, 2.3 to 1.8 million in the popular vote — is too substantial to be plausibly reversed for this exercise. Counterfactualists therefore posit that the Democratic convention nominated McClellan on a war-plank platform rather than the peace plank he was saddled with; or that Sherman failed to take Atlanta before the election; or both.)[30]

Albert Castel, in an essay subtitled "How the South Almost Won by Not Losing," contends that had Atlanta not fallen to Sherman, McClellan would have been elected, in which event he would not have, or could not have, carried on the war. Instead, there would have been an armistice without conditions as called for in the Democratic platform. In *The Jewel of Liberty,* a study of the 1864 election, David E. Long reaches the same conclusion, and details McClellan's probable policies as president. His party's repudiation of Lincolnian war aims, writes Long, would perforce have been honored in full by President McClellan. Hence repudiation of the Emancipation Proclamation, the return of black soldiers to slavery, and a crippling of the Union's armed forces with no doubt widespread mutiny and bloodshed. In any event, Northern soldiers and their officers would already have been demoralized by the electorate's acceptance of the Democrats' "war is a failure" rallying cry. Too, McClellan's election would bring about a reinvigoration of the South's fighting spirit while gravely diminishing the North's will to support the war. A Democratic president and a Republican Congress (even with a November sweep in the congressional races, Democrats would not have regained control of the House and Senate until December 1865) would mean governmental gridlock in prosecuting the war.

William C. Davis, in *his* essay on the 1864 election, titled "The Turning Point That Wasn't," maintains that a McClellan victory in November would have made not the slightest difference in the war's outcome. Lincoln and his generals, Davis feels, would have made extraordinary efforts to put the war beyond McClellan's reach before he could take office. Therefore, upon his inauguration on March 4, 1865, the egotistical, opportunistic McClellan would have made the best of the bargain and leaped at the chance to take credit for presiding over the final victory. In that event, McClellan could rationalize his action to Democrats by pointing to his repudiation of the peace plank the party dissidents had inserted into the platform at the Chicago convention.

Not all the historians in this debate have listened carefully enough to exactly what George McClellan himself had to say about the issues of the war and about his resolve toward these issues. Beginning in the summer of 1862, after the failure of his Peninsula campaign, the general grew increasingly estranged from the Lincoln administration over what he perceived as violations of constitutional precepts and the rules of civilized warfare. He found discreditable, for example, the confiscation acts passed by Congress for dealing with Southerners' property. "Neither confiscation of property, political execution of persons, territorial organization of states or forcible abolition of slavery should be contemplated for a moment," General McClellan told Lincoln in his famous Harrison's Landing letter. His concern here about "forcible abolition" was stated clearly — turning a war for Union into a war for abolition would demoralize and "rapidly disintegrate" the army, for he did not believe his men would willingly go to battle for that objective. This was hardly a reactionary belief, and at the time a great many Northerners agreed with him. As to slavery itself, McClellan went on, military necessity certainly allowed for manumission "within a particular state" — so long as there was compensation.

Conservative constitutional principles were most grossly violated, McClellan thought, by two presidential actions of September 1862, following the Battle of Antietam. These were, of course, the preliminary Emancipation Proclamation, and the proclamation suspending the writ of habeas corpus as applied to those opposing efforts to raise military manpower or otherwise giving aid and comfort to the enemy. In his stand on habeas corpus McClellan was, again, far from being a reactionary and far from being alone. As to the Emancipation Proclamation, what he feared most as its consequence was the outbreak of bloody slave uprisings. "I cannot make up my mind to fight for such an accursed doctrine as that of a servile insurrection — it is too infamous," he told Ellen. He could not imagine any greater violation of the rules of civilized warfare. Yet his basic underlying view was not changed. General Jacob Cox, an admitted antislavery Republican, conversed with McClellan at this time and concluded that the general believed "the war ought to end in abolition of slavery; but he feared the effects of haste, and thought the steps toward the end should be conservatively careful and not brusquely radical."[31]

By the time of the election of 1864, the Emancipation Proclamation had been in effect twenty-two months. Servile insurrections had not marched across the South. The army had not disintegrated or revolted. Black troops — great numbers of them straight from slavery — had poured into the Union ranks. None of McClellan's worst fears, indeed none of the worst fears of a great many Northerners, had materialized. Therefore, to imagine that George McClellan, inaugurated as president, with the war continuing, would in those circumstances have revoked the proclamation and ordered 100,000 black troops disarmed and sent back into slavery is to totally misread the man. To predict *any* return or restoration of slavery under a McClellan administration is equally unimaginable.

Both during the campaign and afterward, General McClellan left not a shred of doubt that if elected he would press the war to a conclusion — a military conclusion — with all possible speed. He did not (as has been thought) hesitate a moment in rejecting the peace plank inflicted on him by the platform committee of the Chicago convention; the delay in his acceptance letter was to try to find a way to paper over the party split that his stand revealed. He had only contempt for those in the peace wing, terming them the "adherents of Jeff Davis this side of the line." During the campaign he made sure officers in the army understood his commitment to seeing the war through to victory. One of his former aides recorded a conversation two weeks before the election "in which the General stated that should he be elected, he expected to be very unpopular the first year, as he should use every power possible to close the war at once, should enforce the draft strictly, and listen to no remonstrance until the rebellion was effectually quashed."[32]

Following his presidential defeat, and with the war over, General McClellan cast a look backward. "Of course I can't tell what the secesh expected to be the result of my election," he told one of his former campaign managers, "but if they expected to gain their independence from me they would have been woefully mistaken. . . ." That, in fact, had been his credo from the moment he accepted his commission, ten days after Fort Sumter. Whether at headquarters or on the battlefield or in the political arena, in defeat and disappointment, George McClellan never wavered in his determination to put down the rebellion. Historians will no doubt continue to debate his exact contribution to that cause, but they have no cause to deny the sincerity of his efforts.[33]

NOTES

1. McClellan to wife, Sept. 20, 1862, George B. McClellan, *The Civil War Papers of George B. McClellan: Selected Correspondence, 1860–1865*, ed. Stephen W. Sears (New York: Ticknor & Fields, 1989), 473; *Springfield Republican*, Nov. 29, 1862; Stephen W. Sears, *George B. McClellan: The Young Napoleon* (New York: Ticknor & Fields, 1988); Joseph L. Harsh, "On the McClellan-Go-Round," *Civil War History* (June 1973).

2. G. S. Hillard, *Life and Campaigns of George B. McClellan, Major-General U.S. Army* (Philadelphia: Lippincott, 1864). Other McClellan campaign biographies are listed in Harsh, "On the McClellan-Go-Round," 102.

3. George B. McClellan, *Report on the Organization of the Army of the Potomac, and of Its Campaigns in Virginia and Maryland* (Washington: GPO, 1864); *New York Times*, Jan. 6, 1864; James Russell Lowell, "General McClellan's Report," *North American Review* (Apr. 1864), 552. Sheldon and Co. published the New York editions of the *Report*.

4. McClellan to wife, July 8, 1862, *McClellan Papers*, 346; and Introduction, x–xi.

5. George B. McClellan, *McClellan's Own Story*, ed. William C. Prime (New York: Charles L. Webster, 1887); McClellan to Prime, Sept. 17, 1865, McClellan Papers, Library of Congress; John C. Ropes in *Atlantic Monthly* (Apr. 1887), 559; Allan Nevins, *The War for the Union: The Improvised War, 1861–1862* (New York: Scribner's, 1959), 294–95n.

6. Stephen W. Sears, "The Curious Case of McClellan's Memoirs," *Civil War History* (June 1988), 101–14; Harsh, "On the McClellan-Go-Round," 112.

7. James B. Fry, "McClellan and His 'Mission,' " *The Century* (Oct. 1894), 931–46; William F. Biddle, "Recollections of McClellan," *United Service Magazine* (May 1894), 460–69; George Ticknor Curtis, *McClellan's Last Service to the Republic* (New York: Appleton, 1886).

8. Peter S. Michie, *General McClellan* (New York: Appleton, 1901), 354, 362. For McClellan at Glendale and Malvern Hill, see Stephen W. Sears, *To the Gates*

of Richmond: The Peninsula Campaign (New York: Ticknor & Fields, 1992), 280–81, 308–9, 330–31.

9. James Havelock Campbell, *McClellan: A Vindication of the Military Career of General George B. McClellan* (New York: Neale, 1916), 228.

10. William Starr Myers, *General George Brinton McClellan: A Study in Personality* (New York: Appleton-Century, 1934), viii.

11. Clarence E. Macartney, *Little Mac: The Life of General George B. McClellan* (Philadelphia: Dorrance, 1940); H. J. Eckenrode and Bryan Conrad, *George B. McClellan: The Man Who Saved the Union* (Chapel Hill: University of North Carolina Press, 1941), vii.

12. James Ford Rhodes, *History of the Civil War, 1861–1865* (New York: Macmillan, 1917); Kenneth P. Williams, *Lincoln Finds a General: A Military Study of the Civil War* (New York: Macmillan, 1949), vol. 2, 479; T. Harry Williams, *Lincoln and His Generals* (Ncw York: Knopf, 1952), 178; Brucc Catton, *Mr. Lincoln's Army* (New York: Doubleday, 1951), 334; Catton, *The Centennial History of the Civil War,* 3 vols. (New York: Doubleday, 1961–65); Allan Nevins, *The War for the Union,* 4 vols. (New York: Scribner's, 1959–71).

13. Warren W. Hassler, Jr., *General George B. McClellan: Shield of the Union* (Baton Rouge: Louisiana State University Press, 1957), xvi; Lowell, "General McClellan's Report," 552.

14. Harsh, "On the McClellan-Go-Round," 117.

15. J. G. Randall, *Lincoln the President: Bull Run to Gettysburg* (New York: Dodd, Mead, 1956), 73; McClellan to Mary Ellen Marcy, c. Dec. 1860, McClellan Papers.

16. Michie, *General McClellan,* 469; Joseph T. Glatthaar, *Partners in Command: The Relationships Between Leaders in the Civil War* (New York: Free Press, 1994), appendix; McClellan to wife, Nov. 7, 1862, *McClellan Papers,* 520.

17. Thomas J. Rowland, "In the Shadows of Grant and Sherman: George B. McClellan Revisited," *Civil War History* (Sept. 1994), 210. Rowland's *George B. McClellan and Civil War History: In the Shadow of Grant and Sherman* (Kent, Ohio: Kent State University Press, 1998), published too late to be examined in this survey, presumably follows the same lines of reasoning as this article.

18. Rowland, "McClellan Revisited," 206.

19. McClellan, "To the Union Men," May 26, McClellan to Lincoln, Aug. 2, 1861, *McClellan Papers,* 26, 72.

20. Charles Sumner to John A. Andrew, May 28, 1862, Andrew Papers, Massachusetts Historical Society.

21. Rowland, "McClellan Revisited," 209; McClellan to wife, July 10, 1862, *McClellan Papers,* 349.

22. Edwin C. Fishel, "Pinkerton and McClellan: Who Deceived Whom?" *Civil War History* (June 1988), 115–42.

23. McClellan to wife, Sept. 18, 1862, *McClellan Papers,* 469.

24. Michie, *General McClellan,* 362.

25. McClellan to S.L.M. Barlow, July 23, 1862, *McClellan Papers,* 370.

26. Lee report, *Official Records* 11:2, 497.

27. Russell F. Weigley in *Civil War History* (Dec. 1989), 332.

28. On this point, a remark by World War II's General George Patton is instructive. After visiting his wounded in a field hospital, Patton entered in his diary his concern that "I might develop personal feelings about sending men into battle. That would be fatal for a General." Quoted in *MHQ* (Winter 1996), 68.

29. McClellan to wife, Sept. 22, 1862, *McClellan Papers*, 477.

30. Recent appraisals of the 1864 election are found in David E. Long, *The Jewel of Liberty: Abraham Lincoln's Re-Election and the End of Slavery* (Mechanicsburg, Pa.: Stackpole Books, 1994); John C. Waugh, *Reelecting Lincoln: The Battle for the 1864 Presidency* (New York: Crown, 1997); William W. Freehling, *The Reintegration of American History: Slavery and the Civil War* (New York: Oxford University Press, 1994); Albert Castel, *Winning and Losing in the Civil War: Essays and Stories* (Columbia: University of South Carolina Press, 1996); William C. Davis, *The Cause Lost: Myths and Realities of the Confederacy* (Lawrence: University Press of Kansas, 1996); Larry J. Daniel, "The South Almost Won by Not Losing: A Rebuttal," *North & South* (Feb. 1998), 44–51.

31. McClellan to Lincoln, July 7, McClellan to wife, Sept. 25, 1862, *McClellan Papers*, 345, 481; Jacob D. Cox, *Military Reminiscences of the Civil War* (New York: Scribner's, 1900), vol. 1, 356.

32. Stephen W. Sears, "McClellan and the Peace Plank of 1864: A Reappraisal," *Civil War History* (Mar. 1990), 57–64; McClellan to William H. Aspinwall, Sept. 6, 1864, *McClellan Papers*, 594; Charles S. Wainwright, *A Diary of Battle: The Personal Journals of Colonel Charles S. Wainwright, 1861–1865*, ed. Allan Nevins (New York: Harcourt, Brace & World, 1962), 477.

33. McClellan to S.L.M. Barlow, Nov. 12, 1865, Barlow Papers, Huntington Library.

[2]

The Ordeal of General Stone

Brigadier General Charles P. Stone

SHORTLY BEFORE MIDNIGHT on Saturday, February 8, 1862, a detail of eighteen men of Company B, 3rd United States Infantry, was mustered for special duty at their barracks on Franklin Square in Washington. To their surprise, they were taken in charge by a full-fledged brigadier general, George Sykes, commander of the City Guard that was responsible for keeping order in the capital. Shouldering their rifles and falling into step behind General Sykes, the regulars set off through the quiet, dimly lit streets.

Their first stop was on H Street, at the home of Lord Lyons, the British ambassador, where a reception was taking place. Sykes went inside but soon returned empty-handed; whoever he was seeking was not socializing with Lord Lyons. Resuming its march, the detail turned into Seventeenth Street. Halfway down the block, Sykes halted the men again and entered a second house. Again he came out alone, but this time he remained in front of the house, pacing expectantly.[1]

In a few minutes a second officer, also wearing the one-star shoulder straps of a brigadier general, came down Seventeenth Street and turned in where Sykes was waiting. The two men greeted each other as friends; they had served together in the same regiment in the old army before the war. Then Sykes drew himself up and said, "Stone, I have now the most disagreeable duty to perform that I ever had — it is to arrest you."

"Arrest me!" exclaimed the newcomer. "For what?" Sykes said he did not know — could not even conceive the reason — except that it was by order of the general-in-chief himself, General McClellan. He added, "I may as well tell you that you are to be sent to Fort Lafayette." Looking back on the moment, Stone remembered his reaction as utter astonishment — "Why, Fort Lafayette is where they send secessionists!" — and then (perhaps embroidering the recollection somewhat) it was his turn to draw himself up: "They are now sending there one who has been as true a soldier to the Government as any in service."[2]

The regulars, waiting at a respectful distance, took all this in and whispered among themselves: That explains it — it must take one brigadier general to arrest another. Flanking the prisoner, they fell into step once more, this time following H Street past Lafayette Park across from the White House. After half a mile they reached the Chain Building, where officers of the City Guard were quartered. The prisoner was locked in a small room on the top floor, with an armed sentry posted outside the door. Early the next morning, permitted pen and paper, he wrote to General McClellan's adjutant general for a copy of "whatever charges may have been preferred against me, and the opportunity of promptly meeting them." He signed himself Charles P. Stone, brigadier general of volunteers. "I supposed there was some strange misunderstanding," he later remembered thinking, "which all connected with the Government & Army would be happy to have cleared up." He received neither answer nor acknowledgment.

That evening, under escort of a lieutenant and two detectives, he was put aboard the night train to New York. At Philadelphia there was some mix-up about the railroad passes, and General Stone ended up paying his own fare for transport to prison. In the small hours of February 10, twenty-four hours after his arrest, Stone was placed in solitary confinement in Fort Lafayette, the military prison at the Narrows of New York Bay.[3]

So began the ordeal of Charles Pomeroy Stone, an ordeal unique in American military history. By the time the ugly, drawn-out scene was done, his reputation both as a soldier and as a patriot was in shreds. In a congressional hearing room and in the nation's newspapers he was charged, tried, judged, and convicted of disgracing his uniform and betraying his country. He was called the Benedict Arnold of the Civil War.

Yet Charles Stone was guilty of nothing whatever. He was not, and never would be, charged with a single violation of either military or civil law. Caught up in a power struggle involving the army, the Congress, and the Lincoln administration, General Stone was destroyed by innuendo and the secret testimony of conspirators.

The Stone case is rich in ironies. The first of these is that at the time of his arrest, no Northern officer had displayed his loyalty more conspicuously and with more dedication, and with better result, than Charles Stone. Indeed, he was the very first soldier to answer his country's call during the secession crisis. On January 2, 1861, he was commissioned by the then general-in-chief, Winfield Scott, to take command of the District of Columbia volunteers and organize them for the defense of the capital. On Inauguration Day, amid reports of secessionist plots to assassinate president-elect Lincoln and overturn the government, Stone and his troops steadfastly stood guard over the change of administrations.

With the coming of war, Stone's excellent military credentials gained him rapid promotion to high command. An 1845 graduate of West Point, he had served with the artillery in the Mexican War, winning two brevets for gallantry. In the peacetime army he was posted on the Pacific Coast as an ordnance officer. Although resigning his commission in 1856, he continued his close relationship with General Scott and in 1861 he hesitated not a moment in answering Scott's call to defend the capital. After Sumter, Stone was appointed colonel of the 14th Infantry, then brigadier general of volunteers. When McClellan was called in to organize the Army of the Potomac after First Bull Run, he chose his old friend Stone to command a division. "He was a most charming and amiable gentleman," McClellan later wrote of Stone, "honest, brave, a good soldier, though occasionally carried away by his chivalrous ideas."[4]

What McClellan termed Stone's devotion to chivalrous ideas is better described as a stiff-necked rectitude toward his soldierly duties. Like most regular officers of the old army (including his chief, General McClellan), Charles Stone displayed a decidedly conservative turn of mind, especially toward politics, the institution of slavery, and the volunteers under his command. These ingredients, when combined with his particular assignment in the Army of the Potomac, made a recipe for serious trouble.

In August 1861 McClellan posted Stone's division along the upper Potomac, making it the extreme right of the Union line guarding Washington. Division headquarters was at Poolesville, Maryland, across the river from Leesburg, Virginia, where the extreme left of the Confederate line was based. Stone's was an assignment that bred problems, for Maryland was a slave state being held in the Union by the iron grip of the Lincoln administration. Runaway slaves frequently appeared in the Federal camps seeking sanctuary, but by the policy then in effect they were to be returned to their Maryland owners, who were (officially at least) loyal citizens of the United States.

Not content with simply following the rules without comment, General Stone went out of his way to settle the whole issue. In a general order to his troops, he warned them against "advising and encouraging insubordination among the negro servants in their neighborhood." They must not disgrace their government by acting the part of "incendiaries."[5] His gratuitous edict was not welcomed by all his soldiers, especially those in New England regiments where abolitionist sentiment was strong. (Stone himself was from Massachusetts, but he took pride in having escaped any taint of abolitionism.) There was much grumbling in the ranks about having to play the role of slave-catching Simon Legrees.

Stone had little enough popularity with his men to begin with. There was a streak of old-army martinet in him, an affinity for unbending, by-the-book discipline that did not sit well with volunteers. An officer who stood by him during his coming ordeal admitted that Stone was "not a man who gets a particular hold on the hearts and enthusiasm of volunteer soldiers."[6] One regiment persistently raised Stone's hackles — the 2nd New York, a militia outfit that in his eyes lacked discipline and most other soldierly attributes. He repeatedly came down hard on the regiment and its officers, which as a group he regarded as poor command material. In due course the 2nd New York would take its revenge on the general.

It was the Battle of Ball's Bluff, on October 21, 1861, that set loose the forces that would destroy Charles Stone. By later Civil War standards, Ball's Bluff was a minor action, with total casualties of fewer than 1,100. By the standards of 1861, however, it was a serious enough affair, and for the Federals, who suffered 85 percent of the casualties, it was a humiliating one as well. Coming three months to the day after Bull Run, it roused an insistent demand, in Congress and across the North, for answers for what had happened and who was responsible. Ball's Bluff roused in the army an equal insistence that these answers not be revealed.

In mid-October, General McClellan had received word that the Confederates were reducing their Leesburg garrison. He decided to see if a threatening move on his part might bluff them into abandoning Leesburg entirely, thus giving up the anchor of their line along the upper Potomac. To be sure, McClellan had no intention of inviting a battle for Leesburg; he believed the Army of the Potomac still too weak in manpower, arms, and training to meet the enemy in open combat. Yet any gain won by maneuvering alone would suit him very well. On October 19 he advanced George McCall's division along the Virginia side of the Potomac to within a dozen miles of Leesburg. On the Maryland side of the river, General Stone was instructed to "keep a good lookout upon Leesburg" to see if McCall's movement might drive the Confederates away. "Perhaps a slight demonstration on your part would have the effect to move them," McClellan added.[7]

In truth, General McClellan was engaging in wishful thinking, waiting hopefully with Mr. Macawber (as he liked to say) "in case anything turns up." He credited the Rebels with an army three times its actual size and substantially larger than his own, and he cannot seriously have expected them to give up Leesburg so obligingly. He must have finally come to that conclusion himself, for on October 20 he ordered McCall and his division back to Washington. He told Stone nothing of this, however. Indeed, he seems to have entirely forgotten about Stone and his "slight demonstration."

On that same day, October 20, Stone dutifully moved his troops up to the Potomac opposite Leesburg and made threatening motions at crossing over to Virginia. During the night, a detachment of the 15th Massachusetts did cross the river, at a place called Ball's Bluff, and made a reconnaissance toward Leesburg. On the morning of October 21, the 15th's Colonel Charles Devens reported that the enemy had spotted him.[8]

Stone, who was at Edwards Ferry, another crossing point four miles downstream, sent Colonel Edward D. Baker to take command at Ball's Bluff. He gave Baker the discretion to withdraw the men from the Virginia shore or to reinforce them, as the situation might dictate. Stone would meanwhile add weight to the demonstration by crossing a brigade at Edwards Ferry. Assuming that McCall's division was then advancing upriver toward Leesburg, Stone expected that these Federal threats to Leesburg from three directions ought to achieve McClellan's purpose very nicely.

Edward Baker was one of the better-known officers in the Army of the Potomac. An old Illinois friend of Lincoln's — the Lincolns named their second son for him — Baker had resigned his congressional seat to raise a regiment in the Mexican War. He had moved west and in 1860 was elected senator from Oregon. After Fort Sumter he raised a regiment for this new war and was commissioned its colonel. In the early months of the war he was partial to appearing in the Senate in full uniform to declaim against secessionists and all their works. Baker was much admired for his oratorical skills but (as events were to prove) he was sadly lacking in comparable military skills. Apparently all he recalled from his Mexican War experience was reckless dash.

When Colonel Baker reached the Ball's Bluff crossing, heavy fire could be heard from across the river. Without going to the scene to investigate, and with only the sketchiest information, he determined to make a battle of it. He ordered three additional regiments to Ball's Bluff, but for some time remained behind to speed the crossing in the few available boats. Finally he crossed and took command. "I congratulate you on the prospect of a battle," he told one of his hard-pressed officers.[9]

Baker's tactical dispositions were as rash as his decision to give battle. Soon the Federals were driven into a meadow at the edge of the bluff, facing a deadly converging fire from the enemy posted in good cover on higher ground. Baker went out front to rally his men by personal example and was in an instant cut down by four bullets. He was dead before he hit the ground.

None of these Yankee troops had been under fire before, all of them could see the trap closing, and Colonel Baker's death was an unnerving blow. Organization began to unravel and then was gone altogether. There was a desperate scramble down the steep bluff to the water's edge. The fugitives found nowhere near enough boats to carry them to safety, and then the largest of the craft was swamped by panicked men and capsized in the swift current, drowning almost everyone in it. Others tried to swim for it, and from the rim of the bluff above, the Rebels poured down a murderous fire until the surface of the river was lashed into white water by the torrent of bullets. Of the 1,700 Federals who had crossed over to Ball's Bluff, fewer than 800 made it back to Maryland. Hundreds were captured, and scores were drowned.[10]

Had he lived, Colonel Baker would certainly have borne primary responsibility for the disaster. He had committed to battle without appraising the situation, failed to take the shortage of boats into account, and on the battlefield handled his troops badly. General Stone could be faulted for giving the inexperienced Baker discretionary rather than positive orders, yet he had no reason to think Baker would so mishandle his part of the demonstration. As McClellan explained to his wife, "the man *directly* to blame for the affair was Col Baker who was killed — he was in command, disregarded entirely the instructions he had received from Stone,

& violated all military rules & precautions." General-in-Chief McClellan officially cleared Stone of culpability: "The disaster was caused by errors committed by the immediate Commander —*not* Genl Stone."[11]

But if Colonel Baker was the immediate cause of the defeat, General McClellan was also culpable. The whole operation had been without point or purpose. His telegraphed orders during the fighting were misleading and confusing. He later insisted he never intended that Stone send a single man across the river, but there was no such stricture in his dispatches. Most serious was his failure to tell Stone that he had withdrawn McCall's division. Everything Stone did was based on the assumption that he was acting in concert with McCall. He never suspected the Confederates were free to concentrate entirely against him. The whole business, a Federal officer wrote home, was "plainly an unpremeditated and unprepared effort, and failed, as nine out of ten such hasty affairs will."[12]

Yet these truths about Ball's Bluff were not easily seen at the time. General McClellan's role was carefully concealed behind a veil of government censorship. Colonel Baker was transmuted into a dead hero, killed in the heat of battle as he rallied his men, his brave sacrifice a bright spot in an otherwise grim story. The first authentic account of Ball's Bluff to penetrate the censorship was Stone's official report, which appeared in the *New York Tribune* on October 30. (Its publication was unauthorized, the *Tribune* reporter having clandestinely made or stolen a copy at Stone's headquarters.) While commending Baker's courage, Stone was unsparing of Baker's failings. Baker's friends in the army, the Congress, and the press rushed to his defense, aiming their shafts at the one visible target, General Stone. "I was bound not to care for the barking of newspaper correspondents and editors," Stone said. He responded with a supplemental report that was even harder on Baker. It was made necessary, he said stiffly, by the "persistent attacks made upon me by the friends (so called), of the lamented late Colonel Baker, through the newspaper press. . . ."[13]

Soon more than Stone's military competence was being questioned. A Massachusetts soldier wrote his governor, John A. Andrew, to complain that his regiment had been forced by Stone's orders to capture fugitive Negroes and send them back into slavery. Governor Andrew publicly protested "such dirty and despotic work. Massachusetts does not send her citizens forth to become hunters of men. . . ." Charles Sumner, the Bay State's celebrated abolitionist senator, was also aroused. "Brigadier General Stone has seen fit to impose this vile and unconstitutional duty upon Massachusetts troops," Sumner announced to the Senate, and he termed it an outrage. Outraged himself now, Stone wrote Sumner a letter that all but challenged the senator to a duel. Stone raised tempers even higher by reissuing his order that had cautioned his troops against "encouraging insubordination" among Maryland's slaves. Charles Stone was certainly treated unjustly, a journalist would later remark, but he had a manner that "provoked injustice."[14]

Congress acted as a forum for debate on the Ball's Bluff disaster. In the House the noisy Roscoe Conkling of New York termed it "the most atrocious military murder ever committed in our history as a people." When General-in-Chief McClellan rejected Congress's call for an investigation, Conkling called it a cover-up. Suppose that General Stone "is a martinet and not a soldier; suppose he turned out to be half-way, either in his soldiership or his loyalty," said Conkling; "is that a reason why investigation should be muzzled or throttled?" Stone sought a military court of inquiry and a chance to rebut "the extraordinary batch of misstatements made by Mr. Conkling." He was warned off by McClellan's staff. "Don't write or say anything now," he was told. "Keep quiet. Your military superiors are attacked."[15]

By the time this exchange took place, in January 1862, a new player had entered the Stone case. Congress had established the Joint Committee on the Conduct of the War to investigate every aspect of military policy and, as Senator Henry Wilson explained it, to "teach men in civil and in military authority that the people expect that they will not make mistakes, and that we shall not be easy with their errors."[16] It was destined to become one of the most notorious investigative committees in congressional history.

Beyond commendable oversight functions — ferreting out waste and corruption in government contracts and inefficiency in military administration — the committee sought to stamp its particularly vehement attitude toward war-making on the army's high command. Under the chairmanship of Senator "Bluff Ben" Wade, a case-hardened radical Republican from Ohio, it pressed for the promotion of generals with proper (i.e., Republican) attitudes and for dismissal of generals exhibiting Democratic leanings. It intruded on military policy-making and pushed the administration to adopt radical measures. Its methods of taking testimony in closed session and browbeating witnesses led opponents to call it a star chamber. Such became the notoriety of the Wade committee that during World War II Senator Harry Truman, heading a similar investigation, was at pains not to model his committee on its predecessor.

Bluff Ben Wade set as his first task to get to the bottom of the Ball's Bluff affair, and a variety of witnesses were called to testify in closed session. Stone testified on January 5, 1862, repeating what he had said in his report that earlier was leaked in the press. He was forbidden by McClellan's express order to reveal anything of the plans or orders of the high command. General McClellan, aware that the committee was making a case against him for the continued inactivity of the Army of the Potomac, was determined to give it no further ammunition by having his own less-than-stellar role in the Ball's Bluff disaster revealed. "They want a victim," he remarked in discussing the committee with one of his officers. "Yes — and when they have once tasted blood, got one victim," the officer warned him, "no one can tell who will be the next victim!" With that McClellan's face flushed and he said nothing more. No doubt the general-in-chief believed Stone innocent "of all improper motives" (as he later put it), yet he had no intention of taking his place on the block.[17]

To this point, despite the restrictions McClellan had placed on his testimony, Stone seemed safe enough in his defense. He might have been slandered in the newspapers and in Congress, as he claimed, but thus far nothing really very damaging to him had come out of the Wade committee's investigation. Then the case took a startling new turn with the testimony of Colonel George W. B. Tomkins, of the 2nd New York militia.

His regiment had not even been at Ball's Bluff, but Colonel Tomkins had a tale to tell anyway. He wanted the committee to know that General Stone was not the loyal Union man he claimed to be — that he communicated with the enemy under flags of truce, and that sealed packages were exchanged on these occasions. The general allowed civilians to pass back and forth across the Potomac. Tomkins claimed that secessionist-minded Marylanders had "a good opinion generally" of Stone. He insisted that not a man in his regiment was willing to fight under the general. Chairman Wade asked if this was because they doubted Stone's ability or his loyalty. They doubted both, replied Tomkins.[18]

Colonel Tomkins was then followed by a parade of other 2nd New York informants — no fewer than ten of the thirty-six witnesses in the Ball's Bluff inquiry were from this one regiment — who painted similar pictures. To be sure, not a single witness could give any actual, direct evidence of General Stone's disloyalty, but all had heard stories of suspicious goings-on with the enemy. They understood, they said, that Stone had even permitted the Rebels to erect a fort guarding Leesburg without interference. These assorted lieutenants and captains, paymasters and quartermasters, enlightened the committee on how Ball's Bluff should have been fought and won.[19]

It is the striking uniformity of this 2nd New York testimony that first suggests a conspiracy, which becomes readily apparent when the witnesses are examined more closely. The ringleader was certainly Tomkins, who, the committee staff reported, came unbidden to the case and "rendered efficient service" in collecting evidence against Stone. His motive is equally clear. Back in September 1861

Stone had brought serious charges against Tomkins, first for filing a false muster — a fraud to gain the pay of nonexistent soldiers — and second for "misbehavior before the enemy" at the Battle of Bull Run. Headquarters affirmed that the misbehavior was cowardice and that Tomkins ought to be cashiered, but to avoid further public "embarrassment" about Bull Run it was suggested that Stone threaten the colonel with court-martial to pressure him into resigning "for the good of the service." The matter was still hanging fire when Tomkins launched his counterattack. Two others among the 2nd New York witnesses had also been brought up on charges by Stone, one for filing a false muster and the other, a quartermaster, for fraud in falsifying his accounts. Both had to be released from arrest to testify before the committee.[20]

General McClellan later claimed that he brought these "disgraceful charges" to the attention of the Wade committee, but if so it went unnoted in the committee's records. The committee also shrugged off the sworn testimony of other witnesses who explained, for example, that flags of truce were perfectly normal between opposing forces, and that what had been exchanged at these meetings was nothing more sinister than packages of letters from prisoners of war. Wade and his colleagues had their teeth into something and would not be deterred. Clearly, General Charles Stone was soft on secessionism as well as slavery, and the disaster at Ball's Bluff had been no accident. Colonel Baker had been the victim not of his own rashness but of a betrayal by his superior officer.[21]

The committee promptly took its evidence impeaching Stone's loyalty to the new secretary of war, Edwin M. Stanton. When Stanton entered the scene, the Stone case had its grand inquisitor. The war secretary, an acquaintance wrote, was a man of grim determination and strong suspicions, "a sleuthhound sort of man who never lost his scent or slackened his purpose." Stanton immediately formed an alliance with the Wade committee, which urged him at least to have General Stone investigated. Stanton went further than that. On January 28, 1862, he ordered McClellan to relieve Stone of his command, arrest him, and hold him "in close custody until further orders."[22]

McClellan did not carry out the order, but instead went himself to the committee to argue that Stone be given the chance to answer the charges against him. The committee agreed to the request, and on January 31 Stone testified for a second time.

He was not, however, permitted to read any testimony or confront any witnesses; it was said that if he knew their identities he might take reprisals. Instead, Ben Wade summarized the case against him. He said that witnesses blamed Stone for the Ball's Bluff defeat, especially for failing to reinforce Colonel Baker from the position at Edwards Ferry. Stone could only repeat that the fight at Ball's Bluff had been made on Baker's responsibility. It would have been "false soldiership" for him to try to break through from Edwards Ferry, even had he known of Baker's crisis; militarily it simply could not be done, since he had lacked both the force and the time. "We are not military men, any of us," Wade told him. "But you judge military men," Stone replied. That was true, Wade said, "but not finally. We only state what, in our opinion, tends to impeach them, . . . and leave it to better judges to determine."

As for his alleged disloyalty, Stone said with rising emotion, "that is one humiliation I had hoped I never should be subjected to." The charge "utterly astounded" him. Were he a traitor, he pointed out, he could easily have turned Washington over to the secessionists during the crisis a year earlier. "And now I will swear that this government has not a more faithful soldier." He insisted that any flag-of-truce dealings he had with the enemy were entirely proper under the usages of war, done only for the benefit of his captured men. As for permitting the Rebels to build fortifications within range of his guns, he said, "That is simply false—it is simply false." (Later, when he read his testimony in the committee's printed report, Stone remarked, "A few strong expressions which I used I notice are not there.") They were not military men, Wade repeated; they only gathered the evidence and let others decide.[23]

There for a time the matter rested. However biased the committee might be and however injudicial its methods, it lacked any actual powers to carry the inquiry further. As Wade pointed out, it only gathered evidence; it would be up to the president or the secretary of war to act. Wade reported the supposed conflicting points in Stone's testimony to Stanton, who found it sufficient to press McClellan again on the arrest order. McClellan cast about for some way to dispose of the explosive situation without additional damage to himself or the army. He was anxious, just then, not to worsen his touchy relationship with Secretary Stanton. He felt he had done all he need do for Stone by getting him, as it were, a second chance. Consequently, when a week after Stone's testimony Allan Pinkerton, his intelligence chief, provided him with a solution to the tangle, he jumped at it.

Pinkerton spent much of his time interrogating those who reached Federal lines "from the other side" — refugees, fugitive slaves, Rebel deserters. One of those he questioned was a Jacob M. Shorb, a refugee from Confederate-held Leesburg who claimed to be a good Unionist at heart. Shorb told of overhearing a Confederate officer call General Stone "a very fine man," and another one comment on the frequency of flags of truce. Someone else told Shorb that the Confederate commander, Brigadier General Nathan G. Evans, was overheard to say "that *General Stone was a brave man and a gentleman.*"

Although even Pinkerton admitted that Shorb, and the thinness of his testimony, "did not impress me very favorably," McClellan was impressed enough to question the man personally. On February 8, satisfying himself that Shorb's story "tended to corroborate some of the charges against General Stone," he showed the report to Stanton. The secretary of war reiterated the arrest order, and this time McClellan obeyed promptly. That night, General Sykes and the detail of regulars arrested Stone. The Pinkerton report that sent him to Fort Lafayette went into the army files labeled "Full account of Gen. Stone's treachery."[24]

The story of Stone's arrest made headlines. Stanton released enough details to leave no doubt that the case involved disloyalty. "Everybody was astounded by the news that General Stone has been arrested," reported the New York diarist George Templeton Strong. "He is now in Fort Lafayette, charged, it is said, with treasonable correspondence. . . . That there has been treason somewhere in high quarters is certain, and if Stone is guilty, I hope he may be speedily hanged." The Washington diarist Elizabeth Blair Lee learned that the arrest was "entirely the act of McClellan & Stanton," and that Senator Wade and his committee "claim to have developed the facts." The *New York Tribune* warned in an editorial, "The knell of traitors within already tolls."[25]

The Articles of War required an officer ordering an arrest to file charges within eight days. That date came and went, and Stone and the counsel he employed dutifully requested copies of the charges from McClellan's headquarters, from the army's adjutant general, from the secretary of war. They met a blank wall. McClellan's staff replied that the case was "still under investigation." Stanton said that charges were being framed and would be filed in good season. The adjutant general did not reply. "Then I began to see that malice and not mistaken justice was at work," Stone said.[26]

The Joint Committee on the Conduct of the War did hear nine more witnesses after Stone's arrest, but they added little that was new. Indeed, more of this testimony supported Stone than condemned him, and the committee ended its inquiry. Pinkerton continued to collect what he labeled "further information concerning Gen. Stone's treachery." There was a remarkable consistency to his reports. Virtually every refugee and fugitive slave interviewed hit on the same phrase to describe how Virginians thought of General Stone — as "a very nice man" — which suggests that each was asked the leading question "Have you ever heard General Stone called a very nice man?" Several were kept close at hand should their testimony be needed against Stone. Jacob Shorb, Pinkerton's main catch from across the river, would remain on the secret service's witness payroll at $3 a day throughout Stone's imprisonment.[27]

As the weeks passed, it became increasingly obvious that no

one in Washington wanted General Stone actually charged and brought to trial. For however long those in the War Department and the army empowered with enforcing the Articles of War chose to ignore them, Stone was helpless. The Joint Committee on the Conduct of the War was satisfied that it had found the truth about Ball's Bluff and in the bargain demonstrated Congress's power to investigate the military. General McClellan was exceedingly anxious not to expose the Ball's Bluff record of either himself or the army to the public scrutiny of court-martial proceedings. McClellan may well have believed in Stone's loyalty, as he later claimed, yet he paid only lip service to getting him his day in court.

For Edwin Stanton, the grand inquisitor, Charles Stone was merely a pawn to be cynically manipulated in a larger game. Possessing one of the best legal minds in the country, Stanton was certainly aware that the case against Stone would never stand up in court-martial. There was not a scrap of direct evidence of his disloyalty. All the testimony was hearsay; the story of every witness would collapse under cross-examination. Yet keeping Stone where he was, uncharged but guilty in the court of public opinion, suited the war secretary's purposes. To Stanton, General Stone's real guilt was his lack of heart for the kind of unsparing war needed to destroy the South and the slave power. So long as Stone was shut away in military prison, incommunicado but for all to see, he was an object lesson to others of his kind (others like General McClellan), a warning that generals must be subservient to the policies and politics of the administration that employed them.

Stone did not lack for defenders during his ordeal. Winfield Scott, his superior in Washington at the outbreak of the war, now retired, was outraged by the arrest. "Why, if he is a traitor," Scott declaimed, "I am a traitor, and we are all traitors." Without Charles Stone, he insisted, the capital would have been lost. A month after the arrest, a petition calling for justice and an immediate trial arrived at the White House from Massachusetts, Stone's home state, signed by first families of the Commonwealth, the mayor and aldermen of Boston, major figures of business and the bar, the

Harvard faculty, and hundreds of others. Stone had enough supporters in the Senate to pass a resolution calling on the president for a report on the arrest.[28]

In this debate, Senator James A. McDougall of California termed General Stone's patriotism above reproach — yet it was said he was a traitor. "Who says it?" McDougall asked. "Rumor says it — the great manufacturer of falsehoods. . . ." Lincoln replied that Stone had been arrested under his "general authority," but it was not now in the public interest "to make a more particular statement of the evidence." The president was keeping his distance, leaving the matter to Stanton. Not for the first time, the secretary of war would serve as the administration's lightning rod.

Senator McDougall went on to call for a court of inquiry in the matter, and he took the Joint Committee on the Conduct of the War to task for its responsibility in the imprisonment of General Stone. Chairman Wade leaped to the committee's defense. "There was, and is, probable cause for the arrest of General Stone," he declared. Wade was scornful of the notion that Stone's constitutional rights had been violated, and he offered a novel defense of the committee's efforts: It should be obvious, he said, "that if people are shut up in dungeons, and restrained of their liberties, it is that the Constitution may live."[29]

After seven weeks in grim Fort Lafayette, Stone was transferred to the less confining Fort Hamilton, but there was no reply to his request to the War Department for a suspension of arrest so that he might serve in the spring campaign beginning in Virginia. In late June he wrote wearily to a friend, "For one hundred and thirty odd days I have been hoping what you have hoped — a trial and acquittal — but up to this time have not advanced so far as to receive any word of charges . . . , so I am in a complete muddle."[30]

Finally, after five long months of captivity, came the break in the Stone case. At Senator McDougall's instigation, a section was inserted in a pending military "pay and emoluments" bill that spoke to the matter of officers under arrest. The accused, it said, must be told the charges against him within eight days of arrest, and was entitled to trial within thirty days. No names were mentioned, of course, but the section contained the key language that it applied to "all persons now under arrest and waiting trial." The bill passed both houses of Congress on July 8, and it was signed into law on July 17.[31]

Vindictive to the last, Secretary Stanton waited until the thirtieth day to acknowledge the new law. Only on August 16, 1862 — after 189 days' imprisonment — did General Charles Stone walk out of Fort Hamilton a free man.

Stone still had to liberate his reputation. In Washington he renewed his call for the charges against him and for a forum in which to refute them. He went to the White House to appeal to the president. Lincoln told him, Stone related, "that if he told me all he knew about the matter he should not tell me much." Henry W. Halleck, the new general-in-chief, said he knew nothing of the case and could find out nothing — nor did he have any orders assigning General Stone to duty. In September, with the Confederates invading Maryland and the military scene in crisis, McClellan sought Stone to command a division of the Army of the Potomac to meet the invaders. Stanton denied the request. Early in 1863, Joe Hooker, the newest commander of the Potomac army, applied for Stone to be his chief of staff. Stanton turned aside that request as "not considered in the interests of the service." The grand inquisitor would not recant.[32]

One of the conspirators, at least, did receive his just deserts. The 2nd New York's Colonel Tomkins, the first conspirator to raise the disloyalty issue against Stone, was subsequently nominated for brigadier general on the recommendation of the Wade committee. General McClellan, however, quietly brought up the matter of the still-pending charge against the colonel for "misbehavior before the enemy." Tomkins's nomination for brigadier was rejected, and on May 26, 1862, he left the service.[33]

At last, late in February 1863, more than a year after his arrest, Charles Stone gained the hearing he sought. The Joint Committee on the Conduct of the War allowed him to read the testimony taken in the Ball's Bluff inquiry and to testify for the third time. Stone went down the list of allegations, thoroughly demolishing each one and discrediting witness after witness. With McClellan gone from the high command and his gag order lifted, he could now detail the orders under which he had acted on that day sixteen months before. Chairman Wade professed astonishment at his testimony. Stone reminded him that against the earlier generalized charges he could make only generalized denials. Six weeks later, the committee published the entire Ball's Bluff inquiry, including (without comment) Stone's most recent testimony. The utter falsity of the case against General Stone, and the injustice of it all, was finally and publicly revealed.[34]

In due course Stone was given a command in the western theater, but in the spring of 1864, on Stanton's order, he was mustered out of the volunteer service, his rank reverting to colonel in the regular army. In August of that year he returned to the Army of the Potomac as commander of a brigade, but after less than a month, still dogged by the rumors of disloyalty and certain he was under surveillance, he resigned his commission. In 1866, recounting his ordeal to Benson Lossing, an early historian of the war, Stone remarked, "If you can make out the *reason* it is more than I have ever been able to do."[35]

Charles Stone would return to military service — albeit foreign — after the war, acting as chief of staff for thirteen years in the army of the khedive of Egypt. He afterward pursued an engineering career, and in a final irony his last project before his death in 1887 was supervising work, within sight of his wartime prison, on the foundation of the Statue of Liberty.

In writing about the first year of the Civil War, Bruce Catton has called it an Era of Suspicion. More than anything else, it was suspicion — laced with conspiracy — that trapped Stone and imprisoned him and destroyed his career. Against the unholy conjunction of conspirators bent on revenge, an unprincipled congressional committee, an inquisitorial secretary of war, and a weak-willed army administration, General Stone had no defense.

"The whole chapter, from beginning to end, has been as impenetrable as the veil of Isis," the *New York Times* editorialized when the Joint Committee on the Conduct of the War published its Ball's Bluff report. "There was *something* behind, but that was all that could be made out. . . . As it is, Gen. Stone has sustained a most flagrant wrong — a wrong which will probably stand as the worst blot on the National side in the history of the war."[36] This was written in 1863 and proved to be prophetic. No doubt that judgment was the only satisfaction Charles Stone ever gained from the affair.

NOTES

1. Robert G. Carter, *Four Brothers in Blue* (Washington: Gibson Press, 1913), 28, 44.

2. Charles P. Stone manuscript, Nov. 5, 1866, Schoff Collection, William L. Clements Library, University of Michigan.

3. Stone to Seth Williams, Feb. 9, 1862, *Official Records* 5, 343; Stone manuscript, Schoff Collection.

4. George B. McClellan, *McClellan's Own Story* (New York: Charles L. Webster, 1887), 139.

5. Frank Moore, ed., *The Rebellion Record: A Diary of American Events* (1861–65), vol. 4, Docs., 11.

6. Henry R. Foote testimony, *Report of the Joint Committee on the Conduct of the War,* vol. 2 (1863), 366.

7. A. V. Colburn to Stone, Oct. 20, 1861, *OR* 5, 290.

8. George A. McCall testimony, *Report of Joint Committee,* vol. 2 (1863), 258; Charles Devens report, *OR* 5, 309.

9. William R. Lee testimony, *Report of Joint Committee,* vol. 2 (1863), 478.

10. *OR* 5, 308.

11. McClellan to wife, Oct. 25, McClellan to division commanders, Oct. 24, 1861, George B. McClellan, *The Civil War Papers of George B. McClellan: Selected Correspondence, 1860–1865,* ed. Stephen W. Sears (New York: Ticknor & Fields, 1989), 111.

12. Alpheus S. Williams, *From the Cannon's Mouth: The Civil War Letters of General Alpheus S. Williams,* ed. Milo M. Quaife (Detroit: Wayne State University Press, 1959), 27.

13. Stone reports, *OR* 5, 293–99, 300–302; Stone manuscript, Schoff Collection.

14. John A. Andrew to Simon Cameron, Dec. 7, 1861, *OR* ser. 2:1, 784–85; *The American Annual Cyclopedia of the Year 1862* (New York: Appleton, 1863), 93; Stone to Charles Sumner, Dec. 23, 1861, Houghton Library, Harvard University;

Moore, *Rebellion Record,* vol. 4, Docs., 11; Edmund C. Stedman, *Life and Letters of Edmund Clarence Stedman,* eds. Laura Stedman and James M. Gould (New York, 1910), vol. 2, 225.

15. Albert G. Riddle, *Recollections of War Times: Reminiscences of Men and Events in Washington, 1861–1865* (New York: Putnam, 1895), 170, 171; Stone to James A. Hardie, Hardie to Stone, Jan. 7, 1862, McClellan Papers, Library of Congress.

16. Henry Wilson quoted in T. Harry Williams, *Lincoln and the Radicals* (Madison: University of Wisconsin Press, 1941), 64.

17. Stone testimony, *Report of Joint Committee,* vol. 2 (1863), 489; Edward Bates, *The Diary of Edward Bates, 1859-1866,* ed. Howard K. Beale (Washington: GPO, 1933), 229; McClellan to Stone, Dec. 5, 1862, *McClellan Papers,* 527.

18. George W. B. Tomkins testimony, *Report of Joint Committee,* vol. 2 (1863), 289–97.

19. The other 2nd New York witnesses in the *Report of Joint Committee* were Downey, De Courcy, Brady, Rea, Berry, Foote, Dimmick, Delany, and Boyle.

20. Thomas T. Gantt to Stone, Sept. 27, 1861, Stone to Seth Williams, Jan. 18, 1862, McClellan Papers.

21. McClellan to Stone, Dec. 5, 1862, *McClellan Papers,* 527; Devens testimony, *Report of Joint Committee,* vol. 2 (1863), 413.

22. Sam Ward to William H. Seward, Jan. 14, 1862, Seward Papers, University of Rochester; Stanton to McClellan, Jan. 28, 1862, *Report of Joint Committee,* vol. 2 (1863), 502.

23. Stone testimony, *Report of Joint Committee,* vol. 2 (1863), 426–33; Stone manuscript, Schoff Collection.

24. Allan Pinkerton to McClellan, Feb. 6, 1862, McClellan Papers; McClellan testimony, *Report of Joint Committee,* vol. 2 (1863), 510.

25. George Templeton Strong, *The Diary of George Templeton Strong: The Civil War, 1860–1865,* eds. Allan Nevins and Milton H. Thomas (New York: Macmillan, 1952), 206; Elizabeth Blair Lee, *Wartime Washington: The Civil War Letters of Elizabeth Lee,* ed. Virginia Jeans Laas (Urbana: University of Illinois Press, 1991), 100; *New York Tribune,* Feb. 12, 1862.

26. Stone manuscript, Schoff Collection.

27. These Pinkerton reports are in the McClellan Papers.

28. Stone manuscript, Schoff Collection; Petition to Lincoln, March 1862, Lincoln Papers, Library of Congress.

29. *Congressional Globe,* 37th Congress, 2nd Sess., Part 2, 1662, 1667; Lincoln to Senate, May 1, 1863, Abraham Lincoln, *Collected Works of Abraham Lincoln,* ed. Roy P. Basler (New Brunswick, N.J.: Rutgers University Press, 1953–55), vol. 5, 204.

30. Stone to Lorenzo Thomas, Apr. 13, 1862, *OR* ser. 2:3, 449; Stone to S.L.M. Barlow, June 20, 1862, Barlow Papers, Huntington Library.

31. *United States Statutes at Large,* 37th Congress, 2nd Sess., Ch. 200.

32. Stone testimony, Halleck to Stone, Sept. 30, McClellan to Stanton, Sept. 7, 1862, *Report of Joint Committee,* vol. 2 (1863), 500, 504, 503; Stephen W. Sears, *Chancellorsville* (Boston: Houghton Mifflin, 1996), 62.

33. Lincoln to Stanton, Mar. 20, 1862, Lincoln, *Collected Works,* vol. 5, 167; McClellan to Stanton, March 24, 1862, Lincoln Papers.

34. Stone testimony, *Report of Joint Committee,* vol. 2 (1863), 486–502.

35. Stone manuscript, Schoff Collection.

36. *New York Times,* Apr. 13, 1863. For an overview of the Wade committee, see Bruce Tap, *Over Lincoln's Shoulder: The Committee on the Conduct of the War* (Lawrence: University Press of Kansas, 1998).

[3]

The Court-Martial of Fitz John Porter

Major General Fitz John Porter

WHEN HE LEARNED the verdict of the court-martial, the New York lawyer George Templeton Strong was deeply saddened by the downfall of an old friend. "But as I look further into the matter . . . ," Strong confided to his diary, "Fitz John Porter's name now seems to me likely to hold the lowest place in our national gallery but one — that of Benedict Arnold." Strong's fellow New Yorker Frederick Law Olmsted was of a like mind. "Fitz John Porter," Olmsted wrote, "needs hanging as much as any other criminal who remains unhung — not that he is a bad man for social purposes — but because he was the worst possible soldier, and in a volunteer army his crime is the most dangerous one and most insidious one possible."[1]

In the Army of the Potomac the message of the Porter court-martial rang loud and clear. Here was one of the best-known soldiers in America, once unofficial second-in-command of the Union's principal army, brought to trial on the gravest of charges, and there was scarcely a man in uniform who did not ponder the verdict. "The evidence leaves little doubt that Porter got 'demoralized,' . . . his frame of mind was un-officer-like and dangerous," Captain Charles Russell Lowell, of the headquarters staff and nephew of the poet, wrote a friend. "This sort of feeling was growing in the army, and the Government and the Country felt that it must be stopped. Porter was made the example." He would always feel sympathy for General Porter, he added, "but I accept the lesson. . . ."[2] The war was now in its twenty-second month, and as Captain Lowell observed, something had gone very wrong in this army. The judges' verdict in the case of Major General Fitz John Porter was calculated to arrest the slide.

The Porter court-martial would continue to echo clangorously through the United States army, and through the White House and the halls of Congress, for almost a quarter of a century. The last army officers of Porter's stature to be convicted by general courts-martial had been Charles Lee, during the Revolution, and William Hull, during the War of 1812; the next one would be Billy Mitchell, the prophet of air power, in 1925. The disparity of opinion in the matter during that quarter-century was great indeed. George Templeton Strong was not alone in ranking Porter at the bottom of the American military pantheon, above only Benedict Arnold. On the other hand, as renowned a soldier as U. S. Grant came to believe that Porter was "a gallant and efficient soldier" who suffered "a very great injustice."[3] As usual in such matters, the truth lies somewhere between the two extremes.

The Porter case properly begins with a letter General Porter wrote on July 17, 1862, to J.C.G. Kennedy, a gossipy Washington insider who worked at the Census Bureau. Just then McClellan's Army of the Potomac, in which Porter commanded the Fifth Corps, was at Harrison's Landing on the James, licking its wounds after the Seven Days' Battles. Off to the north, in the area of the Rappahannock, John Pope was posted with his newly formed Army of Virginia. "I regret to see that Gen. Pope has not improved since his youth," Porter remarked to Kennedy, "and has now written himself down, what the military world has long known, as an ass." Taking his cue from his confidant McClellan, Porter heaped scorn on Pope, predicting that he and his army would never reach Richmond except as prisoners of war. He hoped his views would gain a hearing in Washington, he said, but he warned Kennedy "never to disseminate them as mine." Much to Porter's future discomfort, however, Kennedy could not resist the temptation to peddle some influence. Porter's letter found its way to President Lincoln and Secretary of War Stanton. Stanton, who despised McClellan and all his disciples, passed it on to General Pope. Thus was laid the cornerstone of the case against Fitz John Porter.[4]

At his trial much would be made of Porter's supposed hostility toward Pope, but the examples displayed in court were mild compared to the true measure of his animus toward him, and indeed toward anyone not subscribing to the McClellan catechism of war-making. Porter regularly sent venomous military and political commentaries to Manton Marble, editor of the Democratic *New York World,* the most outspoken critic of the Lincoln administration, with the stated purpose of supplying Marble with ammunition for his editorials. General John Pope, Porter assured Marble, was "a vain man (and a foolish one) . . . who was never known to tell the truth when he could gain his object by a falsehood . . . ," and worse, he was a tool of the radical Republicans and abolitionists dominating the government. On August 10 Porter predicted, "I told you some weeks since Pope would be whipped & expect to hear of it by Tuesday. . . . Would that this army was in Washington to rid us of incumbents ruining our country."[5]

Two weeks after writing this letter, Porter was stunned to find himself under John Pope's command. Over McClellan's vehement protests the Army of the Potomac was ordered up from Harrison's Landing to aid the Army of Virginia. Robert E. Lee was stalking Pope not far from Washington, and one of the first Potomac army units to be fed into the new campaign was Porter's Fifth Corps. Originally, General-in-Chief Halleck had promised McClellan that he would command the combined armies, but Halleck soon enough reneged on the promise and McClellan watched in mounting fury as his army was taken from him division by division. From the field Porter pleaded with his old chief by telegraph, "Can't you get us all away? We pray for it."[6]

At the same time, Porter was telegraphing a running commentary on Pope's operations to Ambrose Burnside, who now held the Federal position on the Rappahannock. The maneuvers of the

Confederates had cut Pope's direct telegraphic link with Washington, and the only news from the battlefront came through the roundabout hookup with Burnside. Porter larded his situation reports with sarcastic swipes at Pope's generalship and regrets at being where he was: "The strategy is magnificent, and tactics in the inverse proportion. . . ." "It would seem, from proper statement of the enemy, that he was wandering around loose, but I expect they know what they are doing, which is more than anyone here or anywhere knows. . . ." "I wish myself away from it, with all our old Army of the Potomac, and so do our companions."

Burnside passed these reports on to Washington, where they went to Lincoln and Stanton — and eventually into the court-martial record. The dispatches (as Porter's prosecutor would phrase it) "express, on the part of the accused, an intense scorn and contempt for the strategy and movements of the Army of Virginia, a weariness and disgust for his association with it, added to a bitter fling at his commanding general. . . ."[7]

Not only were these dispatches crucial to the case against Porter, but without them there is doubt the matter would ever have gone as far as court-martial. Until the president showed them to him, Pope testified, he had not intended bringing charges against Porter. Why Burnside did not simply forward to Washington the military information they contained, cutting out the gratuitous remarks, puzzled even Porter's detractors. Burnside would say that he cautioned Porter about his "indiscreet language," yet he did not feel authorized to edit the dispatches before sending them on. Ambrose Burnside could be exceedingly obtuse at times, and it seems not to have occurred to him that his friend's indiscretions might in due course come back to haunt him.[8]

General Lee determined to move swiftly before the two Federal armies joined forces and made the odds against him too long, and on August 25 he sent Stonewall Jackson with half the army on a wide-sweeping flank march that destroyed Pope's supply base at Manassas Junction, twenty-five miles west of Washington. Pope set his columns to combing the countryside in search of Jackson, who had concealed himself on part of the old Bull Run battlefield of 1861. Lee was meanwhile coming up fast with the other half of his army, under Longstreet. On August 28 Jackson reached out and struck one of Pope's columns, deliberately revealing his position so as to bring on a battle.

Pope had issued a flurry of orders for nighttime marches to bring his army together for an attack that day. The order to Porter specified that he begin his march at one o'clock in the morning. The night was very dark and the road was heavily encumbered by wagon trains and his corps was exhausted from a long day's marching. Porter decided to postpone his departure for two hours in order to rest his men, clear the road, and make better time. Even at that, he could not reach the field before midmorning on August 28.

This was not the only problem General Pope had with his orders that day. The Third Corps' Irvin McDowell, acting on his own, let two of his divisions (led, by a singular irony, by two of the generals who would sit in judgment of Fitz John Porter) fall back from an important position in violation of their orders. McDowell himself then spent the night lost in the woods, unable to command at all. Phil Kearny, a division commander from the Army of the Potomac, received a 1:00 A.M. marching order similar to Porter's. Kearny told the courier, "Tell General Pope to go to hell. We won't march before morning," and was as good as his word.[9] Of these five generals, only Porter would be court-martialed for disobeying his August 28 marching orders.

It was Pope's plan to attack Jackson on August 29 with all the force he could muster before the rest of the Rebel army, under Longstreet, reached the field, which Pope estimated would not occur for another two days. McDowell was to collect his divisions and with Porter's Fifth Corps turn Jackson's right flank while the rest of the army struck his center and left. To effect this, Pope issued a joint order to the two corps commanders, which they received at midday. Its instructions were perplexing: They were to advance to the front along the Gainesville road, halt, and be prepared to fall back at day's end to a defensive position. There was no directive to attack, only an injunction to depart from the order "if any considerable advantages are to be gained."[10] Porter's departure from the joint order earned him a second charge of disobedience.

When by 4:30 that afternoon Porter had not yet joined battle, Pope sent him a peremptory order to attack. Darkness ended the fighting that day with no assault by the Fifth Corps, earning Porter a third charge of disobeying an order. His overall inaction on August 29 resulted as well in three additional charges lodged against him, for misbehavior before the enemy. On August 30, the second day of Second Bull Run, Pope renewed his attack on Jackson, and this time there was no question of the Fifth Corps' being engaged. In severe fighting Porter lost more than 2,100 men, almost a quarter of his force. However, two brigades under his command strayed from the field during the day, bringing him two further charges of disobeying orders.

The Federals were badly defeated on August 30, with Longstreet delivering a devastating flank assault that surprised Pope and drove him from the battlefield. Second Bull Run did not duplicate the rout of the first battle there, yet the demoralization in the ranks was just as severe. The Yankee troops felt betrayed by their high command. They knew they had fought valiantly enough to deserve better; their generals had simply been outgeneraled. In letters and diaries the men of Second Bull Run most often condemned John Pope and Irvin McDowell for their defeat. For McDowell it was all a bad dream, a reprise of his 1861 defeat there.

For his part, Pope insisted to General-in-Chief Halleck that it was the "unsoldierly and dangerous conduct" of generals from McClellan's Army of the Potomac that had caused his downfall. He singled out "one commander of a corps" — Porter was meant, but in this dispatch Pope did not name him — for failing to obey orders to march and for failing to attack when "in plain hearing, at less than 3 miles' distance, of a furious battle, which raged all day." Halleck replied that however that might be, the two armies would be united under McClellan, and Pope was ordered off to the West to fight Indians. Pope complained bitterly that he was deprived of his command "because of the treachery of McClellan and his tools," and to prove his point he saw to it that charges were filed against Fitz John Porter. To John Pope, Porter was merely a proxy for the real villain of the piece, General McClellan, whom he could not reach. That notion would be ever present during the subsequent court-martial.[11]

With Lee now across the Potomac and invading Maryland, McClellan managed to have the charges against his favorite lieutenant suspended so that he might fight in the coming campaign. At Antietam Porter spent nearly the entire battle at McClellan's side, playing the role of most-trusted subordinate. When in November Lincoln at last exhausted his tolerance for McClellan's "slows" and dismissed him, a worried Porter wrote Manton Marble, "You may soon expect to hear my head is lopped. . . ." He explained that his earlier opinion predicting disaster for Pope "is in their possession and brought up against me as proof of intention to cause disaster."[12] On November 25, 1862, army headquarters announced that a general court-martial to try Major General Fitz John Porter would be convened in Washington.

An observer reading the transcript of the Porter court-martial today, without reference to its time and place, is hard put to imagine the court arriving at a verdict of guilty. On all controverted points the defense marshaled not only more witnesses but more authoritative ones. Pope's testimony about what happened at Second Bull Run, and his knowledge of the location of his own troops and those of the enemy, were so clearly faulty that it was obvious he had issued his orders knowing little of the actual situation on the battle lines. The chief prosecution witness, Irvin McDowell, displayed a memory so selective that he must have been intent on saving his own skin rather than seeing justice done the defendant. Other government witnesses gave testimony short on facts and long on impressions.

Factor in the time and the place, and the makeup of the court, however, and the verdict ceases to be surprising. Porter predicted his own fate. On December 29, the sixteenth day of testimony, he wrote a friend, "I have seen sufficient of the court . . . to know their conclusion is a foregone one, if not determined by order or the will of those high in power. . . . I have seen sufficient to convince me of their intent, and no matter what the record may be, to find a verdict against me. . . . I have too many personal enemies and enemies of Gen. McClellan on the court."[13]

Porter recognized that he was on trial for something more than Pope's charges. He was the highly visible representation of McClellanism, the disease the general's detractors defined as bad blood and paralysis infecting much of the officer corps of the Army of the Potomac. Just then McClellanism had become a major issue. Burnside, McClellan's successor, had led the army to disastrous defeat at Fredericksburg, and the officer corps was in revolt. Burnside was undercut from every side by his lieutenants; their cry was for McClellan's return to the command. Among the listeners were the nine generals then sitting in judgment of Fitz John Porter. Their selection had been approved by Secretary of War Stanton, and the selection had not been a random one.

The president of the Porter court-martial was Major General David Hunter, a man of slight military talents but good Republican and abolitionist credentials. He had had a run-in with McClellan early in the war, and McClellan warned Porter, "Hunter I distrust . . . he is an enemy of mine." Major General Ethan Allen Hitchcock, sixty-four and a grandson of Ethan Allen of Revolutionary War fame, was a faint-hearted warrior devoted to alchemy and the occult. He had served on Stanton's War Board and frequently confessed in his diary to being cowed by Stanton's bullying. Hitchcock had opposed McClellan's Peninsula campaign, and Stanton had once tried to make him McClellan's replacement as head of the Army of the Potomac. Silas Casey, too, was a general unpartial to McClellan and his disciples. On the Peninsula Casey's division "gave way unaccountably & discreditably" (as McClellan had put it) at Seven Pines, and McClellan had subsequently demoted Casey to minor behind-the-lines posts.[14]

Napoleon Bonaparte Buford was another general Stanton had once hoped would replace McClellan. Secretary of the Treasury Salmon P. Chase, once a McClellan ally but now vigorously anti-McClellan, was as dedicated to a "correct" verdict in the Porter case as Stanton, and Porter was told during the trial that Chase suborned Buford with promises of promotion and an army posting for his son. The witnesses to this incident were none other than Buford's wife and brother.

Generals Rufus King and James B. Ricketts should have been disqualified from sitting on the Porter court for conflict of interest. Both had served under McDowell at Second Bull Run and both had performed poorly there. King in fact would be charged by a court of inquiry with willfully disobeying orders in withdrawing from a key position during the battle. At one point in the trial, King would step down from the bench to testify in contradiction to one of Porter's witnesses, a gross impropriety even in military law. By contrast, Porter expressed no suspicions about two other generals on the court, Benjamin M. Prentiss and John P. Slough. He described Slough as "friendly," and said of Prentiss that he was "supposed unprejudiced, and acted so."[15]

The ninth judge was Brigadier General James A. Garfield, who would become the twentieth president while the Porter case was still a national issue. Garfield the politician was said by one observer to be "morally . . . invertebrate. He had no bony structure."[16] Garfield the general had displayed middling skills and was well known as a protégé of Secretary Chase. Porter described him as playing the role of prosecutor from the bench. There is no doubt that Garfield was predisposed to convict Porter, and he never changed his view that the verdict was a correct one.

Thirteen judges was the usual complement for a general court-martial, but it was claimed that in this case no more than nine could be assembled "without manifest injury to the service." That meant a simple majority of five to four was needed to convict — a two-thirds majority (six to three) was required to inflict the death penalty — and when the court-martial opened on December 3,

1862, the government had reason to believe it had the votes it needed. Certainly seven of the nine judges were biased to one degree or another in regard to the stated (and unstated) agenda before the court. It was said that when Stanton showed the court listing to Assistant Secretary of War John Tucker, Tucker remarked, "that court will convict General Porter whether guilty or not," and Stanton nodded in agreement. Porter told editor Manton Marble that "proof strong as holy writ will be required to cause a just verdict to be rendered."[17]

Porter was charged under the Ninth Article of War with five instances of disobeying a "lawful command of his superior officer" — failing to obey the 1:00 A.M. march order on August 28, failing to obey both the joint order and the 4:30 P.M. order of August 29, and twice failing to obey the order to bring two of his brigades to the battlefield on August 30. Under the Fifty-second Article of War, misbehavior before the enemy, he was charged under three specifications — failing to engage the Rebels in response to Pope's 4:30 order on August 29, failing to join the battle within his hearing at any time on August 29, and failing to aid Pope but instead retreating when he believed Pope was suffering defeat. Both the Ninth and Fifty-second Articles of War specified the death penalty or "such other punishment" as the court-martial might decree.[18]

In his opening testimony General Pope insisted he could have crushed Stonewall Jackson on August 29, and thus won the battle, had Porter obeyed his orders to attack. He was certain there was nothing that day to prevent an attack by the Fifth Corps. He said he began the campaign convinced he would not have the cordial support of General Porter, having been forewarned by Porter's scornful Kennedy letter shown him in Washington in July. Pope flatly denied the defense's contention that Longstreet was already on the battlefield when he issued his August 29 orders.[19]

General McDowell confessed to the court that he had trouble remembering events unless they were connected to "some important things, such as daylight and darkness." In his testimony he could recall almost nothing the defense wanted him to remember, such as his conversations with Porter and his staff on the critical day of August 29. McDowell's response to the discretionary clause in Pope's joint order had been to take his troops off toward the main army facing Jackson, leaving Porter to advance alone along the Gainesville road for the flank attack. Porter contended that McDowell had told him to stay where he was and that in fact he was already too far advanced. McDowell could not recall saying anything like that.[20]

All McDowell's answers were similarly self-serving, and for good reason. At the same time as the Porter court-martial, and in the same building, McDowell was defending his military record before a court of inquiry, the army's equivalent of a grand jury. To admit Porter's version of events was to admit serious failings of his own, which he was not about to do. (The McDowell court of inquiry recommended no charges be filed.) General McDowell was the most important witness against Porter, who said of him in court, "His testimony, taken as a whole, has astonished me beyond measure." Privately Porter said, with just cause, that much of McDowell's testimony was perjured.[21]

Captain Douglass Pope, the general's nephew, testified that on August 29 he delivered Pope's 4:30 message, for the Fifth Corps to attack, within half an hour or so of its writing, giving Porter plenty of time to launch an assault. Porter, his staff officers, and his field commanders insisted the message did not arrive until sunset, about 6:30, much too late to mount an attack before dark. Porter said he could prove the late hour he received the 4:30 dispatch by a message he sent McDowell that evening, but he had kept no copy and McDowell did not remember such a message. In any event, Porter argued, he could not have attacked at any time that day, regardless of when Pope's orders arrived, because his path was blocked by a superior force of Confederates.[22]

It was the presence (or absence) of this Confederate force, and what Porter did (or did not do) on August 29, that was the crux of the case. His two-hour delay in obeying the 1:00 A.M. marching order was hardly hook enough on which to hang a general court-martial (and might as plausibly be considered within the normal discretion allowed a corps commander); and he produced enough evidence that his two missing brigades on August 30 were misplaced purely by accident that he was acquitted on those two charges. But it was an indisputable fact that the Fifth Corps did not take part in the battle on August 29.

It was quite true, contrary to General Pope's belief, that by noon on August 29 James Longstreet's entire command, 25,000 men, was squarely across Porter's designated line of advance. General Lee was asked after the war what the result would have been had Porter attacked that day. "I suppose we should have cut him to pieces," Lee replied. Yet it was also true that Porter discovered hardly anything about this force in front of him. The moment he sighted dust clouds ahead, he stopped short and deployed his lead troops for what might come. That was as much as he did. He never developed the enemy's position or probed aggressively to discover his strength, and he never reported to the commanding general that day what he had actually encountered. When the next morning he finally met Pope and warned him that Longstreet was on the field, he could furnish no evidence, no concrete details, and Pope refused to believe him. "He put no confidence in what I said," Porter admitted.[23]

Fitz John Porter was handicapped during his court-martial by the military renown in which General McClellan had clothed him. He was McClellan's favorite lieutenant because he did McClellan's fighting for him and so was rewarded with extravagant praise; it was believed that with all that skill his failures at Second Bull Run could only have been deliberate. Yet this reputation was considerably inflated. On this point General Lee's judgment is again instructive. A postwar interviewer recorded Lee's answer to a question about Porter at Second Bull Run: "Porter was not a strong man, would do well enough with somebody to tell him, but rather timid under responsibility."[24] On the Peninsula Porter had indeed done well enough when told to fight defensively (although at Gaines's Mill he was turned out of a very strong position and lost the battle). At Antietam, with the army on the offensive, he hung back and counseled caution to his cautious commander, and in every engagement he wildly exaggerated the strength of the enemy force opposing him. Porter's inaction on the Gainesville road on August 29 was actually very much in character — he was being as hesitant a captain as his old chief, General McClellan.

Porter's attitude, in fact, exactly mirrored McClellan's that day. McClellan had charge of the final 25,000 men of the Army of the Potomac slated to reinforce Pope, and he held off sending them to the battlefield on the principle of not throwing good money after bad. McClellan expected John Pope to be beaten — believed he deserved to be beaten — and wanted to save something from the debacle for the defense of Washington. Consequently, none of the 25,000 men would reach Pope in time to alter the outcome of the fighting. Porter too believed there had to be a better way to fight the battle than Pope's blundering way, and he would not put himself out to contribute to the blundering; the sound of Pope's fight against Jackson on August 29 did not stir him to action. Through the long years of his ordeal, Porter would never lose faith in his innocence of the specific charges against him. That he was guilty of an attitude so contemptuous of his commanding officer that it colored his every action was beyond his admitting.

Small details in the testimony told against him. One man reported that Porter made his headquarters that day fully three miles behind his picket line, and that his troops there had their arms stacked. Another man who came from the front to deliver a message found General Porter "lying down under a shade tree." A third said that when he brought a dispatch from Pope, Porter responded "in a sneering manner, and appeared to me to express a great indifference." When General Burnside testified to the dispatches Porter had sent him, which he then forwarded to Washington, he did Porter's cause little good by remarking that he found nothing unusual about their sarcasms; everybody in the Army of the Potomac had talked that way about General Pope.[25]

The testimony closed on January 6, 1863, and on January 10 the defense presented its closing arguments. The *New York Times* termed it a "masterly address, which was delivered with dramatic effect." In conclusion came Porter's personal testament, read in stentorian tones by his lawyer, Reverdy Johnson. "If the charge had not assumed the solemn form that has been given to it," Porter proclaimed, "it would be received everywhere, where my whole conduct is known, as ludicrously false or the creation of a morbid or distempered brain." This peroration "was patriotic and eloquent, and for thrilling pathos is unsurpassed in the annals of Court-Martial," announced the *Times* reporter, and he thought the summation "made a visible effect upon the Court." To everyone's surprise, the prosecutor presented no summation, and at 2:30 that afternoon the nine judges began their deliberations. Just three and a half hours later, at 6 o'clock, they announced that they had reached a verdict, which would be revealed in good season, after review by President Lincoln. The editorial opinion of the *Times*, published on January 12, was echoed by most observers: "The Court unanimously acquits Gen. Porter of the charges against him." Porter was less sure, writing McClellan on January 13, "the radicals say that the court began to smell your return to power and were influenced by it in their decision."[26]

Much criticism was leveled at the summary of the case prepared for the president by the court-martial's judge advocate, Joseph Holt. "It seems to have been made after the Court [decision] instead of before," Secretary of the Navy Gideon Welles commented in his diary, "and is sent out with it as if in defense of the decision." Holt's summary was a far from impartial document, representing as it did the prosecutor's role Holt had played at the trial—certainly one of the peculiarities of the military justice system. It is doubtful that Lincoln read the voluminous transcript of the entire proceedings, but he probably read at least the defense's summation as well as Holt's paper. However that may be, it is difficult to imagine the president overturning the court-martial verdict. Neither the verdict nor the sentence suggested a blatant injustice, and in any case no one was more aware of the stakes in the Porter case than Abraham Lincoln.[27]

Even as he pondered the Porter matter, the turmoil in the high command of the Army of the Potomac was spilling into the open. Burnside's lieutenants were stepping up their attacks on their chief, even going to the White House to do so. Dissident generals leaked stories to their favorite reporters; among editors it was even money that General McClellan would be called back to pull the Army of the Potomac together once more, or perhaps to return to the post of general-in-chief. The president's need to deliver a message — a warning — an example — to his officer corps was clear. Without delay, Mr. Lincoln approved the findings of the Porter court-martial.

On January 21, in one of the parlors of Willard's Hotel on Pennsylvania Avenue, a *New York Times* reporter found Fitz John Porter and broke the news to him: He was judged guilty under both the Ninth and Fifty-second Articles of War — failure to obey lawful orders, and misbehavior before the enemy. He was sentenced to be cashiered from the army "and to be forever disqualified from holding any office of trust or profit under the Government of the United States." The president, said the reporter, had approved the verdict without comment. "The hounds succeeded at last . . . ," Porter told McClellan two days later. "This is a terrible blow, but my conscious innocence will sustain me, and my indignation will enable me to fight it out."[28]

That fight would consume Porter for the next twenty-four years. If his inflated military reputation had hampered him at the court-martial, his unbridled commitment to the Democratic party would polarize his opposition in these later years. Politics had of course marked the case from the beginning, as McClellanite conservative Democrats rushed to Porter's defense against the radical Republicans seen as persecuting him. In the postwar years, whenever the Porter case stirred the national scene, the politics of the day overwhelmed any plea for simple justice. As one journalist unfriendly to Porter put the matter in 1875, Fitz John Porter had "served the Democratic party when he sacrificed Pope . . . , and whenever the party has the power why should it not serve him by restoring him to the army from which he was dismissed in disgrace." Porter himself advised a supporter, "appear to keep out of politics — but keeping it there is the policy. . . ."[29]

The printing press was the chief weapon in the contest. Even during the trial, pamphlets containing the testimony had been circulated, and after Judge Advocate Holt's summary appeared, Porter's lawyer, Reverdy Johnson, published a lengthy *Reply* of his own. Soon there was a *Reply to the Reply* . . . and then a *Reply to the Rejoinder* . . . , and scores rushed to the presses with appeals and memorials and opinions and articles and legal briefs and statements. Congressmen and senators saw their contributions into print. Second Bull Run became one of the most closely analyzed battles of the Civil War. The *Official Records of the Rebellion* project included a volume on the Porter court-martial. When Porter finally gained a rehearing, the proceedings would fill three large government-issue volumes. A bibliography of the Porter case can now run to a dozen pages.

What Porter sought, from the White House and the Congress, was a new hearing at which to introduce new evidence not available at the original trial. This evidence included newly found battlefield dispatches and, most important, the Second Bull Run testimony of the Confederate generals. Opponents argued this was irrelevant. Porter's actions had been judged — and must only be judged — by what was known at the time. The argument was raised that military law, unlike civil law, was not subject to a review process: The findings of a legally constituted court-martial, reviewed and approved by the president, must not be subject to overturn or the whole system of military discipline would crumble. One secretary of war offered the novel argument that if Porter wanted to be retried and wanted reinstatement in the army if found innocent, he must also be willing to "consent to be shot, should he be deemed guilty."[30]

Porter could expect no relief so long as Edwin Stanton remained secretary of war, but surprisingly he made no better progress after U. S. Grant entered the White House in 1869. Although eventually Grant would become a convert to Porter's cause, as president he applied strict standards to this matter of an officer's battlefield conduct. After all, to the professional soldier obedience to orders and conduct before the enemy were two of the essential rules of war-making, and Porter's fellow soldiers made up his toughest audience during his long fight for restitution. At first Grant's successor, Rutherford B. Hayes, was as unfriendly to Porter as Grant had been. As a regimental officer in 1862, Hayes explained to a Porter ally, "I was an eye witness to the terrible inertia that was exhibited by those officers about me when Pope took command."[31]

Hayes, however, came around to a warmer view of Porter's crusade, and in the spring of 1878 he appointed a three-man board of army officers to rehear the case. The Schofield Board, named for its senior officer, John M. Schofield — the other members were Alfred H. Terry and George W. Getty — was to examine all new evidence and indeed evidence of any kind relating to the Porter case so as to advise the president on whatever action "justice requires." Porter was jubilant to see his turn come at last: "I have stood the kicking so long. I can bear the batting now for a time."

Meeting first at West Point and then in New York City, the Schofield Board re-created the Second Battle of Bull Run virtually minute by minute. Maps were drawn and documents submitted, and 142 witnesses were heard. The case against Porter broke down piece by piece. Douglass Pope, who testified at the court-martial that he had promptly delivered the 4:30 P.M. attack order on August 29, had to admit he could only estimate the delivery time and in fact had gotten lost on the way. The message Porter claimed at the trial he had sent McDowell, proving the late arrival of the 4:30 order, now turned up after fifteen years in McDowell's papers. General Longstreet appeared before the board to confirm that his entire command had been on Porter's front that day. Other witnesses furnished numerous facts that McDowell had failed to remember — and still could not remember in his 1878 testimony. (General Pope strenuously opposed the rehearing and refused to appear before it.) In his summation, Porter lawyer Joseph H. Choate spoke sympathetically of the wartime court-martial judges:

"It was asking more than human judgment, and more than human nature was master of, for them to pass judicially upon the case."

The Schofield Board agreed. Its report, made public in April 1879, was everything Porter could have asked for. On every point, on every charge, the board accepted his contentions. Its sole criticism was the tone of his dispatches to Burnside, which it said "cannot be defended." Schofield wrote privately to Porter, "The cold terms of an official report could but faintly express the feeling which my associates fully shared with me when we fully realized the magnitude of the wrong under which you had so long suffered. . . ."[32]

Porter had won the battle, but there was still the campaign to win. That required seven more years of fighting. The Republican Hayes, having incurred the wrath of many in his party for creating the Schofield Board, prudently passed the buck by submitting the board's report to Congress for action. Year after year, in each legislative session, bills were introduced to provide relief for Porter, and year after year they failed of passage in one house or the other. It was a high exercise in party politics. To restore Porter to the army, Republicans said, was to demean the martyred Lincoln and the Republican wartime leaders who had brought the case, and to reward the McClellanite Democrats who had wanted a divided Union. The bloody shirt was waved early and often. Pass the Porter bill, one Republican senator cried, and "the widow of the North will point to the empty chair at the table where the father once sat who was slain in the battle because Fitz-John Porter lingered and lagged behind and failed to add strength in the conflict." It was charged that ex-Confederates now in Congress were behind the Porter bill, seeking to benefit their warm friend from wartime days.[33]

The elevation of the unrepentant James Garfield to the White House in 1881 was a setback for Porter, but after Garfield's assassination Porter sought the support of the new president, Chester A. Arthur. By a presidential pardon, Arthur lifted the ban on Porter's holding a federal office, but when a relief bill finally passed both houses of Congress in 1884, Arthur remembered his Republicanism and vetoed it. When the Democrats captured the presidency in the election of 1884, Porter's confidence soared. A relief bill passed Congress easily, and on July 1, 1886 — the twenty-fourth anniversary of Porter's finest hour, the Battle of Malvern Hill — President Grover Cleveland signed it. On August 2, Porter's nomination as colonel in the regular army was approved by the Senate. On August 7, he was placed on the retired list. He was vindicated.

Porter had supported himself since the war in various engineering and business capacities and in municipal posts; now, unburdened at last, he returned to his job as New York City's police commissioner. Not until his seventy-fifth year would he retire from active life, and when he entered his last illness, in 1901, he had the satisfaction of knowing he had outlasted all the other main actors in his case.

To acknowledge that injustice was done Fitz John Porter by cashiering him on the specific charges brought by General Pope is not to acknowledge that Porter was innocent on all counts at Second Bull Run. Clearly he was guilty, as Captain Lowell said at the time of the court-martial, of a "frame of mind . . . un-officer-like and dangerous." As the *Springfield Republican* had observed in 1863, "The country does not want soldiers who cannot fight except on particular days and under particular generals." Furthermore, this was an attitude poisoning far too many in the officer corps of the Army of the Potomac, the unhappy legacy of the deposed McClellan. An example had to be made, and General Porter was the not entirely undeserving victim. When everything about that time and place is considered, the judgment of Allan Nevins seems a just one: With his frame of mind, Fitz John Porter "was better out of the army."[34]

NOTES

1. George Templeton Strong, *The Diary of George Templeton Strong: The Civil War, 1860–1865*, eds. Allan Nevins and Milton H. Thomas (New York: Macmillan,

1952), 291; F. L. Olmsted, *The Papers of Frederick Law Olmsted,* ed. Jane Turner Censer (Baltimore: Johns Hopkins University Press, 1986), vol. 4, 640.

2. Edward W. Emerson, *Life and Letters of Charles Russell Lowell* (Boston: Houghton Mifflin, 1907), 231–32.

3. U. S. Grant to Chester A. Arthur, Dec. 22, 1881, Arthur Papers, Library of Congress.

4. Fitz John Porter to J.C.G. Kennedy, July 17, 1862, Porter Papers, Massachusetts Historical Society.

5. Porter to Manton Marble, Aug. 5, 10, 1862, Marble Papers, Library of Congress.

6. Porter to McClellan, Aug. 27, 1862, McClellan Papers, Library of Congress.

7. Porter to Burnside, Aug. 27, 29, 1862, *Official Records* 12:2 Supplement *(Porter Court-Martial),* 1063, 1070; *Porter Court-Martial,* 1113–14.

8. Pope, Burnside testimony, *Porter Court-Martial,* 838, 1003.

9. John J. Hennessy, *Return to Bull Run: The Campaign and Battle of Second Manassas* (New York: Simon & Schuster, 1993), 195.

10. Pope to McDowell and Porter, Aug. 29, 1862, *Porter Court-Martial,* 825.

11. Pope to Halleck, Sept. 1, 1862, *OR* 12:2, 83.

12. Porter to Marble, Nov. 9, 1862, Marble Papers.

13. Porter to S.L.M. Barlow, Dec. 29, 1862, Barlow Papers, Huntington Library.

14. McClellan to Porter, Dec. 19, 1862, McClellan to Stanton, June 1, 1862, George B. McClellan, *The Civil War Papers of George B. McClellan: Selected Correspondence, 1860–1865,* ed. Stephen W. Sears (New York: Ticknor & Fields, 1989), 532, 285.

15. Henry Gabler, "The Fitz John Porter Case: Politics and Military Justice," Ph.D. dissertation (1979), 309–10; Porter to McClellan, Jan. 23, 1863, McClellan Papers.

16. Henry L. Dawes quoted in *Civil War History* (Dec. 1978), 361.

17. *Porter Court-Martial,* 821; Gabler, "Porter Case," 314; Porter to Marble, Dec. 27, 1862, Marble Papers.

18. Stephen M. Weld, "The Case of Fitz-John Porter," *The Virginia Campaign of 1862 under General Pope,* Papers of the Military Historical Society of Massachusetts (1886), vol. 2, 224, 357–58.

19. *Porter Court-Martial,* 834, 840, 852.

20. *Porter Court-Martial,* 904, 909.

21. *Porter Court-Martial,* 1106–7.

22. *Porter Court-Martial,* 875, 1108.

23. J. F. Lee to Porter, July 24, 1870, copy McClellan Papers; Hennessy, *Return to Bull Run,* 312–13.

24. R. E. Lee interview, Feb. 19, 1870, William Allen Papers, Southern Historical Collection, University of North Carolina.

25. *Porter Court-Martial,* 1032, 889, 1006.

26. *New York Times,* Jan. 11, 12, 1863; *Porter Court-Martial,* 1111–12; Gabler, "Porter Case," 285; Porter to McClellan, Jan. 13, 1863, McClellan Papers.

27. *Porter Court-Martial,* 1112–33; Gideon Welles, *Diary of Gideon Welles,* ed. Howard K. Beale (New York: Norton, 1960), vol. 1, 229.

28. Gabler, "Porter Case," 288; *Porter Court-Martial,* 1051; Porter to McClellan, Jan. 23, 1863, McClellan Papers. See "The Revolt of the Generals" elsewhere in this collection.

29. Gabler, "Porter Case," 364, 385.

30. Adjutant General's Office, Record Group 94, National Archives.

31. Gabler, "Porter Case," 374.

32. Gabler, "Porter Case," 379, 412, 413.

33. Gabler, "Porter Case," 443.

34. Emerson, *Lowell Life and Letters,* 231–32; *Springfield Republican,* Aug. 22, 1863; Allan Nevins, *The War for the Union: War Becomes Revolution, 1862–63* (New York: Scribner's, 1960), 400.

[4]

September Crisis

Secretary of War Edwin M. Stanton

WITH THE War Department clamping a blackout on newspaper reporting from the army, blocking the sending of stories by telegraph, reporters had to scramble to file their copy any way they could. Adams Hill, head of the Washington bureau of the *New York Tribune,* resorted to the mails to get background reports to his managing editor, Sidney Gay. In these closing days of August 1862, Federal forces were believed to be fighting a major battle on or near the old Bull Run battlefield, twenty-five miles west of the capital. The rumble of the guns could be plainly heard. At the War Department Hill picked up details on the number of newly arrived recruits "to be relied upon in case of emergency." He sorted through the latest rumors about the failings of certain Union generals. Stopping by the White House, he gathered a particularly juicy tidbit: "The President was never so wrathful as last night against George."[1]

Editor Gay required no last name to identify "George." He could only be George Brinton McClellan, commander of the Army of the Potomac. The general was well known for generating anger. What had moved Mr. Lincoln to wrath, it developed, was a telegram from McClellan dated August 29. He reported on the situation of General John Pope, commanding on the Bull Run field. "I am clear that one of two courses should be adopted," said McClellan. "First, to concentrate all our available forces to open communication with Pope; Second, to leave Pope to get out of his scrape, and at once use all our means to make the capital perfectly safe. No middle course will now answer."

Although the president responded mildly enough that it was the first course that should be adopted, the phrase "leave Pope to get out of his scrape" greatly angered him. For the last week Mr. Lincoln had been closely monitoring telegraphic traffic at the War Department, watching with growing concern as the battle drew near and then erupted. McClellan's offhandedly cruel dismissal of a fellow general caught up in an obviously life-and-death struggle came as a kind of last straw. "The President was very outspoken in regard to McClellan's present conduct," John Hay, Lincoln's secretary, recorded in his diary. "He said it really seemed to him that McC wanted Pope defeated." Lincoln referred specifically to the "get out of his scrape" dispatch, and then went on to catalog the general's other suspect actions over the past few days. General McClellan, Hay decided after hearing all this, "acts as chief alarmist and grand marplot of the Army."[2]

There is no small irony in the fact that the offending phrase, which served to crystallize opposition to the general, had been delivered quite innocently. It was a favorite figure of speech of McClellan's, one he used randomly and without intentional spite, and he would have been astonished at the stir it caused in Washington.

The stir was especially great at the War Department. As *Tribune* correspondent Hill learned from Assistant Secretary of War Peter H. Watson, the issue there had become starkly clear: "Mr. Watson says this morning that if Pope be defeated," Hill wrote his editor on August 29, "McClellan will justly be held responsible, since he received orders to move day before yesterday and had not budged an inch at an early hour this morning. Cause or excuse not stated."[3] Although officially in command of the Army of the Potomac, General McClellan just then was in actual command of only two of its army corps — Edwin Sumner's Second and William Franklin's Sixth, 25,000 men in all — and both corps were under General-in-

Chief Halleck's orders to march to Pope. They had come up from the Peninsula to McClellan's headquarters at Alexandria, a half-dozen miles south of Washington. Although the military situation as seen from the capital was decidedly hazy, there were two things known for certain: Pope's Army of Virginia was confronting the main Rebel army near Manassas and Bull Run, and Pope was supposed to be receiving Potomac army reinforcements from Alexandria in the quickest way possible. It appeared, however, that General McClellan and the War Department had very different definitions of "quickest."

The ugly reality of the matter was that McClellan had no use whatsoever for John Pope. In a letter to Mrs. McClellan he had predicted that Pope's campaign would end in a thrashing: "very badly whipped he will be & ought to be — such a villain as he is ought to bring defeat upon any cause that employs him." Although bitter in his opposition to the evacuation of the Army of the Potomac from the Peninsula, McClellan had taken heart from Halleck's promise that he would have command of both his and Pope's armies when the two were united. Now, on this twenty-ninth of August, even that prospect had evaporated. As McClellan wrote his wife that evening, "I have no command at present . . . & have merely 'turned in' on my own account to straighten out whatever I catch hold of. . . . I have no faith in anyone here & expect to be turned loose the moment their alarm is over."[4]

Franklin's corps finally set off for the front that Friday, but on McClellan's order it stopped short after just seven miles and bivouacked. He held Sumner's Second Corps in the capital's outer fortifications. In the meantime, the heavy rumble of gunfire from Bull Run continued through the day, ceasing only after dark. In official Washington there was consternation and a rising anger at what was widely seen as McClellan's deliberate stalling. Secretary of War Edwin Stanton and Secretary of the Treasury Salmon P. Chase called on General Halleck to demand (as Chase phrased it in his diary) "a report touching McC's disobedience of orders & consequent delay of support to Army of Va."

Typically, General McClellan had created a unique vision of events that was all his own — a vision drawn from his unique view of the enemy. The day before, August 28, he had announced to Halleck that by report "the enemy with 120,000 men" was approaching the fortifications with the intention "of attacking Washington and Baltimore." This more than doubled the actual force with General Lee, but it was a figure that made perfect sense to McClellan. Having previously invented a phantom Confederate army of 200,000 that defended Richmond during the Peninsula operations, he found nothing surprising about Lee's taking 120,000 of that number for this new offensive.

Consequently, McClellan regarded Pope's defeat as inevitable (and richly deserved). Rather than rushing reinforcements to the Army of Virginia as ordered, the prudent course would be to preserve Franklin's and Sumner's 25,000 to anchor the defense of Washington against the invading horde. Somehow the government was failing to grasp his view of the case — he was "heart sick with the folly & ignorance I see around me," he told his wife — but he had no trouble inventing a barrage of excuses for keeping the two corps safe from Pope's certain debacle.[5]

Secretary Stanton saw through this tactic and was infuriated by it. In times like this, Edwin Stanton was given to violent responses. With the distant sounds of battle as accompaniment, he composed a "remonstrance" for fellow members of the Cabinet to sign and present to the president. It charged General McClellan with incompetence, with deliberately disobeying his orders to aid Pope. Lawyer Stanton summed up for the prosecution: "the destruction of our armies, the protraction of the war, the waste of our national resources, and the overthrow of the government, which we believe must be the inevitable consequence of George B. McClellan being continued in command." Stanton was, in short, threatening the breakup of the administration over the issue.[6]

On Saturday, August 30, Stanton opened his campaign in earnest. In reply to the war secretary's earlier demand, General Halleck furnished him specific documentation on McClellan's recent foot-dragging in supporting Pope. His various directives to McClellan, said Halleck, were "not obeyed with the promptness I expected and the national safety, in my opinion, required." In this matter Stanton had already forged a firm alliance with Treasury Secretary Chase, and at the War Department the two of them discussed the remonstrance, made some changes in the wording, and both signed it. They debated the best tactics for presenting it to the other Cabinet members. Secretary of State William Seward was out of town and unavailable (rather conveniently, it was thought). There seemed little point in approaching Montgomery Blair, the postmaster general, who was known to be a McClellan supporter. As for Edward Bates, the conservative attorney general, they deemed it best not to see him until they had at least a majority among the other signers. Secretary of the Interior Caleb Smith had already agreed to sign, but he wanted to wait so the signatures would be in order of rank. That left Secretary of the Navy Welles. Chase, being more of a diplomatist than the abrasive Stanton, volunteered to make their case to Welles.[7]

Gideon Welles, who ran his department with a cool, steady hand and was much respected by the president, balked at the very idea of the remonstrance. In any event, he considered its tone too strong. As he put it in his diary, "I did not choose to denounce McC. for incapacity, or declare him a traitor." Chase replied that it was time the Cabinet acted with "energy and promptitude, for either the Government or McClellan must go down." Welles said that he certainly held no brief for General McClellan, primarily on account of his "dilatory course"; indeed, he agreed that probably it would be best for the country if the general was dismissed. He "should have no hesitation in saying so at the proper time and place," but delivering an ultimatum like this to Mr. Lincoln was not the way.[8]

A disappointed Chase returned the remonstrance to Stanton. They remained one signature short of a Cabinet majority. Stanton said he would take up the matter with Attorney General Bates. It was late afternoon now, and their day's efforts had been energized by the continuing rumble of guns from the direction of Bull Run. A dispatch from the battlefield, written at 5:00 A.M., had finally reached the War Department. In it General Pope described a "terrific battle here yesterday" in which he claimed the advantage. "The news just reaches me from the front that the enemy is retreating toward the mountains. I go forward at once to see."[9]

Stanton, who had vigorously supported bringing Pope to the Army of Virginia command, was much encouraged by this. Should that general, while commanding the combined armies of the Potomac and Virginia, go on to win a great victory at Bull Run, it ought to effectively dispose of McClellan. There might be no need to petition the president after all. That evening Secretary Stanton encountered Lincoln and John Hay at the War Department and (as Hay put it) "carried us off to dinner. . . . Stanton was unqualifiedly severe upon McClellan. He said that after these battles there should be one Court Martial, if never any more. He said that nothing but foul play could lose us this battle & that it rested with McC. and his friends." In his diary Hay caught the optimism of the moment: "Every thing seemed to be going well and hilarious on Saturday & we went to bed expecting glad tidings at sunrise."

At Alexandria that evening, writing his wife, General McClellan was in a very different mood. "I feel too blue & disgusted to write any more now . . . ," he told her. "They have taken *all* my troops from me — I have even sent off all my personal escort & camp guard & am here with a few orderlies & the aides. I have been listening to the distant sound of a great battle in the distance — my men engaged in it & I away! I never felt worse in my life."[10]

At 8 o'clock the next morning, a dark and rainy Sunday, August 31, Mr. Lincoln came to his secretary's room and announced grimly, "Well John, we are whipped again, I am afraid." The report was that the enemy had driven Pope back on Centreville, he went on, "where he says he will be able to hold his men. . . . I dont like to hear him admit that his men need holding." Although obviously disappointed, Lincoln was not despairing. As he went about his duties that day, Hay noted, "The President was in a singularly defiant tone of mind."[11]

When the news reached him, Secretary Stanton, dour but with renewed resolve, took up his remonstrance again. He understood that for much or all of the Bull Run fighting, three of McClellan's principal lieutenants — Fitz John Porter, William Franklin, and Edwin Sumner — had taken no part at all. Stanton conferred at length with Attorney General Bates, who said he was in basic agreement with the purpose of the remonstrance but thought it much too strong in tone. Rather than including a bill of particulars against McClellan, he said, it ought simply to express the signers' conviction that the general should be relieved of his command. The reasons could then be given in detail if the president asked for them. Bates agreed to revise the remonstrance in his own hand, to give it the weight of an opinion by the president's chief legal adviser. Stanton concurred, and a new, milder remonstrance was soon committed to paper. The undersigned in this crisis, wrote Bates, were performing "a painful duty in declaring to you our deliberate opinion that, at this time, it is not safe to entrust to Major General McClellan the command of any Army of the United States." The signatures were those of Stanton, Chase, Caleb Smith, and Bates.[12]

In the capital it was a Sunday of suspenseful waiting. Little was known, and much was feared. The wounded from the battlefield began streaming into the city. With them came a veritable army of stragglers, spreading tales of defeat and demoralization. It was reported that Franklin's and Sumner's reinforcements from the Army of the Potomac had only reached the field in time to help pick up the pieces of the badly battered Army of Virginia. At Centreville General Samuel Sturgis, commanding a reserve division, encountered a dejected General Pope. "Too late, Sammy, too late!" Pope called out. Sturgis offered him no comfort. "Damn it," he said, "didn't I tell you that all it was necessary for you to hang yourself was to give you plenty of rope!"

At his headquarters in Alexandria, General McClellan was feeling helpless and useless. A private message from his confidant Fitz John Porter told of being driven from the field and of the danger of being cut off. "The men are without heart — but will fight when cornered," Porter said. To give himself something to do, McClellan inspected the city's outer fortifications. "I feel in that state of excitement & anxiety that I can hardly keep still for a moment," he told his wife. Mrs. McClellan was summering in Connecticut, and had written him repeatedly of her concern about the possessions in their house in Washington should the Rebels break into the city. He promised he would "quietly slip over there" and see to the safety of at least their silver. In his present circumstance of suspended animation he thought there ought to be plenty of time for that.[13]

For General-in-Chief Halleck, at the War Department, August 31 found each new dispatch from the front grimmer than the one before. Right up to the last minute Halleck had entertained the hope that the army corps of Franklin and Sumner he had ordered to Pope would reach the field in time to seal a victory. Now Pope could tell him only that things might indeed have been different had Franklin and Sumner reached him three or four days before. But they had not; consequently he telegraphed, "I should like to know whether you feel secure about Washington should this army be destroyed." By nightfall, after a steady diet of such messages, Halleck was in a state of virtual collapse. He implored McClellan, "I beg of you to assist me in this crisis with your ability and experience. I am utterly tired out." As McClellan explained it to his wife, he was just finishing "a very severe" application for an extended leave of absence "when I received a dispatch from Halleck begging me to help him out of the scrape." He arranged to go up to Washington the next morning to see the general-in-chief.[14]

In his diary for Monday, September 1, Secretary Chase wrote, "This has been an anxious day." Stanton now had the signatures of a majority of the Cabinet members on his remonstrance. Seward was still absent, and Montgomery Blair was still thought to be in the McClellan camp. To further strengthen his hand, Stanton decided to try again for Gideon Welles's signature. When his ally Chase showed the revised remonstrance to the navy secretary, however, Welles again balked. Chase sought to argue with him that the case was unique: "he deliberately believed McClellan ought to be shot," Welles wrote. Welles repeated that he would not hesitate to say in council that he believed McClellan ought to be relieved, but to put the case in this manner was disrespectful to the president "and would justly be deemed offensive."

At this, Stanton and Chase elected to go ahead with what they had — the signatures of four of the seven Cabinet members, while holding a fifth name, Welles's, in a sort of reserve. They intended to present the softened remonstrance to Mr. Lincoln at the Cabinet meeting scheduled for the next day.[15]

McClellan reached Halleck's office in the War Department at midday that Monday, where he found the president as well as the general-in-chief waiting for him. As McClellan described the meeting for his wife, he said of course he could not refuse Halleck's invitation to help him out of the scrape, "so I came over this morning, mad as a March hare, & had a pretty plain talk with him & Abe." Plain talk was very likely delivered by Mr. Lincoln as well. His secretary reported the president telling him that morning, "Mr. Hay, we must whip these people now." Pope must fight, he went on, and if the enemy proved too strong, he must retire in good order to the Washington fortifications. "If this be not so, if we are really whipped and to be whipped, we may as well stop fighting."

McClellan was ordered to take charge of Washington and its defenses and its garrison, presumably with the injunction to "whip these people now." The decision was apparently proposed by Halleck and seconded by the president. Privately McClellan expressed himself reluctant to take on this new assignment. It seemed a thankless task, "for things are far gone." He told Mrs. McClellan that although he would do all he could during the immediate emergency, "If when the whole army returns here (if it ever does), I am not placed in command of all I will either insist upon a long leave of absence or resign. . . ." Thus, unbeknownst to President Lincoln, as of September 1 there were two major ultimatums that it appeared he would have to contend with — one about to be delivered by his Cabinet, and the second by his highest-ranking general.[16]

A dispatch now reached the War Department, after McClellan was sent on his way, in which General Pope unburdened himself of all the supposed treacheries heaped on him over the past week or so. He saw it as his duty, Pope said, to call Halleck's attention "to the unsoldierly and dangerous conduct of many brigade and some division commanders of the forces sent here from the Peninsula." He said it was their "constant talk, indulged in publicly and in promiscuous company," that the Army of the Potomac was demoralized and would not fight. Without naming him, Pope left no doubt he believed McClellan to be behind all this. "You have hardly an idea of the demoralization among officers of high rank in the Potomac Army, arising in all instances from personal feeling in relation to changes of commander-in-chief and others. . . . Its source is beyond my reach, though its effects are very perceptible and very dangerous." It was his advice to withdraw the combined armies behind the Washington fortifications and then rearrange and reorganize them totally. "You may avoid great disaster by doing so."[17]

However much — or little — truth there was to Pope's charge, it had the effect of a bombshell. No more grave accusations had ever been made against the Army of the Potomac's officer corps. McClellan was promptly summoned to a second meeting with Lincoln and Halleck. The president told him there was reason to believe that the Potomac army (as McClellan later recorded it) "was not cheerfully co-operating with and supporting General Pope." Lincoln asked him to "rectify the evil" by telegraphing his confidant Porter to "try to do away with any feeling that might exist." McClellan's is the only account of the meeting, and he has Lincoln requesting his help "as a special favor." Upon his agreeing to do so, the president "thanked me very warmly, assured me that he could never forget my action in the matter, &c., and left."

Considering the gravity of Pope's charge, and John Hay's description of the president that day being "in a singularly defiant tone of mind," it seems safe to assume that Mr. Lincoln took a considerably harder line during this meeting than McClellan admitted. It was, after all, an extraordinary comment on the times that in a major crisis one Union army reportedly scorned aiding another. It is most likely that Lincoln *ordered* McClellan to take the action he did, for the very act of it was at least tacit acknowledgment that there was something behind Pope's accusations. In any event, McClellan telegraphed Porter, "I ask of you for my sake, that of the country, and of the old Army of the Potomac, that you and all my friends will lend the fullest and most cordial co-operation to General Pope in all the operations now going on . . . , the same support they ever have to me." McClellan added that he was now in command of the Washington defenses — which was surely the only good news of the day so far as Porter was concerned — "and am doing all I can to render your retreat safe. . . ." During this exchange, and no doubt lending urgency to the moment, came the sounds of renewed battle from the west, from the direction of Chantilly.[18]

It was a night of anguish for the president. Colonel John C. Kelton of Halleck's staff, sent to the front for a report on the situation independent of Pope, returned with ill tidings. As Kelton told one of McClellan's generals at Centreville, he "found matters very different" from the understanding at Washington based on Pope's dispatches. The president should know, said Kelton, that all the roads leading to the capital were clogged with stragglers, perhaps 30,000 in number. Furthermore, those troops, and their officers, still standing with their commands were severely demoralized. On the evidence of his tirade earlier that day against McClellan's officer corps, it appeared that General Pope, too, was demoralized. The army was beaten and the capital threatened. Never had the Union cause looked so desperate.

It may be that an undated musing by Lincoln from this period was written that night. "In the present civil war," the president observed, "it is quite possible that God's purpose is something different from the purpose of either party. . . . I am almost ready to say this is probably true — that God wills this contest, and wills that it shall not end yet. . . . He could have either *saved* or *destroyed* the Union without a human contest. Yet the contest began. And having begun He could give the final victory to either side any day. Yet the contest proceeds."[19]

The immediate contest would proceed under a different leader, however. The president rose early on Tuesday, September 2, and with General Halleck walked the few blocks to McClellan's quarters on H Street. It was 7:00 A.M. when they found McClellan at the breakfast table. McClellan, again, has left the only account of the meeting. He wrote his wife a few hours later that Mr. Lincoln "expressed the opinion that the troubles now impending could be overcome better by me than anyone else." Pope had been ordered back to the Washington fortifications, "& as he reenters everything is to come under my command again! . . . I only consent to take it for my country's sake & with the humble hope that God has called me to it — how I pray that he may support me! . . ."[20]

It is clear from his later comments that Lincoln made this decision himself — Halleck concurred in it, but certainly he did not take the lead in proposing it — and that he decided on this course only with the greatest reluctance. No doubt he was cordial enough — so McClellan described the scene at his quarters — in turning over command of the joint armies, and of course he would have made it clear to the newly appointed general commanding that he had full presidential support. Yet to give that command to a general he judged had acted treacherously toward Pope and his army (among numerous other failings) surely made this the most agonizing military-command decision that Lincoln had to make during the war.

Interestingly, General Orders No. 122 read, as first drafted, "By direction of the President, Major General McClellan will have command of the fortifications of Washington, and of all the troops for the defense of the capital. By order of the Secretary of War." When the order was published, however, the phrases "By direction of the President" and "By order of the Secretary of War" were deleted, and it was signed, "By command of Major-General Halleck." This left Halleck solely responsible before the country for the change of command. In this Lincoln and Stanton were deliberately distancing themselves from a decision that promised political as well as military consequences. (Officially, of course, McClellan had never been removed from the command of the Army of the Potomac, and in that sense G.O. 122 simply gave him the Army of Virginia too. But to everyone concerned, then and later, the practical consequence of G.O. 122 was that it took the Army of the Potomac away from John Pope and gave it back to George McClellan.)[21]

The Cabinet meeting at noon that day was perhaps the most unusual of the war. "There was a more disturbed and desponding feeling than I have ever witnessed in council," Gideon Welles recorded in his diary. The first arrivals, before Lincoln and Stanton came in, discussed the critical military situation. Montgomery Blair, who as a West Pointer was respected for his military opinions, said he knew Pope well and would describe him as a braggart and a liar, "with some courage, perhaps, but not much capacity." Blair was not much surprised at Pope's reverses. It was generally agreed, however, that for all that, Pope had not been supported as he should have been by McClellan and his Potomac army generals, especially Franklin and Porter. As Welles phrased it, "Personal jealousies and professional rivalries, the bane and curse of all armies, have entered deeply into ours." Blair, a long-time McClellan supporter, confessed that even he now thought that general should not be trusted with the chief command of the army. That change of heart put the entire Cabinet, absent Seward, into the anti-McClellan column.

When Stanton arrived he was in a state of barely suppressed rage. It was being told at the War Department, he announced, that McClellan had just been ordered to take command of all the forces defending Washington. "General surprise was expressed," Welles noted. Much excited comment followed. The president now came in and confirmed McClellan's appointment, saying it had been his decision, with which Halleck agreed, and that he would be responsible for it to the country. (The subsequent alteration of G.O. 122 suggests his second thoughts in that regard.) With that, the discussion became heated. Stanton and especially Chase registered strong objection. According to Chase, McClellan's failure to reinforce Pope during the Bull Run fighting on Friday and Saturday had made him "unworthy of trust." As everyone knew, he had once sponsored McClellan, Chase said. Now, "I could not but feel that giving the command to him was equivalent to giving Washington to the rebels." Attorney General Bates remarked that if General-in-Chief Halleck could not defend Washington with even 50,000 men, "he ought to be instantly broke." Should the capital fall, Bates went on, "it would be by treachery in our leaders, not by lack of power to defend."

At some point, according to Bates's notes on the meeting, Lincoln saw, or was read, the Stanton-Chase remonstrance. It left the president, Bates noted, "in deep distress . . . ; he seemed wrung by the bitterest anguish — that he felt almost ready to hang himself. . . ." He was so greatly disturbed, according to Bates, "precisely because he knew we were earnestly sincere." Lincoln said he knew of no other general who could do the work needed as well as McClellan. His task was the defense of the capital. He pointed to McClellan's skills as an engineer and an organizer, and his familiarity with the city's defenses. They had, after all, been built under his direction. He admitted that McClellan had the "slows" and was "good for nothing in a forward movement." Yet above all, he said, General McClellan had the confidence of the army. That fact, by all reports, was far more important than anything else just then.

At length, wrote Secretary Chase bitterly, "the meeting broke up, leaving the matter as we found it." Attorney General Bates, hardly containing his anger, immediately sat down to write a friend, "The thing I complain of is a criminal tardiness, a fatuous apathy, a captious, bickering rivalry, among our commanders who seem so taken up with their quick made dignity, that they overlook the lives of their people & the necessities of their country." The day before, when he tried to persuade Welles to sign the remonstrance, Chase had made a prediction. Welles recorded it in his diary: "Conversations, he said, amounted to but little with the President on subjects of this importance. It was like throwing water on a duck's back." And so it seemed. By presidential fiat, General McClellan, for good or ill, virtually without a friend in the administration, was back in command of the Army of the Potomac at the very center of the Union's greatest crisis.[22]

In conversation the next day with John Hay, Lincoln revealed the depth of his anger at McClellan and suggested what it had cost him to reinstate the general. "The Cabinet yesterday," he admitted to Hay, "were unanimous against him. . . . Unquestionably he has acted badly toward Pope! He wanted him to fail. That is unpardonable. But he is too useful just now to sacrifice." General McClellan, the president summed up, "has acted badly in this matter, but we must use what tools we have."[23]

As for McClellan, he was clearly galvanized by his reinstatement. In the letter he dashed off to his wife at midday on September 2, announcing that he was in command again, McClellan told her, "I am too busy to write any more now." He meant it. There was nothing that General McClellan did better than administer an army and organize a defense. He sent off to alert the Washington outposts to cover the entry of Pope's columns. Guards were posted on all the roads to corral stragglers. The army's trains were hastened into secure locations. "I have been & am busily engaged in transmitting the necessary orders & obtaining the requisite information," McClellan assured the president that afternoon. "If Pope retires promptly & in good order all will yet go well. . . . You may rest certain that nothing I can think of shall be left undone." In a dispatch to Pope (accompanied by Halleck's order placing the Washington defenses, and all the troops, in McClellan's charge), McClellan directed that the various units be marched to their old encampments around the city. In those familiar settings, he thought, they would be ready to turn quickly on the enemy should he pursue.[24]

All this comprised an essential first step. With the troops, especially the veteran troops, about to man the parapets, there appeared to be little chance of the enemy storming right into Washington on their heels. However encouraging that might be, it was entirely dependent on a crucial second step. The army must be told who its commander was. There were genuine fears in the capital that the troops might not again willingly fight under John Pope or his second-in-command, Irvin McDowell. Fitz John Porter, reviewing the debacle of the Second Bull Run fighting, had given it as his opinion to McClellan that the only way the men would fight now was if they were cornered. Pope himself, just that morning, warned Halleck, "Unless something can be done to restore tone to this army, it will melt away before you know it." With his unsurpassed sense of theater, General McClellan knew just how to pass the word that he was back. At 4 o'clock that afternoon, September 2, he wrote a brief note to his wife: "I am just about starting out to pick up the Army of the Potomac. . . ."[25]

What happened next became legendary in the annals of the Potomac army. Nothing like it had ever happened before; nothing like it would happen again. With a few aides and a small cavalry escort, McClellan rode out to the city's westernmost fortifications, and there on the turnpike to Alexandria he reined up his little cavalcade to await the first troops from the battlefield. This turned out to be McDowell's corps of the Army of Virginia, with Pope riding alongside McDowell at the head of the column. McClellan cantered out to meet them. After an exchange of salutes, he formally presented Pope with the order from Halleck putting the defenses and all the troops under McClellan's command. There was a brief discussion of troop dispositions. One of those listening to the exchange was Brigadier General John Hatch, whom Pope had recently demoted from a cavalry command to the infantry. Hatch turned back to the column, carefully staying within earshot of Pope, and shouted, "Boys, McClellan is in command again! Three cheers!"

A moment of stunned silence, then the column exploded with

cheers, repeated and echoing. As word spread, the cheering rolled down the length of the column like serial bursts of cannon fire. These were not even Army of the Potomac troops, but instead men of the Army of Virginia who had never served under McClellan on the Peninsula. That suggested the depth of their hatred for their superiors. "You cannot conceive of the intense feeling against Pope, McDowell, and Stanton," one man wrote home. McClellan then rode on to the next column and the next, and before long that evening the cry "Little Mac is back!" had reached out to every unit and every bivouac.

For a man in Porter's Fifth Corps the moment was still vivid two decades later. ". . . Tired fellows, as the news passed down the column," he wrote, "jumped to their feet, and sent up such a hurrah as the Army of the Potomac had never heard before. Shout upon shout went out into the stillness of the night; and as it was taken up along the road and repeated by regiment, brigade, division, and corps, we could hear the roar dying away in the distance." The effect, he remembered, "was too wonderful to make it worth while attempting to give a reason for it."[26]

It is beyond any doubt that before that moment the armies of Virginia and the Potomac were seriously, even severely demoralized. The futility of all Pope's marching and countermarching throughout the campaign had been painfully evident to even the lowliest rear-rank private. His persistent battle tactics of frontal assault drained the confidence of both officers and men. Their confidence was further diminished when Pope allowed himself to be surprised and flanked at the climax of the fighting on August 30. Having to leave their wounded behind was still another blow to morale. The consistent theme of their letters home in these days was that they had not been so much outfought as outgeneraled. Thus *any* command change would have helped morale. As it happened, the reversion of command to General McClellan sent morale skyrocketing, so great was his appeal to the rank and file.

To be sure, there remained much to be done before this force — actually a mismatched aggregation of half a dozen once-independent commands — could be regarded as an army ready to take the field. Then, just as McClellan turned his considerable energies to this task, General Lee abruptly raised the stakes. On September 3, the day after McClellan took command of the combined armies, it was reported that the enemy, baffled in his attempt to capture Washington, "will cross the Potomac, and make a raid into Maryland or Pennsylvania. A movable army must be immediately organized to meet him again in the field."

This directive, sent to McClellan by Halleck, was the general-in-chief's response to an earlier order Lincoln had issued to him. Halleck, said the president, was, "with all possible dispatch, to organize an army for active operations, . . . when such active army shall take the field." General Halleck, in short, was being invited to lead the combined armies into the field after Lee. That General Halleck would not do. He promptly assigned McClellan the task of preparing "a movable army." In reply to McClellan's query, Halleck said it had not yet been decided who would command that army when it went on campaign.[27]

Once the troops were safely back behind the Washington fortifications and the commissary and quartermaster departments began to operate properly again — just then a major problem in the beaten armies was hunger — the next step was to sort out the great mass and miscellany of units. McClellan ordered generals to his Alexandria headquarters to confer with them personally about what needed to be done. Units were called on for returns so as to appraise the manpower situation. Provost marshals and cavalrymen were sent to round up the stragglers and the wanderers and head them back to their proper commands. Generals and their staffs took hold, building order out of confusion. Discipline and military routine brought cohesion to broken companies and regiments. Such was the progress that as early as September 3 McClellan could write his wife confidently, "All is quiet today, & I think the Capital is safe."[28]

The process of sorting out would take longer. It was apparent to McClellan in those first crucial hours that the most reliable anchor for the defending forces would be Sumner's Second Corps and

Franklin's Sixth, from the Army of the Potomac. Thanks to his delaying efforts over the past few days, both corps were intact and neither had been engaged, nor had they even done very much marching. Indeed, they had hardly been out from under McClellan's control. The Second and Sixth corps therefore became the core around which a new army was to be built.

For the task ahead McClellan was quick to strengthen both these corps. A division of the Fourth Corps, under Darius Couch, newly arrived from the Peninsula, was temporarily attached to Franklin's corps in order to give it three full divisions. A third division was also grafted onto Sumner's corps and put under one of Sumner's brigadiers, William H. French. This new division of French's was a hastily thrown-together patchwork — one brigade of raw levies fresh from Northern recruiting stations, one brigade of garrison troops untested in combat, and a brigade made up of one new regiment and three regiments of veterans from the Shenandoah campaign.

McClellan, however, discovered severe problems with the two Army of the Potomac corps that did fight under Pope. An inspection left him much moved. "It makes my heart bleed to see the poor shattered remains of my noble Army of the Potomac . . . ," he told his wife on September 5. "I hear them calling out to me as I ride among them — 'George — don't leave us again!' 'They *shan't* take you away from us again' etc. etc. I can hardly restrain myself when I see how fearfully they are reduced in numbers. . . ." It was, he thought, further damning evidence in his indictment of Pope and McDowell.

He found Samuel Heintzelman's Third Corps all but wrecked. One of the two divisional commanders, Phil Kearny, had been killed in the fighting at Chantilly on September 1. The other division, under Joe Hooker, was (as Hooker put it) "in no condition to engage the enemy. . . . Kearny's is not much better." The damage was too great for quick repair, and McClellan elected to hold Heintzelman's corps in the Washington defenses and not make it a part of the field army.[29]

Fitz John Porter's Fifth Corps had also been badly hurt in the recent battle, and for the moment McClellan delayed deciding on its future role. Just then holding Washington was the paramount issue, and McClellan wanted Porter, his favorite lieutenant, available for its defense. As it gradually became clear that Lee's objective was north of the Potomac, the redeployment of Porter's corps began — now McClellan wanted Porter at his side should he have to give battle in the field. First, George Sykes's division, made up largely of regulars, was assigned as escort for McClellan's headquarters. A second Fifth Corps division was shifted to another corps and its place taken by a division of new recruits under Andrew Humphreys. In due course Humphreys, along with Porter's remaining division under George Morell, would be called up to the field army in Maryland.

Meanwhile, John Pope was relieved of his command and summoned to the War Department for reassignment — which was to fight the rebellious Sioux in Minnesota. Pope did not leave gracefully. In long angry letters to General Halleck and various other authorities, he raged at the perpetrators of his downfall. "The greatest criminal of all is McClellan," he insisted to Halleck, and he warned, "The *Praetorian system* is as fully developed and in active operation in Washington as it ever was in Ancient Rome."

Before he departed, Pope did manage to create a momentary upheaval in McClellan's command scheme by arranging for charges to be filed against Generals Franklin, Porter, and Charles Griffin, one of Porter's brigade commanders, alleging misconduct in the recent campaign. Pending a court of inquiry in their cases, the War Department ordered all three relieved of their commands. McClellan was quick to use the incident to test the waters with the administration. Seeking a suspension of the order, he went first to his archenemy, Secretary Stanton. As McClellan explained smugly to the president, "The Secretary of War (with whom I had a very pleasant interview) promised me that he would cheerfully agree to anything of this kind that I regarded as necessary." Stanton had apparently decided to grit his teeth and make the best he could of his unhappy situation. With Stanton's agreement in hand, McClellan took his appeal to Mr. Lincoln, asking for the restoration of Franklin, Porter, and Griffin "until I have got through with the present crisis." The president referred him to General Halleck for the final decision. The general-in-chief had no difficulty seeing what course he was expected to take and promptly restored the three generals to their commands.

John Pope, still snarling, pointing to this as a prime example of the Praetorian system at work, went off to his new command. In time, Pope would gain a measure of revenge and see Porter court-martialed and cashiered for misconduct at Second Bull Run. In the immediate September crisis, however, McClellan had gained his way.[30]

Yet he failed to gain his way when on September 7 he petitioned Stanton to allow General Charles P. Stone "to serve with the Army during the impending movements." Stone, falsely accused of disloyalty, had been freed from imprisonment three weeks before, and McClellan wanted him to fill one of the divisional vacancies in the combined armies. The ever-suspicious Stanton would not hear of it, and Stone's once-promising military career continued to languish.[31]

Although not officially announced until September 12, the Army of Virginia actually ceased to exist the moment McClellan took command. Pope's army was never very well unified to begin with. It had been assembled in late June from three independent commands — those of John Charles Frémont, Nathaniel Banks, and Irvin McDowell — that had chased Stonewall Jackson all over the Shenandoah Valley that spring with notable lack of success. Frémont refused to serve under Pope, and by the time of Second Bull Run that command was numbered First Corps of the Army of Virginia, led by Franz Sigel. Neither its commander nor its troops were highly regarded, and when it was renumbered Eleventh Corps, Army of the Potomac, McClellan marked it for the defense of Washington.

Banks's Second Corps under Pope had suffered heavy losses at Cedar Mountain, and when it was rechristened Twelfth Corps in the Army of the Potomac, it was with substantial changes. The corps was judged by McClellan to have enough good troops and subordinate officers to be a part of the field army. Banks, however, was a political general with a very checkered military record, and McClellan sought some way to avoid using him on campaign. His being a major general with considerable seniority suggested a solution, and Banks was "promoted" to command of the Washington defenses when McClellan left the capital to lead the Potomac army into Maryland. In Banks's place went Joseph K. F. Mansfield, an earnest old regular in his first combat command. Alpheus Williams, a first-rate divisional commander, would often be placed in temporary command of the Twelfth Corps — during the Antietam fighting, for example, after Mansfield was killed — but his lack of a West Point education kept him from the permanent corps command he deserved. Williams's two brigades were understrength and had to absorb half a dozen raw new regiments during the army's reorganization. On the way to battle, his fellow divisional commander, George Sears Greene, had to break in new commanders for all three of his brigades. The smallest corps in the army, the Twelfth was fated to see some of the campaign's hardest fighting.

Irvin McDowell's Third Corps, Army of Virginia, was also deemed fit for field service in the Army of the Potomac, and for that purpose was renumbered First Corps. It would make the shift without McDowell, however. He had come under a storm of abuse for Second Bull Run, and was in any case much distrusted by General McClellan. McDowell realized that he had no future under McClellan, and on September 6 he was relieved at his own request. He would demand and receive a court of inquiry to investigate his actions at Second Bull Run. The court found in his favor, but McDowell played no further significant role in the war. "Pope & McDowell have morally killed themselves," McClellan told his wife with satisfaction, "— & are relieved from command — a signal instance of retributive justice."

Perhaps because of his scorn for McDowell, McClellan did not at first rate this newly designated First Corps very highly. He was satisfied in general that the men of this army would fight well, he told Mrs. McClellan. "The only doubtful ones are McD's old troops, who are in bad condition as to discipline & everything else." To remedy this situation, he reached into Heintzelman's corps manning the Washington forts for divisional commander Joe Hooker and made him head of the First Corps. McClellan had learned to respect Hooker's experience and his fighting qualities on the Peninsula, and he predicted that Hooker would soon bring McDowell's troops "out of the kinks, & will make them fight if anyone can." The other important command change in the First Corps was the replacement of Rufus King as a divisional head. King was relieved to await a court of inquiry, which would find him guilty of "grave errors" at Second Bull Run. King's replacement was the veteran Abner Doubleday.[32]

In the ongoing effort to strengthen as many of the army corps as possible before the next fighting began, the First Corps gained the division of Pennsylvania Reserves under much-respected John Reynolds. The Reserves had served capably in the Fifth Corps during the Peninsula campaign, and fought attached to McDowell's corps during the Second Bull Run operations. In a matter of pure political expediency, General Reynolds was soon transferred right out of the campaign. With rumor multiplying Lee's forces and his intentions, Pennsylvania's Governor Andrew Curtin mobilized his state's home guards and demanded from the War Department an experienced Pennsylvania native son to command them. Logically enough, the governor called loudly for the head of the Pennsylvania Reserves. Outspoken Joe Hooker tried to argue otherwise — "a scared Governor ought not to be permitted to destroy the usefulness of an entire division," he said, and added, "the rebels have no more intention of going to Harrisburg than they have of going to heaven."[33] However, the administration could not afford to offend the very influential governor of Pennsylvania, and Reynolds was dispatched to lead the state's militia. Hooker's fears proved unfounded, for Reynolds's replacement as head of the Reserves was the highly capable George Gordon Meade.

Still another piece of the Army of the Potomac needing assembly for the new campaign was the Ninth Corps. This corps, under Ambrose Burnside, had been pulled together in July from the various detachments stationed on the North Carolina and South Carolina coasts. Two divisions, led by Jesse Reno, had been engaged in Pope's operations. A third division came up afterward from Fredericksburg, and a fourth, Jacob Cox's Kanawha Division, joined up from western Virginia. At Chantilly one of these Ninth Corps divisional commanders, Isaac Stevens, had been killed, and Orlando Willcox appointed in his place. On September 3, in a second divisional change, Isaac Rodman replaced John Parke after Parke was named to Burnside's staff. Then, four days later, Samuel Sturgis took over the division of Jesse Reno, and Reno was moved up to the command of the Ninth Corps.

As these Ninth Corps changes suggested, there was little that was routine and nothing seamless about the pace and process of reorganizing the Union forces after Second Bull Run. It had to be accomplished under the extreme time pressures applied by General Lee. Units, ready or not, had to be started northward in pursuit of the enemy. Indeed, changes were still being made after the shooting started. Along the way there were detours and false starts. In a matter of days, Joe Hooker, for example, went from leading a division in Heintzelman's corps to commanding Fifth Corps when Fitz John Porter was suspended from duty, to commanding newly numbered First Corps after Porter was reinstated. Jesse Reno exercised joint command of two Ninth Corps divisions during Pope's operations, was put in charge of Third Corps, Army of Virginia, when McDowell resigned, then returned to command his old Ninth Corps division, and finally rode into Maryland as head of Ninth Corps. All the while, no fewer than thirty-six new regiments were being sorted out and assigned, and before long the roads running northwest from the capital were jammed with recruits hurrying to catch up with their new commands already on the march.

In order to better control the army on the march — which he seems to have assumed from the first that he would lead — McClellan determined to superimpose on it a new set of subcommanders. He recast the Army of the Potomac into a triad structure. The right wing, Hooker's First Corps and Reno's Ninth Corps, he put under Burnside's command. The center, Sumner's Second Corps and Mansfield's Twelfth Corps, was directed by Sumner. The right wing, Franklin's Sixth Corps with Couch's attached Fourth Corps division, was commanded by Franklin. Porter's Fifth Corps was designated the army's reserve.

The Maryland campaign is well remembered as George McClellan's campaign, as indeed it was. But it is often forgotten that it was a campaign in which well over half his troops — new men and men from other commands — were strangers to his battlefield leadership. Only eight of these eighteen divisions had served under McClellan on the Peninsula. General McClellan always liked to speak of the Army of the Potomac as "his" army, yet on this campaign at least it may be better described as in large part an adopted army.

It is in that respect that the burgeoning of morale in the ranks is all the more remarkable. "Everything now is changed," wrote General Meade; "McClellan's star is again in the ascendant, and Pope's has faded away." General Alpheus Williams, who had suffered the many misfortunes of the Shenandoah and Second Bull Run campaigns, was another who sensed the change, and, more, the promise of the new regime. "There will be a great battle or a great skedaddle on the part of the Rebels," he predicted. "I have great confidence that we shall smash them terribly if they stand, more confidence than I have ever had in any movement of the war."[34]

While the president remarked approvingly that McClellan was "working like a beaver" in these hectic days, there still remained for Mr. Lincoln (if not for General McClellan) the agonizing question of who should command the Army of the Potomac when next it went on campaign. With the latest reports locating the Rebel army across the Potomac and well into Maryland, that question now became paramount. General Lee, by his election not to attack the Washington defenses, was forcing a decision on the administration.

On the morning of September 5, for the second time in three

days, the president and General Halleck appeared unannounced at McClellan's quarters on H Street. There was not much in the way of preliminaries. As Halleck recalled it, Lincoln simply announced to McClellan, "General, you will take command of the forces in the field." There was no written order; an implied command function was being confirmed by the commander-in-chief. Although the matter had been under discussion for two or three days, said Halleck, it was entirely the president's decision and that moment was the first he knew of it — officially at least. In any event, for a decision as major as this one, it was delivered utterly without fanfare.

While certainly not revealing his mood to McClellan or Halleck that morning, Lincoln seems once again to have been in a "defiant tone of mind." Soon after leaving McClellan's quarters, he sought to undo this decision he had apparently made against his better judgment. He called in Ambrose Burnside and offered *him* command of the Army of the Potomac. Lincoln had pressed the command of the Potomac army on Burnside once before, following the Peninsula campaign, and Burnside had refused it. With refreshing candor, he admitted he was not general enough for such an important post. In any case, said he, no one was better for it than his friend McClellan. Now, for the second time, General Burnside repeated his litany. That settled the matter. "We must use the tools we have," the president had said, and so it appeared.[35]

As was the case earlier when appointing him to command the forces at Washington, the president deliberately distanced himself from the decision to put McClellan in charge of the field army. Lincoln told Gideon Welles privately, and repeated to the assembled Cabinet, that it was General Halleck, not he, who had sent McClellan on campaign that day. "I could not have done it," Welles quoted him as saying, "for I can never feel confident that he will do anything." He said he acquiesced because he did not want to undermine Halleck's authority.

This is exactly contrary to Halleck's account of the incident, but surely Halleck's version is the correct one. In these weeks the general-in-chief had displayed a continual aversion to making major decisions, and here on September 5 was a decision far too important for him to have taken on his own initiative. It appears that Mr. Lincoln, having earlier assured his rebellious Cabinet that he only intended for McClellan to guard Washington, elected not to deepen his split with the Cabinet by letting it be known that it was he who had sent McClellan off to do battle. Pending the outcome of that battle, the president preferred to let his advisers think the fateful decision was General Halleck's.[36]

For General McClellan, the president's directive, delivered to him personally, to take the field against the enemy host was a dramatic and emotional moment. "Again I have been called upon to save the country," he confided to his wife shortly after Lincoln and Halleck left him that morning; "— the case is desperate, but with God's help I will try unselfishly to do my best & if he wills it accomplish the salvation of the nation." He collected his staff and issued movement orders to his lieutenants, and on Sunday, September 7, scheduled the shift of his headquarters from Washington north into Maryland. Much remained to be done to organize the army and its command, but Lee's invasion left him no choice but to begin the pursuit. The labors would have to continue on the march.

"I leave in a couple of hours to take command of the army in the field . . . & start out after the rebels tomorrow," he wrote Mrs. McClellan that afternoon. The occasion caused the Young Napoleon to feel very Napoleonic: "I have now the entire confidence of the Govt & the love of the army — my enemies are crushed, silent & disarmed — if I defeat the rebels I shall be master of the situation. . . ." Next came a Napoleonic gesture. At the White House, at the home of Secretary of State Seward, and at the offices of Secretary of War Stanton and General-in-Chief Halleck McClellan left calling cards bearing his name and the initials P.P.C., *pour prendre congé,* French military parlance for formal leave-taking to go on campaign.[37]

That evening, out for a stroll along Pennsylvania Avenue, Navy

Secretary Gideon Welles encountered General McClellan and his finely turned-out escort departing for the new seat of war to the north. Spotting Welles, the general signaled a halt and rode over to bid him farewell.

Where was he bound, asked Welles. To take command of the onward movement, McClellan told him.

"Well, *onward,* General, is now the word — the country will expect you to go forward."

"That is my object," said McClellan.

"Success to you, then, General, with all my heart," said Welles.

A quick salute, and then with a clatter and a spatter of dust the general commanding and his escort rushed off for Maryland.[38]

NOTES

1. Adams Hill to Sidney H. Gay, Aug. 31, 1862, Gay Papers, Columbia University.

2. McClellan to Lincoln, Aug. 29, 1862, *Official Records,* 11:1, 98; Lincoln to McClellan, Aug. 29, 1862, McClellan Papers, Library of Congress; Sept. 1, 1862, John Hay, *Inside Lincoln's White House: The Complete Civil War Diary of John Hay,* eds. Michael Burlingame and John R. Turner Ettlinger (Carbondale: Southern Illinois University Press, 1997), 37.

3. Hill to Gay, Aug. 29, 1862, Gay Papers.

4. McClellan to wife, Aug. 10, 29, 1862, George B. McClellan, *The Civil War Papers of George B. McClellan: Selected Correspondence, 1860–1865,* ed. Stephen W. Sears (New York: Ticknor & Fields, 1989), 389, 418–19.

5. Aug. 29, 1862, Salmon P. Chase, *The Salmon P. Chase Papers,* ed. John Niven (Kent, Ohio: Kent State University Press, 1993), vol. 1, 366; McClellan to Halleck, Aug. 28, 1862, *OR* 12:3, 710; McClellan to wife, Aug. 29, 1862, *McClellan Papers,* 417.

6. Cabinet remonstrance (Stanton), Benjamin P. Thomas and Harold M. Hyman, *Stanton: The Life and Times of Lincoln's Secretary of War* (New York: Knopf, 1962), 220.

7. Halleck to Stanton, Aug. 30, 1862, *OR* 12:3, 739; Aug. 30, 1862, *Chase Papers,* vol. 1, 366–67.

8. Aug. 31, 1862, Gideon Welles, *Diary of Gideon Welles,* ed. Howard K. Beale (New York: Norton, 1960), vol. 1, 93–95.

9. Aug. 30, 1862, *Chase Papers,* vol. 1, 367; Pope to Halleck, Aug. 30, 1862, *OR* 12:3, 741.

10. Sept. 1, 1862, Hay, *Inside Lincoln's White House*, 37; McClellan to wife, Aug. 30, 1862, *McClellan Papers*, 419.

11. Sept. 1, 1862, Hay, *Inside Lincoln's White House*, 37–38.

12. Cabinet remonstrance (Bates), Stanton Papers, Library of Congress.

13. Quoted in Allan Nevins, *The War for the Union: War Becomes Revolution, 1862–1863* (New York: Scribner's, 1960), 184; Porter to McClellan, Aug. [31], 1862, *OR* 12:3, 768; McClellan to wife, Aug. 31, 1862, *McClellan Papers*, 423–24.

14. Pope to Halleck, Aug. 31, 1862, *OR* 12:2, 80; Halleck to McClellan, Aug. 31, 1862, *OR* 11:1, 103; McClellan to wife, Sept. 2, 1862, *McClellan Papers*, 428; McClellan to Halleck, Aug. 31, 1862, *OR* 12:3, 773.

15. Sept. 1, 1862, *Chase Papers*, vol. 1, 367; Sept. 1, 1862, Welles, *Diary*, vol. 1, 100–102.

16. McClellan to wife, Sept. 1, 2, 1862, *McClellan Papers*, 427, 428; Sept. 1, 1862, Hay, *Inside Lincoln's White House*, 38.

17. Pope to Halleck, Sept. 1, 1862, *OR* 12:2, 82–83.

18. McClellan, *Report on the Organization of the Army of the Potomac, and of Its Campaigns in Virginia and Maryland* (Washington: GPO, 1864), 183; Sept. 1, 1862, Hay, *Inside Lincoln's White House*, 38; McClellan to Porter, Sept. 1, 1862, *OR* 12:3, 787–88.

19. Porter Second Bull Run memorandum, n.d., McClellan Papers; "Meditation on the Divine Will," [Sept. 1862], Abraham Lincoln, *The Collected Works of Abraham Lincoln*, ed. Roy P. Basler (New Brunswick, N.J.: Rutgers University Press, 1953), vol. 5, 403–4.

20. McClellan to wife, Sept. 2, 1862, *McClellan Papers*, 428.

21. G.O. 122 (draft), Sept. 2, 1862, RG 94, National Archives; G.O. 122, Sept. 2, 1862, *OR* 12:3, 807.

22. Sept. 2, 1862, Welles, *Diary*, vol. 1, 104–6, 102; Sept. 2, 1862, *Chase Papers*, vol. 1, 368–69; Bates notes, Cabinet remonstrance, [Sept. 2, 1862], Lincoln Papers, Library of Congress; Bates to Francis Lieber, Sept. 2, 1862, Lieber Papers, Huntington Library. Neither Welles nor Chase mentions Lincoln's being shown the remonstrance, but that action is mentioned twice in Bates's notes on the Cabinet meeting. Lincoln's seeing it would also explain his unusual emotional stress on this occasion.

23. Sept. [3], 1862, Hay, *Inside Lincoln's White House*, 38–39. Although the Burlingame-Ettlinger edition of the Hay diary dates this entry September 5, that appears to be a misreading. The entry's contents can only refer to a dating of September 3.

24. McClellan to wife, Sept. 2, McClellan to Lincoln, Sept. 2, 1862, *McClellan Papers*, 428, 428–29; McClellan to Pope, Sept. 2, 1862, *OR* 19:1, 38; Halleck to Pope, Sept. 2, 1862, *OR*, 12:3, 797.

25. Porter to McClellan, Aug. [31], Pope to Halleck, Sept. 2, 1862, *OR* 12:3, 768, 797; McClellan to wife, Sept. 2, 1862, *McClellan Papers*, 431.

26. Jacob D. Cox, *Military Reminiscences of the Civil War* (New York: Scribner's, 1900), vol. 1, 245; Stephen M. Weld, *War Diary and Letters of Stephen M. Weld* (Boston: Massachusetts Historical Society, 2nd ed., 1979), 137; William H.

Powell in *Battles and Leaders of the Civil War* (New York: Century, 1887–88), vol. 2, 490.

27. Halleck to McClellan, Lincoln to Halleck, Sept. 3, 1862, *OR* 19:2, 169; McClellan testimony, *Report of the Joint Committee on the Conduct of the War,* vol. 1 (1863), 438–39.

28. McClellan to wife, Sept. 3, 1862, *McClellan Papers,* 431.

29. McClellan to wife, Sept. 5, 1862, *McClellan Papers,* 435; Joseph Hooker to R. B. Marcy, Sept. 5, 1862, *OR* 19:2, 184.

30. Pope to Halleck, Oct. 20, Pope to Richard Yates, Sept. 21, 1862, Pope Papers, Chicago Historical Society; S.O. 223, Sept. 5, McClellan to Halleck, Sept. 6, 1862, *OR* 19:2, 188, 189–90; McClellan to Lincoln, Sept. 6, 1862, *McClellan Papers,* 437–38. See "The Court-Martial of Fitz John Porter" elsewhere in this collection.

31. McClellan to Stanton, Sept. 7, 1862, *McClellan Papers,* 437. See "The Ordeal of General Stone" elsewhere in this collection.

32. McClellan to wife, Sept. 7, 12, 1862, *McClellan Papers,* 437–38, 450.

33. Hooker to Seth Williams, Sept. 12, 1862, *OR* 19:2, 273–74.

34. George G. Meade, *The Life and Letters of George Gordon Meade* (New York: Scribner's, 1913), vol. 1, 307; Alpheus S. Williams, *From the Cannon's Mouth: The Civil War Letters of General Alpheus S. Williams,* ed. Milo M. Quaife (Detroit: Wayne State University Press, 1959), 120–21.

35. Sept. 1, 1862, Hay, *Inside Lincoln's White House,* 38; Halleck, Burnside testimony, *Report of Joint Committee,* vol. 1 (1863), 451, 453, 650; Orville H. Browning, *The Diary of Orville Hickman Browning,* eds. Theodore C. Pease and James G. Randall (Springfield: Illinois State Historical Library, 1925), vol. 1, 589–90. Burnside reached Washington the morning of September 5 and reported to McClellan; Halleck would tell Pope he remembered seeing Burnside leaving McClellan's quarters just as he and Lincoln arrived there that morning (Pope to V. B. Horton, Mar. 25, 1863, New-York Historical Society). It is therefore evident that it was only after seeing McClellan that Lincoln offered Burnside the command.

36. Sept. 8, 10, 12, 1862, Welles, *Diary,* vol. 1, 116, 122, 124; Pope to V. B. Horton, Mar. 25, 1863, New-York Historical Society; Halleck testimony, *Report of Joint Committee,* vol. 1 (1863), 451, 453.

37. McClellan to wife, Sept. 7, 1862, *McClellan Papers,* 437–38; McClellan in *Battles and Leaders,* vol. 2, 552.

38. Sept. 7, 1862, Welles, *Diary,* vol. 1, 114–15.

[5]

Last Words on the Lost Order

President Lincoln and General McClellan,
on the Antietam battlefield

THE LOST ORDER is one of those Civil War incidents that, when viewed in retrospect, seems to expand almost exponentially into a pivotal event, a golden opportunity, a turning point. Francis W. Palfrey, author of the first full account of the Battle of Antietam, in 1882, stated the case with stark simplicity. The Lost Order, said Palfrey, "placed the Army of Northern Virginia at the mercy of McClellan. . . ."[1]

At the time, however, there was an astonishing lack of interest in how the Lost Order was lost, in how it was found, even in what it meant in the larger scheme of things. To be sure, it proved indeed to be a pivotal event, one on which the course of the war turned, yet it was some time before that notion sank in. Even now it remains a story marked by misunderstanding and a certain mystery.

Special Orders No. 191, to give the Lost Order its official designation, was key to Robert E. Lee's strategic plan for the fall campaign of 1862. He composed S.O. 191 on Tuesday, September 9, at his headquarters at Frederick in western Maryland, where he was resting his invading army and contemplating nothing less than winning independence for the Confederacy. General Lee was on a winning streak. In June he had beaten George McClellan in front of Richmond. In August he had beaten John Pope at Bull Run in front of Washington. Now, in September, learning that McClellan was back in command and opposing him, he fully intended to deliver a knockout blow on Northern soil. His intuitive reading of his opponent was an important element in his planning. Only the day before he was heard to describe McClellan as "an able general but a very cautious one." (On another occasion, he labeled McClellan "timid" rather than "cautious.") Lee's entire design, as he worked it out that Tuesday, was carefully calculated with General McClellan's shortcomings in mind.

It was Lee's intention, in crossing the Potomac into Maryland, to draw the Army of the Potomac after him and away from its Washington base. In due course, somewhere off to the north and west in the Cumberland Valley of Pennsylvania, he would maneuver McClellan into a finish fight. He was very clear on that point. "I went into Maryland to give battle," he said in recalling the campaign after the war; had it all gone as he planned, "I would have fought and crushed him."[2]

To clear the way for this march westward, Lee had to establish a new line of communications back to Virginia through the Shenandoah Valley, and to do that he had to dispose of the Federal garrisons guarding the Shenandoah at Harper's Ferry and Martinsburg. S.O. 191 was designed for that purpose. He assigned six of his nine infantry divisions to the operation, under the overall command of Stonewall Jackson. In thus dividing his army in the face of superior forces Lee was violating the military canon, but it gave him no concern. He had done it twice before, against McClellan in June and against Pope in August, and twice it had brought him victory. The Federals were reported to be advancing from Washington with great caution and were several days' march away. Jackson should be back and the army reunited before McClellan caught on to what was happening. In ten days they would be in Pennsylvania, said Lee, with "a very good army, and one that I think will be able to give a good account of itself."[3]

During the afternoon of September 9 the Confederate headquarters staff busied itself making copies of S.O. 191 for the generals involved and dispatching them by courier. The army was well closed up, and there was no particular challenge in this procedure. Each copy was on a single sheet, written front and back, and listed in detail the assignment of every major command in the Army of Northern Virginia. Each was marked "Confidential" and signed "by command of Gen. R. E. Lee" with the name of R. H. Chilton, Lee's chief of staff. Each was delivered in an envelope that was to be signed by the recipient and returned to headquarters by the courier as proof of delivery.[4] All the deliveries but one were made without event. The exception was the copy addressed to General D. H. Hill, which someone at headquarters had wrapped around three cigars for the general, who was known to enjoy a good smoke. The packet with Chilton's copy of S.O. 191 never reached Hill or anyone at his headquarters with the authority to sign for it.

What General Hill received instead that day was a copy of S.O. 191 in the handwriting of Stonewall Jackson himself. Thus far in the campaign Hill had been under Jackson's orders, but now he was reassigned to be the army's rear guard. Consequently, when Jackson received the copy of S.O. 191 addressed to him, he made a copy of it to inform his erstwhile subordinate of the change. Hill thus received his new orders from the same source he had been receiving orders for the past week, and thought nothing of it — and so everyone on Chilton's list now had his orders. For some reason that no one at Lee's headquarters could ever explain, no alarm was raised on September 9 over the lack of a delivery receipt for the copy of S.O. 191 Chilton had addressed to D. H. Hill. No one in the Confederate chain of command that Tuesday suspected, as Hill later phrased it, "that there was something wrong in the manner of transmitting it. . . ."[5]

The next morning, September 10, at his customary starting time of first light, Stonewall Jackson led the way westward on the National Road out of Frederick and over South Mountain. Through the day the rest of the army followed, division by division, until only a cavalry picket remained at Frederick. Over the next three days, three of Jackson's divisions, varying their march route from what was specified in S.O. 191, crossed the Potomac back into Virginia at Williamsport and, pushing the Yankee garrison from Martinsburg ahead of them, closed in on Harper's Ferry from the west. Jackson's two other columns — adhering exactly to the plan — marched by separate routes to complete the encirclement of Harper's Ferry.

Meanwhile, in a second change from S.O. 191's order of march, Lee took James Longstreet's two divisions with him to wait at Hagerstown, near the Pennsylvania border. D. H. Hill's single division remained at Boonsboro, on the National Road beyond South Mountain, to act as rear guard. Jeb Stuart's cavalry patrols, continuing to watch the Federal movements, reported nothing untoward. Except for the fact that it was running twenty-four hours behind schedule, the Harper's Ferry expedition was proceeding smoothly.[6]

"As soon as I find out where to strike I will be after them without an hour's delay," General McClellan had promised Washington when he moved into Maryland on the trail of the enemy. Finding out where to strike, however, was proving uncommonly difficult. His cavalry under Alfred Pleasonton was unable to break through Stuart's troopers for a firsthand look at the Army of Northern Virginia. Pleasonton's intelligence-gathering was therefore limited to interrogating Rebel prisoners and deserters and questioning civilians who had picked up what they knew from Confederate soldiers passing through their towns or stopping at their farms. The result was an intelligence babel. Reports handed to McClellan had enemy columns marching toward every point of the compass — even eastward straight toward him, which caused him to halt his own columns for a time and prepare to receive an attack. The Confederates planted stories wherever they went, so that Stonewall Jackson was "reliably reported" to be where he was and where he wasn't in about equal measure.

Mixed in with these tales from talkative clergymen and boastful prisoners and credulous country folk was some highly accurate intelligence, but all of it arrived at headquarters in an indiscriminate jumble. McClellan could make little sense of it. As late as

September 12 it was his best guess, he told his wife, that "secesh is skedadelling & I don't think I can catch him. . . . I begin to think that he is making off to get out of the scrape by recrossing the river at Williamsport. . . . He evidently don't want to fight me — for some reason or other." On that day, as on previous days, the average march in the Army of the Potomac was just six miles.

McClellan was especially befuddled about the size of the enemy's army. It was an article of faith with him that he was fated to be the underdog in any contest with Lee, and the intelligence reaching him in Maryland reinforced that delusion. He finally settled on a count for "the gigantic rebel army before us" of 120,000 men, "numerically superior to ours by at least twenty-five percent." That this calculation tripled the size of Lee's army was a truth quite beyond his imagining. On Saturday morning, September 13, when he arrived in Frederick with the Potomac army's headquarters, he was acting every inch the cautious captain that General Lee believed him to be.[7]

The Federal Twelfth Corps also advanced to Frederick that morning, with the 27th Indiana regiment in the lead. The column splashed across the Monocacy River at Crum's Ford and went on two miles along a back road to the outskirts of town. There the order came back to halt and make camp. Company F of the 27th appropriated a clover field alongside the road for its bivouac. Later it would be said that this was the field where D. H. Hill's division had camped during the occupation of Frederick, but that was pure speculation. Hill's division had actually been posted several miles away on the Monocacy. There is no certain evidence that any Confederate troops had camped in this particular clover field.

Company F had the odd distinction of having the largest contingent of tall men in the 27th Indiana — two-thirds of the company stood six feet or more — and the unique distinction of having the tallest man in the entire Union army, Captain David Van Buskirk, who was half an inch shy of being seven feet tall. Corporal Barton W. Mitchell was about to give Company F another mark of distinction.

Corporal Mitchell was himself unusual in that he was much

older than almost all his fellow soldiers. He was a man in his forties, a farmer in civilian life from Putnam County, Indiana, who had volunteered to go to war in 1861 despite having a wife and four children to support. Patriotism ran strongly in the Mitchell family; his oldest son had recently enlisted in another Indiana regiment.

Company F stacked arms and Mitchell was relaxing and chatting with Private John Campbell when he noticed a bulky envelope in the clover nearby. Curious, he picked it up and found that it contained a document of some sort wrapped around three cigars. The cigars were a find enough, but Corporal Mitchell had the intelligence and the maturity to investigate as well the document they were wrapped in. While he read it through, Private Campbell (as he later testified) "looked over his shoulder and read it with him." The paper was marked "Confidential" and was headed "Hd Qrs Army of Northern Va Sept 9th 1862 Special Orders No 191." It was studded with names and places Mitchell immediately recognized: Jackson, Longstreet, Stuart, Lee, Harper's Ferry, Martinsburg, Boonsboro. It was signed by R. H. Chilton and labeled "For Maj Gen D. H. Hill, Comdg Division." By sheer chance, by fantastic good fortune, Corporal Mitchell had in his hand the missing copy of S.O. 191. Furthermore, he recognized it as something important.[8]

Mitchell took his find to his first sergeant, John M. Bloss, and together they went to the company commander, Captain Peter Kopp. Kopp took one look at the paper and told them to find the regimental commander, Colonel Silas Colgrove. Colgrove read it and, as he later said, "was at once satisfied that it was genuine." He sent Mitchell and Bloss back to their company — presumably with thanks, but apparently not with the cigars; Colgrove's recollection is the last mention of them, and who finally smoked them will probably never be known — and set off for higher command.

Colgrove skipped brigade and division, the next links in the chain of command, and rode straight to Twelfth Corps headquarters and Brigadier General Alpheus S. Williams. Williams and his adjutant, Colonel Samuel E. Pittman, scanned the paper. As Colgrove remembered their conversation, Pittman said he had served with R. H. Chilton in the old army in Michigan before the war and recognized his handwriting, but Colgrove's recollection was faulty. Pittman had entered the army only in September 1861, six months after Chilton resigned his U.S. commission to join the Confederacy. By Pittman's own postwar recollection, he simply recognized Chilton's name as the army paymaster stationed in Detroit when he had lived there. In any event, General Williams was convinced that the order was genuine. He sent Pittman with it to army headquarters, along with a brief note for General McClellan: "I enclose a Special Order of Gen. Lee commanding Rebel forces which was found on the field where my corps is encamped. It is a document of interest & is also thought genuine." In a footnote Williams added, "The Document was found by a corporal of 27 Ind. Rgt, Col. Colgrove, Gordon's Brigade."[9]

Colonel Pittman delivered the envelope containing the Lost Order, along with General Williams's covering note, to McClellan's adjutant, Seth Williams. McClellan was in his headquarters tent discussing details of the army's occupation of Frederick with a delegation of local citizens when adjutant Williams interrupted to hand him the find. McClellan scanned the paper and the note with it and suddenly, according to one of his visitors, threw up his hands and exclaimed, "Now I know what to do!"

This description of his reaction is entirely creditable in light of the telegram he sent a few minutes later, at noon, to President Lincoln. No doubt he first ushered his visitors out with the explanation that he had urgent army business to attend to. Usually McClellan's dispatches to Lincoln were stiff and militarily formal, for usually the two were at odds over one thing or another, but this dispatch was like none he had sent before. "I think Lee has made a gross mistake and that he will be severely punished for it," he boasted. ". . . I hope for a great success if the plans of the Rebels remain unchanged. . . . I have all the plans of the Rebels and will catch them in their own trap if my men are equal to the emergency." In his elation he became almost giddy, presenting his respects to Mrs. Lincoln and exclaiming over the enthusiastic greeting he had received from the ladies of Frederick that morning. "Will send you trophies," he promised.[10]

What so excited McClellan about the Lost Order was its revelation that Lee had divided his army into four widely scattered segments, at least two of which appeared to be so isolated from the others as to be fair game for destruction. (In fact, the Rebel army was even better game than he imagined, for Longstreet's move to Hagerstown had divided it into five segments, the largest of which were twenty-five miles and a river crossing apart.) No general could even dream of knowing more about his opponent's most secret plan — McClellan knew Lee's objective, knew his dispositions for taking that objective, knew his routes of march, knew his timetable, and, most important, knew how vulnerable he was to a strategy of divide and conquer.

There can be no doubt that McClellan grasped his unique good fortune. That evening he would take the Lost Order out of his pocket and tell General John Gibbon, "Here is a paper with which if I cannot whip Bobbie Lee, I will be willing to go home. . . . Castiglione will be nothing to it."[11] Castiglione was the 1796 military classic in which Napoleon crushed Wurmser's divided and overextended Austrian army. To act on his opportunity, however, required General McClellan for once in his life to throw caution to the winds. Time was critical; the Harper's Ferry operation described in S.O. 191 was already in its fourth day.

His time clock of opportunity began ticking at noon on September 13, when he sent his exuberant telegram to President Lincoln. Sounds of gunfire could be heard from Harper's Ferry, indicating that the Confederates were still engaged there. The Lost Order told McClellan that one Rebel division had crossed the Potomac to invest Harper's Ferry on the south and east. Two more divisions, under command of Lafayette McLaws, were still in Maryland, holding Maryland Heights overlooking the town on the north. Jackson's "command," its forces unspecified, was according to S.O. 191 at Martinsburg, eight miles beyond the Potomac, to prevent the Yankee garrison from escaping to the west. At Boonsboro, across South Mountain from Frederick, the Lost Order placed D. H. Hill's division and Longstreet's "command," his forces like Jackson's unspecified. Just then at Frederick McClellan had four army corps — thirteen divisions — with which to cross South Mountain and fall on Hill and Longstreet at Boonsboro, fifteen miles distant. A half-dozen miles south of Frederick was the army's left wing, three divisions under William Franklin; it too was fifteen miles distant from its potential quarry, McLaws's two divisions at Maryland Heights.

It might be supposed that any commanding general presented with such an opportunity would put his troops on the march without a moment's delay, taking advantage of the seven hours of daylight remaining that Saturday to close up to the base of South Mountain and so be ready to force the passes in the range at dawn the next morning. General McClellan marched to a different drummer. He could never act until all plans were complete, all details accounted for, all potential surprises disarmed before they occurred, and the more he studied the Lost Order the more uneasy he became. He later testified that he gave no thought to its being a *ruse de guerre* — it explained too much to be a plant, and General Williams's note suggested that it was discovered by accident rather than by enemy design — yet he began having increasingly worrisome second thoughts about it. He must ponder the whole matter before acting.[12]

The Lost Order confirmed some of the intelligence received over the past few days, yet seemed to contradict other reports. He had been told of a substantial Rebel force at Hagerstown, and of a major crossing of the Potomac at Williamsport, but neither place was on the routes of march specified in S.O. 191. He had told Mr. Lincoln he hoped for success "if the plans of the Rebels remain unchanged." Now it looked as if they had been changed. He worried that question for three hours, then at 3:00 P.M. sent a copy of S.O. 191 to his cavalry chief, General Pleasonton, with instructions to find out if the routes of march it contained had actually been followed. Pleasonton knew little enough about the matter but replied that he thought Lee's instructions had been adhered to. That was the wrong answer, but it reassured McClellan; thereafter he regarded everything in the Lost Order as gospel. With that settled, McClellan determined to begin his movements the next morning, September 14. "My general idea," he told General Franklin, "is to cut the enemy in two & beat him in detail." Reaching that decision cost eighteen hours of his golden opportunity.[13]

The other factor giving him pause that September 13 was the enemy's numbers. In a dispatch to Washington that night he listed eight generals in Lee's army, commanding a total of "120,000 men or more . . . & they outnumber me when united." From the Lost Order and other sources he knew that six of these generals led single divisions, and that gave him a problem with his arithmetic. His solution was to give the two "commands" of Jackson and Longstreet a kind of "grand corps" rating, so that in advancing across South Mountain to do battle with Longstreet and Hill at Boonsboro he anticipated meeting a substantial force. That prospect instilled in him further caution. Give me two days' hard marching, he told General Gibbon that evening, and "I will put Lee in a position he will find hard to get out of." By that timetable he budgeted an additional forty-eight hours to gain his reward from the Lost Order. If the loss of Lee's orders "was a shabby trick for fate to play us," as Confederate Porter Alexander put it, fate contrived to even the balance by handing S.O. 191 to General McClellan.[14]

It might also be supposed that army headquarters, with General Williams's note as a guide, would have made an effort to identify the discoverer of the Lost Order and to reward him — a field promotion, a mention in dispatches, perhaps nomination for the newly authorized Medal of Honor. Instead, the discovery went entirely unremarked; literally no one gave it another thought. When he was asked about it after the war, General McClellan confessed that he knew next to nothing about how the Lost Order reached him.

Only in 1886, twenty-four years after the event, was an account of the finding published in *The Century* magazine, whose editors had sought the details from Colonel Colgrove for their "Battles and Leaders of the Civil War" series. There for the first time Barton Mitchell was identified as the finder of S.O. 191 — and in Colgrove's account, demoted to private. In 1892 Sergeant Bloss, to whom Mitchell had taken his find, further diminished Mitchell's role by manufacturing an account in which *he* was the actual discoverer — he had merely asked Mitchell to pick up the envelope and hand it to him. Bloss had risen in the world to be a school superintendent and his self-importance rose as well.[15]

This credit, imperfect as it was, came too late for poor Corporal Mitchell. For him the Lost Order was simply an ill omen. The fruit of his discovery, the Battle of Antietam, was fought four days later, and in it he suffered a severe leg wound from which he would never really recover. (Antietam cut a terrible swath through the 27th Indiana — 209 casualties — and especially through Company F. Of those linked to the Lost Order, Corporal Mitchell, his friend Private Campbell, and Sergeant Bloss were all wounded. Captain Kopp, to whom they took the find, was killed. In all, Company F suffered 40 percent casualties at Antietam.) After eight months in the hospital Mitchell was forced by disability to transfer to the ambulance corps. After his discharge in 1864 his disability grew progressively worse until it left him bedridden. He died early in 1868, not yet fifty. His widow did not succeed in obtaining a survivor's pension until 1890. The army's Pension Office was not moved to act any sooner on her claim by the fact that it was her husband who had found the famous Lost Order.[16]

If it is clear enough how S.O. 191 was found, it is still not clear exactly how it was lost. One certainty is that D. H. Hill was innocent in the matter. Hill spent a quarter of a century vigorously defending himself against those who tried to make him the scapegoat. In 1867, for example, a Richmond editor, E. A. Pollard, charged him with tossing the order away in a fit of petulance at its contents. In 1876 the Count of Paris, pretender to the French throne, wrote in his history of the Civil War that Hill carelessly left his copy of S.O. 191 on a table in his headquarters. In 1884 former Confederate general Bradley T. Johnson retailed the story that the paper was seen to fall from Hill's pocket as he rode through Frederick. Where Pollard and Johnson and the count heard these tales is anyone's guess. All of them were demolished by publication of the *Century* article and by Hill's repeated declaration that he never saw the copy of S.O. 191 that the Federals found; he had instead, and carefully preserved, the copy Jackson sent him.[17]

What these theories (and others like them, then and since) fail to account for is the fact that the Chilton copy of S.O. 191 addressed to Hill was found by Corporal Mitchell still in its envelope — the envelope the courier was supposed to return to headquarters as proof of delivery. When Hill learned after the war that McClellan had preserved in his private papers both the Lost Order and the envelope in which it left Lee's headquarters that September 9, he put the case with perfect clarity: "If the envelope was with it," he told McClellan, "the paper was never received."[18] The fact that the order was found not in Hill's former encampment but some miles from it is further evidence that it never reached its destination. Finally, the fact that the discovery represented the workings of pure chance — that the envelope containing S.O. 191 and the three cigars could just as easily have been overlooked as it lay in that clover field outside Frederick on September 13 — is evidence that its loss was as much an accident as its finding.

Before the account of Mitchell's discovery appeared, General Hill suggested treachery as the cause of its loss. He was supported in this by his wartime adjutant, Major J. W. Ratchford, who recalled that soon afterward, during the Harper's Ferry operation, a headquarters courier was unmasked as a Yankee spy and hanged from the nearest tree. The problem with this treachery theory is the place were the Lost Order was found. Surely a traitor to the Confederate cause would have devised a better way to make certain so important a piece of secret intelligence as S.O. 191 reached General McClellan than to drop it in a meadow alongside a back road — not even along one of the major highways in the region — in the hope that at some future time the Federals might just come that way, discover the packet, recognize its importance, and get it to the high command in time to do some good. It is impossible to imagine so naive a spy, or (as it turned out) one so lucky.[19]

In 1897 former Confederate cavalryman Thomas L. Rosser, in delivering a talk on the late war, offered the speculation that the party guilty of losing the Lost Order had been a member of Stonewall Jackson's staff. While Rosser thereby absolved D. H. Hill of guilt, his account is seriously muddled as to fact and fails to overcome the illogic of anyone from Jackson's headquarters having any reason to handle the copy Chilton had addressed to Hill.

Far and away the most likely explanation for the loss of S.O. 191 is also the simplest one — that it was accidentally dropped by the courier from Lee's headquarters while on his way to deliver it to D. H. Hill. The identity of that courier remains a mystery. A dozen years later, explaining to Jefferson Davis the routine of delivering such a dispatch to Hill, Chilton admitted, "I could not of course say positively that I had sent any particular courier to him after such a lapse of time."[20]

Whoever the courier may have been, at some point he would have discovered his loss and probably backtracked in search of it. Perhaps he continued his search as far as Hill's headquarters and learned that Hill already had his orders (unbeknownst to the courier, from Stonewall Jackson). Perhaps (greatly relieved) he therefore assumed that the envelope he had lost had been found and delivered. However that may be, back at army headquarters the courier must have invented some excuse for lacking a delivery receipt; perhaps he even forged a receipt. Possibly in this busy time headquarters was careless about routine and did not carefully check delivery receipts. That is not unlikely, for Robert Chilton was not known for being meticulous about his paperwork. On the Peninsula and, later, at Chancellorsville he made serious errors in the transmission of General Lee's orders. In time he would leave Lee's service to return to Richmond's army bureaucracy.[21]

However it happened, it must have happened something like this, and the courier, thinking or hoping that no real harm had been done, covered his tracks well enough to escape detection and punishment. Just then he was the only one who knew that anything had gone amiss. No general on Chilton's list would make complaint about not receiving his marching orders. Remarkably, there is no record of General Lee or anyone at his headquarters ever investigating the matter, even after, some months later, it was learned that a copy of S.O. 191 had reached enemy hands. Ultimate responsibility for not discovering the loss the day it occurred, on September 9, lay with Colonel Chilton. General Lee realized this well enough, and it may be one reason he began easing Chilton out of his chief-of-staff duties.

Nothing in the tangled story of the Lost Order is more misunderstood than just when General Lee did discover that his opponent had a copy of S.O. 191. Many historians have assumed, following the lead of Douglas Southall Freeman in *Lee's Lieutenants,* that within some twelve hours of the time McClellan was handed the Lost Order, Lee learned that he had it. This is a false assumption, however. One of the highest trump cards that fate dealt General McClellan that day was the advantage of surprise, for at no time during the Maryland campaign did Lee (or any other Confederate general) know about the Lost Order. It was not until January 1863 at the earliest, and probably several months after that, that he learned of the loss, and the finding, of S.O. 191.

When he did learn it, it was through the Northern press. The Lost Order first appeared in print (based on a copy made by General McClellan himself) in the New York *Journal of Commerce* on January 1, 1863. Then, in March, McClellan testified to a congressional committee that "at Frederick we found the original order issued to General D. H. Hill by direction of General Lee, which gave the orders of march for their whole army, and developed their intentions." A month later McClellan's testimony was put into print by the committee and by the newspapers. General Lee, always a careful reader of Northern papers passed through the lines, thus learned for the first time of the loss of S.O. 191.[22]

However, Lee might very well have learned exactly that fact just forty-eight hours after General McClellan did. In yet another strange twist to the story, the Northern press was guilty of exposing the whole secret of the Lost Order to the enemy. This greatest intelligence coup of the war was revealed on the front page of the nation's largest newspaper. In its morning edition of Monday, September 15, 1862, two days after Corporal Mitchell's discovery, the *New York Herald* printed a bulletin, datelined September 14, from its Washington correspondent: "Officers who left Frederick this morning report that a general order of General Lee was found there, directing that two columns of the rebel army should proceed by way of Middletown, one of them destined for Greencastle, Pa., with all possible expedition, and the other to proceed by way of Williamsport or Shepherdstown, at discretion, to engage the Union forces at Harper's Ferry."

Earlier in the war, Northern journalists and editors had on occasion been careless about military secrets, but this leak was something special. It took place in special circumstances. The War Department, in its anger over press reporting of the recent Second Bull Run campaign, had instituted a press blackout. Correspondents were ordered out of the army in the field. Censorship of any news sent by telegraph grew oppressive. Government handouts were empty of news content. The consequences were chaotic. The press gag demonstrated that in a news vacuum rumor will rush in to fill the void. The papers were reduced to filling their pages, in this time of crisis and Confederate invasion, with whatever reporters could lay their hands on, from any source, and there was no knowing where rumor ended and truth began. It is therefore not surprising that the *Herald*'s Washington correspondent would jump at the chance to report whatever these talkative officers just in from Frederick had to say. The press blackout erased all the rules.[23]

The officers from Frederick had to be on McClellan's staff, or had close access to his staff, to know about the finding of S.O. 191. Even though their reporting of the Lost Order's contents was somewhat garbled, there is no question that if General Lee had seen the *Herald* for that Monday he would have immediately recognized that his Special Orders No. 191 had been compromised.

But he did not see it. During this invasion of enemy territory, he had outrun his usual sources for collecting Northern newspapers. He was also ill served that day by the Confederate signal corps' "secret line" that was supposed to gather intelligence from New York and Washington papers; somehow it failed to turn up this nugget in the *Herald*.[24] By all rights, then, courtesy of the North's largest newspaper, General Lee should have discovered before the fighting began at Antietam that his opponent knew all about his divided forces. That he did not is further evidence that the fates seemed to be smiling on General McClellan.

The confusion among historians about when Lee *did* learn of the Lost Order stems from a misreading of what Lee said about the matter after the war. In 1868, in reviewing the Maryland campaign, Lee recalled that on the night of September 13–14 he received a dispatch from Jeb Stuart with information from a civilian who had been at General McClellan's headquarters in Frederick that morning. The civilian, a Confederate sympathizer, said that during their meeting McClellan was handed a paper by an aide and seemed excited by it and exclaimed, "Now I know what to do!" The man hurried off to find Stuart, to tell him of McClellan's response and to report that something — he could not say exactly what — was energizing the Federals; on his way, he had seen Yankee troops advancing beyond Frederick toward South Mountain. (In fact this was only a routine movement, ordered some hours earlier, but the civilian tied it to what he had seen at McClellan's headquarters.) Stuart reported this development to Lee at Hagerstown.[25]

In recounting the story, Lee phrased it as McClellan's reaction to being handed the Lost Order, which was true enough but was a fact supplied by Lee from hindsight knowledge. The amateur spy did not know — could not have known — that the paper McClellan read in his presence was a copy of Lee's plans. Neither McClellan nor his staff would have been so careless of security as to reveal that fact to a civilian, particularly a civilian in Maryland, where loyalties were known to be divided. (That reticence evaporated, however, when certain staff members talked the next day to the *New York Herald.*) Stuart made no mention in his official report of any Confederate plan, lost or found; Lee said nothing of it to Longstreet that night when they discussed their next move. Most telling is the testimony of Lee's aide Charles Marshall, who was explicit about the matter. "I remember perfectly," Marshall would tell D. H. Hill, "that until we saw that report" — McClellan's March 1863 report of the finding of the Lost Order — "Gen. Lee frequently expressed his inability to understand the sudden change in McClellan's tactics which took place after we left Frederick. He regarded the finding of that order by McClellan as a complete and satisfactory explanation of the change."[26]

As important as anything else, Lee's actions over the next several days were hardly those of a general who knew his opponent had all his plans. Rather than ordering Jackson to give up the siege of Harper's Ferry and find safer ground, he allowed him to continue it. Rather than instantly marching from Hagerstown to block the South Mountain passes, he waited until morning to move. Rather than prudently withdrawing across the Potomac to unite his scattered forces, he ran an immense bluff by standing at Sharpsburg and then by challenging McClellan to fight there. Lee's actions were simply those of a general reacting to an opponent who was now advancing (as he told Jefferson Davis) "more rapidly than was convenient. . . ."[27] To be sure, the Army of Northern Virginia survived these various perils to fight again on other fields, but it survived only because McClellan threw away his golden opportunity. However little General Lee thought of McClellan's abilities, not even he would have dared to count on that happening.

On Sunday, September 14, D. H. Hill had time enough to cobble together a defense of Turner's Gap in South Mountain, with assistance late in the day from Longstreet's column from Hagerstown, against McClellan's belated offensive. To the south, at Crampton's Gap, Franklin's equally sluggish advance got no farther that day than the crest of South Mountain. McClellan proclaimed a great victory, but his dream of cutting the enemy in two and beating him in detail — of winning another Castiglione — was fading rapidly.

The next day, September 15, Lee with Hill and Longstreet fell back behind Antietam Creek at Sharpsburg. Lee took his stand that day with hardly 15,000 men of all arms, but McClellan's pursuit was slow and cautious. According to the headquarters journal kept by his brother, Arthur McClellan, the general commanding believed he was facing 50,000 Rebels.[28] Franklin's feeble effort to advance toward beleaguered Harper's Ferry was blocked by McLaws. On September 15, too, General McClellan put the Lost Order aside. Whatever advantage he thought he had gained from it, he now decided its usefulness was at an end.

The narrator of this final twist in the Lost Order story is Captain William Palmer, who visited McClellan's field headquarters a mile or so from Antietam Creek the night of the fifteenth. Palmer, a scout for Pennsylvania's militia forces and easily the best intelligence gatherer on the Federal side, had an inside look at the view from headquarters. General McClellan, Palmer reported to Pennsylvania's governor, believed that the Harper's Ferry garrison had surrendered to the Rebels that morning, and that by nightfall "Jackson re-enforced Lee at Sharpsburg. . . . Rebels appear encouraged at arrival of their re-enforcements."[29] By McClellan's train of thought, the scattered elements of the Army of Northern Virginia were now reunited, he was once more outnumbered, and the Lost Order was no longer of any use as a blueprint for his opponent's operations.

This final twist is the final irony as well, for it was thanks to the Lost Order that General Lee was granted a final reprieve. McClellan concluded, despite conflicting evidence, that Jackson spent the siege of Harper's Ferry on guard duty at Martinsburg, where S.O. 191 placed him, and that on learning of the garrison's surrender on the morning of the fifteenth he made the easy march from Martinsburg to Sharpsburg to join Lee. To be sure, McClellan had not a scrap of evidence to confirm this — he had none for there was none; even the cheering he supposed had greeted Jackson's arrival was merely Lee's men reacting to news of the capture of Harper's Ferry — but simply deduced it from his blind faith in the Lost Order. The first of Jackson's footsore troops did not reach Sharpsburg until noon on September 16, and they continued trailing into the lines throughout the afternoon. Even then, just three of Jackson's divisions were at hand. Fully a third of Lee's army was still absent. Two more divisions would reach the field at dawn on September 17, the day McClellan finally determined to offer battle, and the last division would arrive only at the last moment during the battle. Meanwhile, General McClellan spent September 16 pondering the daunting odds facing him and letting his golden opportunity slip farther and farther away.

In the end, the single fruit left him from the finding of the Lost Order was the Battle of Antietam. For four days McClellan had wasted glittering chances to divide and conquer the Army of Northern Virginia, yet at Antietam he still had odds greatly in his favor. By Lee's own testimony, he fought there with fewer than 40,000 men, leaving him outnumbered two to one. Lee's position was a good one, but his back was to the Potomac, inviting almost certain destruction if his lines were breached and he had to fall back. But at this climactic moment General McClellan could not rid himself of his fears and his delusions; on September 17 he could not force himself to seek victory for fear of courting defeat. And so it ended: in the bloodiest single day of the war he did not win the victory, but he was not defeated, either.

After defiantly holding his lines for another day, Lee returned with his battered army to Virginia. At Antietam he had inflicted one-fifth more casualties than he suffered, and in the Maryland campaign as a whole he showed a profit — 27,000 Federals (including the Harper's Ferry garrison) and substantial captures of arms and supplies against a loss of 14,000. But he failed to achieve the task he had set for himself. At best he might claim Antietam as a narrow tactical victory, at worst as a draw, but he did not win a campaign decisive for the war.

That, finally, is how the impact of the Lost Order is measured.

Lee termed the loss of S.O. 191 "a great calamity"; to his mind, it was of crucial importance to the Maryland campaign because it enabled General McClellan "to discover my whereabouts . . . and caused him so to act as to force a battle on me before I was ready for it." Had S.O. 191 never been lost, it is permissible to speculate (as General Lee speculated) that sometime during the latter half of September 1862 a great battle would have been fought in the Cumberland Valley of Pennsylvania — the Battle of Greencastle, perhaps, or the Battle of Chambersburg, or even the Battle of Gettysburg — in which "I would have had all my troops reconcentrated . . . , stragglers up, men rested and I *intended then to attack McClellan. . . .*" It was "impossible to say that victory would have certainly resulted," Lee admitted, but on one point he was clear: "the loss of the dispatch changed the character of the campaign."[30]

NOTES

1. Francis W. Palfrey, *The Antietam and Fredericksburg* (New York: Scribner's, 1882), 22.

2. John G. Walker in *Battles and Leaders of the Civil War* (New York: Century, 1887–88), vol. 2, 606; E. C. Gordon to William Allan, Nov. 18, 1886, in Douglas Southall Freeman, *Lee's Lieutenants: A Study in Command* (New York: Scribner's, 1942–44), vol. 2, 716–17.

3. Walker in *Battles and Leaders,* vol. 2, 605.

4. Charles Marshall to D. H. Hill, Nov. 11, 1867, Hill Papers, Virginia State Library.

5. D. H. Hill, "The Lost Dispatch," *The Land We Love* (Feb. 1868), 274, 275.

6. S.O. 191 is printed in the *Official Records* 19:2, 603–4.

7. McClellan to Halleck, Sept. 8, McClellan to wife, Sept. 12, McClellan to Halleck, Sept. 10, 1862, George B. McClellan, *The Civil War Papers of George B. McClellan: Selected Correspondence, 1860–1865,* ed. Stephen W. Sears (New York: Ticknor & Fields, 1989), 439, 449, 445.

8. E. R. Brown, *The Twenty-Seventh Indiana Volunteer Infantry in the War of the Rebellion* (Monticello, Ind., 1899), 22, 228; R. H. Chilton to Jefferson Davis, Dunbar Rowland, ed., *Jefferson Davis, Constitutionalist: His Letters, Papers and Speeches* (Jackson: Mississippi Department of Archives and History, 1923), vol. 7, 412–13; Barton W. Mitchell pension record, National Archives. The Lost Order is in the McClellan Papers, Manuscript Division, Library of Congress.

9. Silas Colgrove in *Battles and Leaders,* vol. 2, 603; Samuel E. Pittman pension record, National Archives; Pittman in *Detroit Free Press,* June 20, 1886; Alpheus

S. Williams to McClellan, Sept. 13, 1862, McClellan Papers. General Williams was in temporary command of Twelfth Corps pending the arrival of J.K.F. Mansfield.

10. McClellan to D. H. Hill, Feb. 1, 1869, Hill Papers, Virginia State Library; E. C. Gordon memorandum, Feb. 15, 1868, in Freeman, *Lee's Lieutenants*, vol. 2, 718; McClellan to Lincoln, Sept. 13, 1862, *McClellan Papers*, 453.

11. John Gibbon, *Personal Recollections of the Civil War* (New York: Putnam's, 1928), 73.

12. McClellan to D. H. Hill, Feb. 1, 1869, Hill Papers, Virginia State Library.

13. McClellan to Lincoln, Sept. 13, McClellan to Franklin, Sept. 13, 1862, *McClellan Papers*, 453, 455; Marcy to Pleasonton, Sept. 13, 1862, *OR* 51:1, 829; Pleasonton to McClellan, Sept. 13, 1862, McClellan Papers.

14. McClellan to Halleck, Sept. 13, 1862, *McClellan Papers*, 456–57; Gibbon, *Personal Recollections*, 73; E. Porter Alexander, *Fighting for the Confederacy: The Personal Recollections of General Edward Porter Alexander*, ed. Gary W. Gallagher (Chapel Hill: University of North Carolina Press, 1989), 141.

15. McClellan to D. H. Hill, Feb. 1, 1869, Hill Papers, Virginia State Library; Silas Colgrove in *Battles and Leaders*, vol. 2, 603; John M. Bloss, "Antietam and the Lost Dispatch," *War Talks in Kansas* (Kansas MOLLUS, 1906), 77–91; Bloss pension record, National Archives.

16. *OR* 19:1, 198; Brown, *Twenty-Seventh Indiana*, 252; Mitchell pension record.

17. D. H. Hill, "The Lost Dispatch," 273; Count of Paris, *History of the Civil War in America* (Philadelphia: Porter & Coates, 1875–88), vol. 2, 318; Bradley T. Johnson in *Southern Historical Society Papers*, vol. 12, 520. The copy of S.O. 191 Jackson made and sent to D. H. Hill is in the Hill Papers, North Carolina State Archives.

18. D. H. Hill to McClellan, Apr. 17, 1869, McClellan Papers.

19. D. H. Hill, "The Lost Dispatch," 275; J. W. Ratchford to D. H. Hill, Hill Papers, North Carolina State Archives.

20. Thomas L. Rosser account: Thomas Jackson Arnold in *Confederate Veteran* (Aug. 1922), 317; Chilton to Davis, Dec. 8, 1874, Rowland, *Jefferson Davis*, vol. 7, 413. Accepting the cloudy and undocumented Rosser account, Wilbur D. Jones, Jr., has built a case for indicting Henry Kyd Douglas for losing S.O. 191. However, there is no actual evidence to support such a case, and too many illogical assumptions have to be made for Douglas's involvement (for just one example, that he would have dared to open and read *any* orders sent to the ultrasecretive Jackson) for his guilt to be credible: Jones, "Who Lost the Lost Orders?" *Civil War Regiments* (5:3), 1–26.

21. For Chilton's failings, see Stephen W. Sears, *To the Gates of Richmond: The Peninsula Campaign* (New York: Ticknor & Fields, 1992), 268, 317; and Sears, *Chancellorsville* (Boston: Houghton Mifflin, 1996), 250, 283.

22. *Journal of Commerce*, Jan. 1, 1863 (from McClellan's copy of S.O. 191, McClellan Papers); McClellan testimony, *Report of the Joint Committee on the Conduct of the War*, vol. 1 (1863), 439.

23. *New York Herald*, Sept. 15, 1862; Stephen W. Sears, "The First News Blackout," *American Heritage* (June 1985), 24–31.

24. For the Confederates' "secret line," see William A. Tidwell, James O. Hall, and David Winfred Gaddy, *Come Retribution: The Confederate Secret Service and the Assassination of Lincoln* (Jackson: University Press of Mississippi, 1988), 87–90.

25. E. C. Gordon memorandum, Feb. 15, 1868, in Freeman, *Lee's Lieutenants,* vol. 2, 718–19.

26. Marshall to D. H. Hill, Nov. 11, 1867, Hill Papers, Virginia State Library.

27. Lee to Davis, Sept. 16, 1862, *OR* 19:1, 140.

28. Arthur McClellan diary, Sept. 15, 1862, McClellan Papers.

29. William Palmer to A. G. Curtin, Sept. 16, 1862, *OR* 19:2, 311.

30. Lee to D. H. Hill, Feb. 21, 1868, Hal Bridges, "A Lee Letter on the 'Lost Dispatch' and the Maryland Campaign of 1862," *Virginia Magazine of History and Biography* (Apr. 1958), 164; E. C. Gordon memorandum, Feb. 15, and William Allan memorandum, Feb. 15, 1868, in Freeman, *Lee's Lieutenants,* vol. 2, 717, 721.

[6]

The Revolt of the Generals

Major Generals William F. Smith
and William B. Franklin

THE GENERALS' REVOLT was an amorphous sort of thing, ill defined and hard to pin down, but for some ten months it was always there, lurking somewhere in the dark corners of the army. The participants varied, shifting and changing, rarely emerging into the open. Sometimes it could be dismissed as just loose talk. At other times it seemed genuinely threatening, or at least so newspaper correspondents thought. "The army is dissatisfied and the air is thick with revolution," a breathless reporter assured his editor at one point in the fall of 1862.[1] Yet however difficult it might be to define, the revolt of the generals is something to be reckoned, for it reshaped one campaign and was instrumental in the dismissal of two commanding generals of the Army of the Potomac.

It began in the officer corps as rising discontent rather than actual revolt. In the wake of defeat on the Peninsula and debacle at Second Bull Run, generals were heard to grumble about interference from Washington. The Potomac army, they said, was not being allowed to manage its own affairs. Its generals' hands were tied by inept civilians. Calls for reinforcements went unanswered; correct strategies were sidetracked; radical pressures for abolition and confiscation demoralized both officers and men. This was General McClellan's message to his supporters on the home front during that summer of 1862. His disciples among his lieutenants, notably Fitz John Porter, helped him insure that anti-administration newspapers had the message.[2]

Taking all this in were impressionable young bloods on the headquarters staff. Their indignation boiled over at an evening bivouac in mid-September while the army was pursuing Lee into Maryland. Colonel Thomas M. Key, a former Ohio legislator and judge and long-time McClellan aide, now the Potomac army's acting judge advocate, heard their talk and was dismayed by its vehemence. Afterward he recounted the episode to Nathaniel Paige, a lawyer friend who was a correspondent for the *New York Tribune.* Key told him, Paige later wrote, "that a plan to countermarch to Washington and intimidate the President had been seriously discussed the night before by members of McClellan's staff. . . ." These dissident officers, he said, appeared to be fighting more for a boundary than for the Union, and they were contemptuous of the president, Secretary of War Stanton, and General-in-Chief Halleck, calling them "the old women at Washington." Colonel Key made strenuous objection at this point, and thought he had stopped at least the conspiracy if not the talk. He added that General McClellan knew nothing of the scheme.[3]

Discontent of this kind in the army's high command, or at least the rumors of it, was not in fact silenced, and after the Battle of Antietam it grew loud enough to reach the ears of the president. Lincoln determined he must do something about it, and a week or so after the battle an opportunity offered. Secretary of the Interior Caleb Smith reported to him a conversation he had had with Levi C. Turner, judge advocate at the War Department in Washington. Turner, it seems, had asked a member of General Halleck's staff, Major John J. Key, about what happened after the Battle of Antietam. With all of McClellan's talk about his great victory in Maryland, why had he not pursued and "bagged" the Rebel army? "That is not the game," Major Key explained. "The object is that neither army shall get much advantage of the other; that both shall be kept in the field till they are exhausted, when we will make a compromise and save slavery."

Major John Key was the brother of Colonel Thomas Key of McClellan's staff, who earlier had also demonstrated an ear for army conspiracies. Turner was shocked enough by Major Key's novel theory of war-making to mention the incident to Secretary Smith, and Smith, one of the more outspoken anti-McClellan members of the Cabinet, thought Mr. Lincoln should know about it. If any army officer had used such language, the president remarked to his secretary, "his head should go off." On September 27 Key, along with Turner, was called to the White House to explain himself. Lawyer Lincoln made a careful record of the hearing that he conducted personally. In his testimony, Turner repeated Key's explanation for the failure to bag Lee's army after Antietam. He added that this had been a private conversation, and that he had never heard Key express disloyal sentiments. "Major Key did not attempt to controvert the statement of Major Turner," the president recorded, ". . . but simply insisted, and sought to prove, that he was true to the Union." Lincoln continued, writing in the third person, "The substance of the President's reply was that if there was a 'game' ever among Union men, to have our army not take an advantage of the enemy when it could, it was his object to break up that game."

Lincoln's endorsement on the record of the hearing was blunt: "In my view it is wholly inadmissible for any gentleman holding a military commission from the United States to utter such sentiments as Major Key is within proved to have done. Therefore let Major John J. Key be forthwith dismissed from the Military service of the United States." He later explained to John Hay, "I dismissed Major Key for his silly treasonable talk because I feared it was staff talk & I wanted an example." No doubt an injustice was done to the hapless Major Key, but as a signal to officers of the Army of the Potomac it was unmistakable. The officer corps was not going to dictate any contrary military policy to the administration so long as Mr. Lincoln had anything to say about it — and he would definitely have his say.[4]

General McClellan was said by common report to be in on the

game Major Key had described. "In high circles," the Washington tipster T. J. Barnett wrote a friend on September 23, ". . . it is whispered that McClellan is of a school & with a party who, of purpose, desire to exhaust the sections by war with a view to reconstruction." Consequently, those who did their best to influence the general made a point of mentioning the Key affair to him. On September 27, the day he determined to dismiss Key, the president mentioned the case (probably deliberately) to Montgomery Blair, supposedly McClellan's one friend in the Cabinet. Blair wasted no time writing the general to inform him of Key's fate, and to suggest that he distance himself from (as Blair put it) "such a compromise as Maj. Key has mentioned." The country wanted to hear from the commanding general of the Army of the Potomac, he said, that while the object of the war was the maintenance of the government, the "natural result" would be the extinction of slavery. With such a statement "you would head off your opponents very clearly."[5]

Advice such as this reached McClellan just as he was pondering what stand he should take in regard to Lincoln's recent announcement of the preliminary Emancipation Proclamation. Emancipation was too radical a step for him, yet at the same time he dared not be seen as allying himself with those dissident officers in his army who, by report at least, were looking for a military compromise — fighting only for a boundary — that would end up preserving slavery in the South. It had all become infernally complicated. General McClellan did not want to support abolitionism, yet he did not want to appear soft on putting down the rebellion. Finally he issued a general order reminding the army of the "true relation" between soldiers and the government they served. The only remedy for political error, he pointed out, was action at the polls. The general's order, the *New York Tribune* said approvingly, ought to be a rebuke to the "zanies and their more dangerous ringleaders" in shoulder straps who were "raving and foaming over the country, threatening the most unutterable vengeance of 'the Army' on 'the Abolitionists' if they don't 'stop interfering with Gen. McClellan!' "[6]

William Swinton, the veteran military correspondent of the *New York Times,* carefully observed the reaction in the Army of the Potomac when McClellan was relieved of his command in November and took his leave of the troops in an elaborate ceremony. Although Swinton believed the emotion and affection of the men in the ranks for their general was genuine enough, he decided that the farewell ceremony itself was "of the nature of scenic effect, prepared by the hand of the cunning artificer." Afterward he heard much loud talk in the officer corps. One brigade commander was of the opinion that the army would all go home as well within a short time, led by its officers. "We have only two or three days more to serve in the Army of the Potomac," he prophesied. Another general, apparently a well-read one, pointed to McClellan and declaimed, "Why does he not take us down with him to Washington, and clear out the Abolition crew, as Cromwell did the Rump Parliament?" While much of this sort of talk might seem perilous to the republic, Swinton wrote, "I feel every assurance that the effervescence will presently die away. . . ."[7]

Swinton was quite right to assume that all the high talk of a march on Washington behind the Young Napoleon would soon enough evaporate. But as far as fidelity to General McClellan within the Potomac army's officer corps was concerned, that by no means was immediately weakened. Scarcely a month after McClellan's dismissal there arose a full-fledged generals' revolt aimed at bringing him back to the command.

In addition to this newly energized generals' revolt, there was — and had been for some time — also a single general's revolt seething within the army. This singular rebellious officer was Joe Hooker, who was convinced that the only fully qualified general for command of the Army of the Potomac was . . . Joe Hooker. Ever since the Peninsula campaign Hooker had been campaigning for the post by undermining the general commanding. McClellan, he told a Senate supporter, "is not only not a soldier, but he does not know what soldiership is." In testimony before Congress's Joint Committee on the Conduct of the War, where he proved to be a great favorite, Hooker claimed that early on in the Peninsula campaign, immediately after the fight at Williamsburg, had McClellan any backbone the army could have marched straight into Richmond "without another gun being fired."

Hooker increased his sniping after Antietam. He was wounded in the foot in that battle, and afterward in his convalescence he held court for visitors in the well-appointed doctors' quarters at Washington's insane asylum. The president and members of the Cabinet called on him, to whom he was generous with his advice on how the war should be conducted. Hooker formed a particular alliance with Secretary of the Treasury Salmon P. Chase, who visited frequently, along with his beautiful daughter Kate, and brought baskets of fruit for the gallant invalid. To them Hooker confided his stories of McClellan's many failings on the Peninsula. At Antietam, he said, there ought to have been a total victory had only McClellan showed the enterprise to follow up on what he, Joe Hooker, had begun: "I had already gained enough and seen enough to make the rout of the enemy sure."[8]

What his biographer would term Hooker's Washington campaign seemed to be making progress, and the betting in the officer ranks made him the leading candidate to replace McClellan, should that momentous event come to pass. Before long the newspapers were on the story. On October 22 the *New York Express* announced the rumor that the Cabinet had unanimously "resolved to remove McClellan, and that Hooker should succeed him." The Washington tipster T. J. Barnett, at about the same time, had Lincoln initiating a more complex scheme. General Halleck would be transferred to a command in the western theater, to make room for McClellan to resume the post of general-in-chief. That, in turn, would make way for Joe Hooker to take over the Army of the Potomac.

This scheme was indeed under serious consideration, with McClellan making every effort he could to reclaim the general-in-chief post. Hooker expressed confidence that the army command would soon be his. In the end, however, the president seems to have balked at keeping General McClellan in his administration in any capacity; their policy differences had grown too great to manage the war in partnership. On November 5 Lincoln ordered the Army of the Potomac turned over to Ambrose Burnside. Hooker contended that Halleck, an old enemy from before the war, had blackballed him. Certainly Halleck did oppose Hooker, but that this had influenced Lincoln's decision is doubtful. It may be that there was a bit too much partisanship, a bit too much salesmanship, in Joe Hooker's Washington campaign. And, too, perhaps Lincoln still considered Hooker too rash. "I fear he gets excited," he had recently observed to Gideon Welles. As for Hooker, since he thought even less of Burnside than he had of McClellan, he believed his turn would not be long in coming.[9]

The disastrous battle at Fredericksburg, on December 13, set off the revolt of the generals in full cry. With the exception of Joe Hooker's individual efforts, this was the first time that the dissidents' aim was actually to unseat the general commanding. Fredericksburg was certainly not the Army of the Potomac's first defeat, but it was the first defeat to be so obvious and so obviously blamable. McClellan had managed (at least to the satisfaction of the officer corps) to disguise the reverses of the Seven Days and to shift responsibility and lay the blame on shoulders other than his own. At Second Bull Run John Pope and Irvin McDowell were the handy — and largely deserving — scapegoats, and both were now gone from the army. But, in effect, Fredericksburg left Ambrose Burnside nowhere to hide. Nor did he even try. In a statement that he made sure was distributed to the newspapers, he took full responsibility for the defeat. This was the manly thing to do, but it did not enhance his credibility among his fellow generals. To admit poor generalship was no good way to rebuild support for his leadership among his lieutenants. "There is no confidence in Gen. Burnside in that Army," General Samuel Heintzelman confided to his diary. "I am not surprised, when he publishes to the country that he has no confidence in his abilities to command so large an army."[10]

Leadership of the anti-Burnside forces was taken in hand by two of the more senior generals in the Potomac army, Major Generals William B. Franklin and William F. Smith. Franklin headed one of the three Grand Divisions into which Burnside had subdivided his army; Smith led the Sixth Corps under Franklin. The two were old and tried friends. On campaign they shared a tent and a common mess, and they shared a like view of the proper way to conduct the war. As Smith remembered it, "there was never the slightest disagreement between us as to plans or details. We worked harmoniously for the same end and with unparalleled serenity." Franklin and Smith concluded after Fredericksburg that everything about Burnside's campaigning was wrong, but instead of taking their ideas to the general commanding as army protocol dictated, they went over Burnside's head, silently and without notice, to the president. By Smith's description, General Burnside held no views or opinions "save the reflection from the last person with whom he had talked. With all this there was the intense stubbornness which sometimes takes hold of weak minds. . . ."[11]

On December 20, 1862, a week after the Fredericksburg disaster, Franklin and Smith jointly signed a long letter to Mr. Lincoln that called for the Army of the Potomac to abandon the Rappahannock line for a return to the Peninsula, where McClellan had unsuccessfully campaigned for five long months. They prefaced their proposal with the flat assertion "that the plan of campaign which has already been commenced cannot possibly be successful. . . ." They argued instead that it would be easy to gather and concentrate forces on the James River, establishing the army within twenty miles of Richmond "without the risk of an engagement." The navy would assure adequate and secure communications. Their arguments, presented in close detail (including, for example, the issuance to each soldier of one pair of socks and one pair of drawers), echoed those of General McClellan the previous February. Even if their campaign did not result in the destruction of the enemy's army, it would surely capture the enemy's capital, "and the war will be on a better footing than it is now or has any present prospect of being."[12]

It was clear enough by implication that Burnside, architect of the recent disastrous Rappahannock campaign, should not be anyone's choice — he was certainly not Franklin's and Smith's choice — to lead a new campaign on the Peninsula. Franklin was not unaware that he had been spoken of as commanding-general material, which was no doubt one motive behind his proposal. He was also probably hoping it might divert attention from a growing undercurrent of complaint that Franklin's Left Grand Division had not done its full duty at Fredericksburg. Burnside had expected a powerful flank attack by Franklin, and it never quite materialized. "Baldy" Smith, in addition to attaching himself firmly to Franklin's coattails, was further motivated by contempt for the general commanding. "Smith was one of those personalities," General McClellan would later explain, "who must always intrigue the acts of all above him. He did much harm in that way."

Whatever their innermost hopes may have been, Franklin and Smith were realists. They clearly recognized that the most popular choice to replace Burnside in command of any new campaign would be the deposed McClellan. That was perfectly acceptable to them. As the cynical Smith afterward wrote, whatever McClellan's failings, "he never was so mediocre as any of his successors even at their highest." McClellan surely was the choice within the high command. Two days before the Franklin-Smith letter went to the president, Gouverneur Warren of the Fifth Corps wrote home, "We *must* have McClellan back with unlimited and unfettered powers. His name is a tower of strength to everyone here. . . ."[13]

The president had never favored McClellan's Peninsula plan over what seemed to him the simpler and more direct approach of challenging the Confederate army then at Manassas, within easy striking distance from Washington. In his reply to the two generals, Lincoln said the issue was the "old question of preference" between the line of the Peninsula and the present position of the army. "But now, as heretofore, if you go to James River," he pointed out, "a large part of the army must remain on or near the Fredericksburg line, to protect Washington. It is the old difficulty."

In a rather lame response, Franklin said that he and Smith had assumed a sufficient garrison for Washington in their plan. He did not explain how the Army of the Potomac might safely disengage itself from Lee's army facing it at Fredericksburg and then shift to the Peninsula.[14]

On December 29 Burnside issued orders for an advance to begin on twelve hours' notice, and it became clear to the two dissident generals that their scheme to change the line of campaign was not working. They would have to try something else to thwart the army commander — something that was more direct yet at the same time disguised their own roles in the affair.

They had also to act quickly, and so the next morning, two generals from their command were hurried off to Washington to carry out their secret bidding. Theirs was a carefully calculated pairing. Brigadier General John Newton, leading a division in Smith's Sixth Corps, was a career soldier who had ranked second in the West Point class of 1842. A native Virginian, Newton had stayed with the Union in 1861 and gone on to compile a solid if unspectacular record as one of Franklin's brigade commanders. With Franklin's advancement to Grand Division before Fredericksburg, Newton had moved up to divisional command. It was as Franklin's protégé that Newton seems to have been tapped for this scheme — and the reason he dutifully accepted. Although acknowledged to be a thoroughgoing professional soldier — and, with his erect carriage and steely gaze, decidedly looking the part — Newton was not exactly a stranger to Washington politics. His father, Thomas Newton, had served twenty-nine years in the Congress from Virginia.

Newton's companion in this adventure was a soldier only by the uniform. Brigadier General John Cochrane, dumpy and baggy-eyed, was a pure example of political general, a canny veteran of New York's Mozart Hall political wars to whom Washington was a second home. He had served two terms in Congress as an archconservative Democrat defending Southern causes. When secession converted him into a patriot, he recruited the 65th New York regiment and was welcomed into the army as a War Democrat courted by the Republican administration. Although he had been in the service for eighteen months and now commanded a brigade in Newton's division, Cochrane's sole action had been at Seven Pines on the Peninsula. He functioned primarily as what a later generation would term a political fixer. General McClellan had employed him for his good connections in the capital. Back in October, when he was seeking reinstatement as general-in-chief, McClellan dispatched Cochrane to Washington to plead his case. Cochrane did his best in a losing cause, buttonholing Treasury Secretary Chase and President Lincoln on McClellan's behalf, and even enlisting the support of the *New York Herald.*[15] Cochrane's purpose on this new Washington trip was (along with Newton) to rid the Army of the Potomac of General Burnside — and then, if all went well, to see him replaced by General McClellan.

Generals Franklin and Smith would later profess ignorance, or forgetfulness, of the Newton-Cochrane mission. However, for a general of division and a general of brigade in the Sixth Corps to head off to Washington, with the army under marching orders, had obviously required their superiors' permission. And with equal certainty, undertaking so bold a mission as theirs would hardly have occurred spontaneously to these two officers. John Newton and John Cochrane were where they were on this December 30, 1862, because the two ringleaders of the generals' revolt had instructed them and sent them on their way.

Cochrane took charge upon their arrival in Washington. He would later explain to the Joint Committee on the Conduct of the War that his intent in the capital had been no more ambitious than a meeting with two members of Congress — Henry Wilson, head of the Senate's Committee on Military Affairs, and Congressman Moses F. Odell, a member of the Joint Committee — for the purpose of confiding to them the low morale of the soldiers of the Army of the Potomac, so these facts might "be weighted at their true value." Wilson and Odell were found to be absent from the city, however, Congress being on its holiday recess — "a fact which had not before occurred to me," said Cochrane. Only then did he decide to seek an audience for himself and Newton with President Lincoln.

That two-term Congressman Cochrane was unaware that the Congress recessed in December is no more credible than his pleading of entirely innocent motives in coming to Washington. Only Lincoln had the authority to carry out the change in the army's high command that Franklin and Smith were seeking. Senator Wilson and Congressman Odell would have been of only marginal help at best. Consequently, the generals' instructions to Cochrane surely directed him to make first-priority use of his political connections to gain entrance to the White House.[16]

That, in any event, is exactly what Cochrane did. Encountering Secretary of State Seward, a political acquaintance from his New York days, he persuaded Seward to obtain an appointment for him with the president. In midafternoon that Tuesday, with Newton in tow, Cochrane hurried to the White House and the president's office.

General Newton, the senior officer and displaying the more stalwart military presence of the two, made the presentation. It was a vexing, rather delicate moment for Newton. Should he phrase the opposition to Burnside in such a way that it appeared he was contriving to have his superior officer relieved (which, of course, was precisely the dissidents' intention), he could be court-martialed and cashiered under the Articles of War. As Newton later recounted the conversation for the Joint Committee on the Conduct of the War, he dared not come out and baldly announce, "Mr. President, the army has no confidence in General Burnside; that is the whole trouble down there." To say that would be "manifestly improper," although it was in fact what he believed. What Newton did attempt to say, by talking his way with great caution all around the subject, was that the troops under Burnside's command were demoralized. Another campaign like the last one would produce not merely a defeat but the destruction of the army.

Lincoln soon enough saw through Newton's evasions, and went

at him. "At first the President misunderstood our object in coming there," was how Newton phrased it, "and thought we were coming to injure General Burnside, and even to suggest somebody for commander of the army." The crestfallen Newton hastened to explain that, no indeed, they had no one in mind for the command; "our sole intention was to express the facts as to the condition of the army."

At this awkward turn, the more adept Cochrane stepped in to pour oil on the roiled waters. In phrases soothing and politic, "with much feeling," he confirmed, from his personal observation, everything Newton had said of the demoralization within the ranks. In so doing (as he told the Joint Committee), "I deemed it the best evidence of patriotism and of my loyalty to the government that I could give." Having thus raised the tenor of the conversation to these rarefied heights, Cochrane noted that the president "resumed his ordinary manner." As he showed the two generals out, Cochrane remembered, Lincoln said "he was glad that we had visited him, and that good would come of the interview."[17]

This White House interview, as related by the two generals in their testimony to the Joint Committee, was incomplete in at least one respect, and probably deliberately so. It did not include what was for the president just then the most important, and disturbing, factor in the increasingly tortuous command structure of the Army of the Potomac. Whether directly or by implication, what Lincoln took away from this meeting with Newton and Cochrane was that Burnside had lost the confidence of his own lieutenants. This bespoke the gravest of consequences.

Having seen through his visitors' subterfuge and recognized who probably put them up to their tale-bearing mission — after all, just ten days before, the pair's immediate superiors, Franklin and Baldy Smith, had reached out to the White House over Burnside's head to try and redirect the army's strategy — Lincoln no doubt made a quick head count. Of Franklin, Hooker, and Edwin Sumner, the Army of the Potomac's three Grand Division commanders — Burnside's chief lieutenants — only old Sumner (as always) could be counted on for unquestioning loyalty to his superior. Hooker made no secret of his attitude toward Burnside. Now Franklin was apparently revealing his true colors. If, in addition, at least three of the principal generals under Franklin's command were following his lead, it strongly suggested a growing rot within the army's high command.

At 3:30 that afternoon of December 30, shortly after Generals Newton and Cochrane left the White House to return to their commands, a telegram was sent over the War Department wires to General Burnside's headquarters on the Rappahannock: "I have good reason for saying you must not make a general movement of the army without letting me know." It was signed "A. Lincoln."

The preliminary moves for a full-army advance had already begun. Burnside telegraphed that he would call a halt, rescinding "some orders that had already been given," and come up to Washington the next day to confer. His aborted battle plan would most likely have gone into the history books as Second Fredericksburg. This time the main Rappahannock crossing for the army, rather than being right at Fredericksburg, was to have been some distance downstream. A feint was scheduled for upstream. The cavalry was meanwhile to make a deep strike to the south to cut Lee's communications. If nothing else, this December 30 plan was a good deal more imaginative than Burnside's earlier effort. Its cancellation was the first bitter fruit of the revolt of the generals.[18]

On December 31 Burnside met with the president in his White House office and was astonished to learn that two of his generals — Lincoln would not tell him their names — had been in that office the day before and predicted defeat and disaster if the army should go to battle. Lincoln went on to say, as Burnside remembered it, "that he had understood that no prominent officer of my command had any faith in my proposed movement." (Newton and Cochrane on their own would not have had nerve enough to claim to know any such unanimous opinion by the army's high command, further evidence that it was Franklin and Smith who had fed them their lines.) Burnside defended his battle plan, but the president said it must wait until he had discussed it with his advisers. Considerably distraught by this time, Burnside said that if his general officers had so lost confidence in him, it was best that he resign his command. Lincoln asked him to return the next day and they would discuss the whole matter.[19]

New Year's Day 1863 may have been a high point for President Lincoln, with his signature putting the Emancipation Proclamation into effect, but for the Army of the Potomac it was the worst of days. The president's conference that morning with General-in-Chief Halleck, Secretary of War Stanton, and General Burnside produced nothing by way of agreement on anything. What it did produce was letters of resignation by Mr. Lincoln's two foremost generals.

The conference began with Burnside handing the president his letter of resignation. "Doubtless this difference of opinion between my general officers and myself," he had written, "results from a lack of confidence in me." He could therefore no longer conscientiously retain his command. Having gone that far, he then went farther, observing that neither Secretary Stanton nor General Halleck any longer held the confidence of either the army or the country. While Burnside did not come right out and say it, his implication was clear — if there was reason enough for him to resign, there were equally valid reasons for Stanton's and Halleck's resignations as well.

Lincoln read the letter and without comment handed it back to Burnside. The president's silence seemed to inspire Burnside to something of an act of contrition. He blurted out for Stanton's and Halleck's benefit that he was hereby offering to resign his command. They should also know, he went on, that he had given the president his opinion that neither of them any longer had the confidence of the army or of the country. With Lincoln refusing to be drawn into any discussion of resignations, Burnside's remarks no doubt hung like a dark cloud over the rest of the conference.

There followed a squabble over the identity of the talebearers of two days before, with Halleck joining Burnside in insisting that the two deserved to be cashiered. Lincoln, however, withheld their identities. The discussion of Burnside's plan of campaign went nowhere either. Considering all the talk of lack of confidence that he was hearing, Burnside demanded from Halleck and Stanton a specific vote of confidence for the battle plan that was then hanging fire. Both men backed away from a commitment, saying any advance was Burnside's responsibility. They would agree only in the most general terms to an offensive strategy. On that indecisive note the meeting ended. "No definite conclusion was come to . . . ," said General Burnside bitterly, "in reference to the subject of a movement."[20]

Lincoln was equally frustrated by this outcome, and he soon vented that frustration in a letter to Halleck. Burnside's chief lieutenants were apparently opposed to his campaign plan, the president said. It was to resolve just such a difficulty as this that he had brought General Halleck to Washington. He wanted the general-in-chief to go to the Rappahannock, inspect the ground, confer with the generals there, and pass judgment on the proposed movement — "tell Gen. Burnside that you *do* approve, or that you do *not* approve his plan. Your military skill is useless to me, if you will not do this."

Halleck refused to rise to the challenge. Indeed, he seems to have seized on this letter of Lincoln's as an opportunity to get out of a posting he despised. Halleck was serving as general-in-chief only out of a sense of duty, and his concept of the job was so restrictive that he had become little more than a glorified chief clerk for the army. His response to the president's letter was prompt and to the point: "I am led to believe that there is a very important difference of opinion in regard to my relations toward generals commanding armies in the field. . . . I therefore respectfully request that I may be relieved from further duties as General-in-Chief."

However tempting it might have been to accept this second resignation of the day — it was, after all, not the first time Lincoln had found Halleck's military skills elusive — the president had no one of any stature to replace him. Militarily the war was stalled on dead center, and no general had risen high enough above the average to seem an alternate choice for general-in-chief. Certainly, despite all the pressures, the president was not ready to entrust the post to McClellan again. Consequently, on the file copy of his letter to Halleck, he wrote, "Withdrawn because considered harsh by General Halleck." The tally for the day was two resignations offered and two refused, and one campaign plan aborted. January 1, 1863, was (to repeat) not a good day for the Army of the Potomac.[21]

When Burnside returned to his Falmouth headquarters, he was by turns furious and bewildered. It seemed he was the victim of a conspiracy, but he knew not where to turn to fight it. One thing he did not try to do was keep his troubles quiet. He was almost compulsive about relating his experiences in Washington. Before long he had confided in virtually every senior commander in the army (including the conspirators), even displaying his resignation letter that the president had returned to him. This was, once again, an instance of Burnside being manly and painfully honest, yet it did nothing to inspire confidence among his lieutenants in his leadership. One of his first confidants was General George Meade, and on January 2 Meade wrote his wife with all the details, and all the frustrations, Burnside had experienced in the capital: "Finding he could get nothing out of any of them, he came back, and thus matters stand. Burnside told me all this himself this morning, and read me his paper, which was right up and down. . . . God only knows what is to become of us and what will be done."

The army command became the chief topic of interest and gossip within the officer corps. Generals Franklin and Smith, having been successful in blocking Burnside's campaign plan, went about planting their seeds for raising an alternate strategy and at the same time recruiting allies to unseat the general commanding. In the same letter that described Burnside's Washington experiences, Meade wrote, "I had a long talk with Franklin yesterday, who is very positive in his opinion that we cannot go to Richmond on this line, and hence there is no object in our attempting to move on it." One of the more outspoken recruits in the conspiracy, Baldy Smith's divisional commander W.T.H. Brooks, long known in the old army as "Bully" Brooks for his ill-mannered ways, was so loud in his denunciations that Burnside had him arrested for insubordination and "using language tending to demoralize his command."[22]

It did not take long for the capital's network of gossip to unravel the story of the talebearers who had been to see the president. As early as January 5 General Heintzelman, in command of the Washington defenses, recorded in his diary, "Gen. Burnside wanted to cross the Rappahannock when two Generals came to town, saw Mr. Lincoln & he sent orders not to do it. I heard later that Genls. Newton & Cochrane who got leave from Gen. Franklin were the officers." A few days later Heintzelman was visited by one of the capital's prime purveyors of gossip, the Polish Count Adam Gurowski, who had it that Franklin had not just given Newton and Cochrane leave to visit Washington, but had actually sent them. "It is monstrous," Heintzelman sputtered. "Can we hope to do anything, when such conduct is tolerated?"[23]

Joe Hooker refused to join with the Franklin-Smith band of conspirators to seek Burnside's overthrow. He preferred to go his own way with confidence in his own individual goal. He would of course be as happy as the others to see Burnside displaced, but he ardently wanted Burnside's replacement to be Joe Hooker rather than George McClellan. He was also a good deal more open and candid about his ambition than Franklin and Smith and their followers were about theirs.

Hooker consistently made his case against Burnside out loud and without subterfuge, as in his testimony to the Joint Committee on the Conduct of the War investigating Fredericksburg — testimony where in the bargain he also took aim at Franklin, a potential rival for the army command. Senator Zachariah Chandler of the committee wrote afterward, "I believe in Hooker & have no faith in Franklin. He was & is one of the McClellan worshippers *& not to be trusted.*" Thus Hooker made no common cause with the other intriguers. Indeed, he would later describe Baldy Smith as the "evil genius" behind Franklin and Newton and the other plotters. Once Smith was exorcised — which he would do when he achieved the command — he thought the others might be rehabilitated.[24]

The debate over blame for Fredericksburg and the infighting and intrigue concerning the Potomac army command were widely leaked to the newspapers, further poisoning the atmosphere at Falmouth headquarters and in Washington. "The persistent attempts made by certain Presses and parties to use the disaster of Fredericksburgh as a lever for the overthrow of the Secretary of War and General-in-Chief, if not of the Government, cannot have failed to attract the attention of thoughtful minds," wrote a correspondent of the *New York Times.* "Many of these attacks are obviously and avowedly made in the interest of the late Commander of the Army of the Potomac." The reporter went on to speak of the "deliberate and malicious misrepresentations" of nearly everyone involved. "The interests engaged in the onslaught err not so much from want of knowledge as from design. . . ."[25]

It was inevitable that the poisons being generated in the high command would leach down into the lower ranks. The combination of battlefield defeat and incompetence in the army administration was already having a disastrous effect on morale. Desertion was growing at an alarming rate. Now, as confidence in their generals plummeted, deeper demoralization among the troops was the inevitable result. In letters home the men poured out their disillusion. Edward H. Taylor, a Michigan soldier in the Fifth Corps, echoed any number of letter writers when he wrote, "We think Burnside 'played out.' We know he is no general for such a command. Will the Government take warning in time or will they continue as they have begun? Must the Army mutiny before they understand that we are not in 'excellent spirits' and 'thinking to be led against the enemy' under such men as Burnside? Poor weak-minded fool he!"[26]

Against this enveloping storm Burnside stubbornly lowered his head and ordered yet another offensive. Concluding that the attack scheme in his December 30 plan had by now been compromised, he elected to march the whole army upstream for a crossing at Banks's Ford in the hope of outflanking the Confederate defenses. When he announced his intentions, Generals Franklin and Smith went to his headquarters on January 19 and spent the entire evening in a fruitless effort to talk him out of the movement. Hooker added his protest, as did Daniel Woodbury of the army's engineering brigade. Burnside would not listen. The order for the new advance stood. Joe Hooker unburdened himself to William Swinton of the *New York Times.* According to Swinton, the general "talked very openly about the absurdity of the movement . . . , denounced the commanding general as incompetent, and the President and Government at Washington as imbecile and 'played out.' Nothing would go right, he said, until we had a dictator, and the sooner the better."[27]

It had become virtually open rebellion in the high command. Nothing like this had ever happened before in the Army of the Potomac. This generals' revolt continued to center in Franklin's Left Grand Division. The best description of its workings is in the diary of Charles Wainwright, commanding the artillery of the First Corps in Franklin's Grand Division. He was at Franklin's headquarters on January 19, the day before the operation was scheduled to begin. "Both his staff and Smith's are talking outrageously," he wrote, "only repeating though, no doubt, the words of their generals." Whatever might be thought of Burnside and of his plan, Wainwright felt, "his lieutenants have no right to say so to their subordinates. As it is, Franklin has talked so much and so loudly to this effect . . . that he has completely demoralized his whole command, and so rendered failure doubly sure. . . . Smith and they say Hooker are almost as bad."

Nature now intervened in the form of a winter nor'easter, the consequence of which became infamous in the Army of the Potomac as the Mud March. The whole offensive sank forlornly in a sea of mud. Finally Burnside recognized the hopelessness of it all and ordered a return to Falmouth. In the midst of this chaos Colonel

Wainwright again made his way to Franklin's headquarters, "where I found him, Smith, and their staffs, in quite a comfortable camp; doing nothing to help things on, but grumbling and talking in a manner to do all the harm possible. . . . His staff talks very freely about Franklin's having command of the army in Burnside's place." None of this was lost on Ambrose Burnside at *his* headquarters, and he determined to stamp out this revolt of his generals for good.[28]

By now Burnside had learned the identity of the two talebearers who visited the president, resulting in the cancellation of his earlier offensive. The leadership of the conspiracy was becoming clear to him as well. Traveling with him during the movement was Henry J. Raymond, editor of the *New York Times,* and Raymond shared with the general the considerable amount he had learned about the dissident generals. He passed on, for example, correspondent Swinton's account of Hooker's diatribe against Burnside (and everyone else) of a few days earlier. Armed with all this information, and in high temper, Burnside on January 23 composed General Orders No. 8, a document unique in the history of the Army of the Potomac.

The first target on Burnside's list was Joe Hooker. Declaring that general "guilty of unjust and unnecessary criticisms of the actions of his superior officers, and of the authorities," and a catalog of similar offenses, Hooker was to be dismissed from the military service of the United States. W.T.H. Brooks, whom Burnside had arrested earlier for insubordination and demoralizing language, was also to be dismissed. Warming to his task, Burnside turned to the two talebearers, Newton and Cochrane, and ordered them dismissed. As for Generals Franklin and Smith, and Colonel Joseph H. Taylor, Sumner's chief of staff, it "being evident" that said officers "can be of no further service to this army," they were to report to Washington for reassignment. Now confused as well as angry, Burnside listed two additional generals for reassignment, a decision he later admitted was taken in error.[29]

In thus ordering out of the Army of the Potomac these seven

dissident officers, Burnside was ridding himself of two of his three Grand Division chiefs (along with the third Grand Division's chief of staff), one corps commander, two division commanders, and one brigade commander. He showed the order to editor Raymond, who complimented him on "the best step taken during the war." Raymond asked if Burnside thought there was any danger that Hooker might challenge his dismissal by leading a mutiny. Let Hooker make such a move, said Burnside, and he personally would "swing *him* before sundown." In that fighting mood, he told his adjutant to issue General Orders No. 8. At that, Burnside's medical officer, Dr. William Church, who had also been shown the order, pointed out to the general that such dismissals were subject to Mr. Lincoln's approval. And only the president could issue a peremptory dismissal. With that, Burnside telegraphed the president that he was on his way to Washington with "some very important orders, and I want to see you before issuing them."[30]

At the White House the next day, January 24, General Burnside presented Lincoln with two documents — G.O. 8, and his resignation of his major general's commission. It was not his intention to challenge or in any way embarrass the president, Burnside said, but he could no longer command the army with these generals in it. Either they, or he, must go.

Lincoln cannot have been entirely surprised by this ultimatum and its implications for the Army of the Potomac. The goings-on at Falmouth had hardly escaped his notice. Just that day he was handed a warning by General Carl Schurz that spoke of dire straits within the army. The worst consequence of the turmoil, said Schurz, was that "the spirit of the men is systematically broken by officers high in command." And just three days earlier, Mr. Lincoln had sent out a warning signal of his own to the officer corps by approving the court-martial verdict against Fitz John Porter. Interested observers could not have helped pondering the consequences visited upon Porter for his "intense scorn and contempt" toward a general commanding, in that case John Pope.

Lincoln told Burnside he wanted to consult with his advisers, and asked him to return the next day. That evening editor Raymond, who had come up with Burnside from Falmouth, encountered the president at a White House reception. The editor, it appears, was eager to put in a bad word for Joe Hooker. He recounted for Lincoln that general's conversation with correspondent Swinton, to the effect that the administration was imbecile and played out, and what the country needed, and soon, was a dictator. The president sighed and acknowledged that General Hooker did talk badly. "But the trouble is," he added, "he is stronger with the country to-day than any other man." Subsequently, Raymond was probably the least surprised person in Washington when the news broke the next day of a new commander for the Army of the Potomac.[31]

The following morning, January 25, the president met first with Stanton and Halleck, explained briefly the choice Burnside had given him, and announced that Joe Hooker was to be the new commander of the Potomac army. He did not ask for advice or invite discussion. Lincoln already knew that Halleck and Hooker were locked in an apparently intractable feud, and certainly he recalled the general-in-chief's recent refusal to apply his military skills to the army's problems on the Rappahannock. In this matter he placed little value on Halleck's opinion, and apparently he held the same view of Stanton's. It is safe to say that Mr. Lincoln recognized that he was the only one even qualified to take such a decision.

The decision no doubt came as a relief to poor Burnside. He had never believed himself qualified for the army command, and the events of the past weeks signaled all too clearly that his lieutenants were of the same mind. The president refused his resignation, granted him a thirty-day leave, and promised him a post befitting his rank. In due course that would be the Army of the Ohio. To soften public reaction to the command change, it was no one's intention that either General Orders No. 8 or Burnside's proffered resignation should become known. (That hope would be dashed when Hooker discovered a carelessly left copy of G.O. 8 at Falmouth headquarters and leaked it to the *New York Herald,* intending to make Burnside, he said sarcastically, "more conspicuous than he had ever been before.")[32]

The revolt of the generals must be credited with two major successes. The dissidents were wholly responsible for blocking Burnside's battle plan of December 30. Then, within less than a month, they were so successful in undermining confidence in the general commanding that he was goaded into military self-immolation. Where the Franklin-Smith cabal failed, of course, was in dictating or influencing the choice of Burnside's successor.

In the matter of McClellan, its favorite, the cabal quite misread the portents. That winter of 1862–63 was not only the nadir for the Army of the Potomac; in many respects it was also the nadir for the Union cause. To Mr. Lincoln, General McClellan was more than simply a failed general who might be reshuffled into perhaps a more successful posting. He had become, or had let himself become, a well-recognized symbol of opposition, a magnet attracting the elements within the country in dissent against the administration's war policies. To put McClellan back in command of the Army of the Potomac, or to make him general-in-chief, would in effect be confessing the failure of those policies. The president was hardly ready to confess that, and so the conspirators had to suffer Joe Hooker in the command.

These dissenting generals gained neither profit nor honor from their efforts. The army would prove unforgiving of their intrigue. Baldy Smith spoke for them all when he said ruefully, "the results followed me through the war."

On the same day that Hooker took over, William Franklin was relieved of his Grand Division command. He would serve with a signal lack of success in the western theater and would spend the last year of the war awaiting orders. Hooker disposed of "evil genius" Baldy Smith by putting him in temporary command of the Ninth Corps when that corps was detached from the Army of the Potomac. The Senate allowed Smith's appointment as major general to expire in March. He served for a time in the West, and again in the East in the 1864 campaigns, but his intrigues and quarrelsome nature caused him, like Franklin, to sit out most of the last year of the war.

Bully Brooks was put for a time in a behind-the-lines command, in Pittsburgh, and saw his major general's commission revoked in 1864. After divisional command in the Potomac army that spring, he resigned in July 1864, citing poor health. John Newton, after commands at Chancellorsville and Gettysburg, was transferred to the western theater. Like Brooks, he had his major general's commission revoked the next year, and he ended the war in a backwater command in the Florida Keys. Political general Cochrane, foreseeing an empty military future for himself, resigned just a month after the command change (claiming ill health) in order to return to political warfare in New York. Chief of staff Joseph H. Taylor, a lieutenant colonel in January 1863, was still a lieutenant colonel at war's end.

With the conspirators either excised from the Potomac army or with their identities revealed, comparative calm would settle on the high command for some three months. Joe Hooker — brashly outspoken, of raffish reputation, a well-known intriguer — may be said to have lacked any sort of constituency among his fellow generals. The president, too, went out of his way to warn his new commanding general just how much he disapproved of the unbounded ambition Hooker had displayed in undercutting Burnside. Still, Hooker's important administrative reforms and his obviously positive impact on morale in the ranks gained him at least temporary respect among his colleagues. Second Corps commander Darius Couch, soon to be a Hooker archenemy, wrote of this period before Chancellorsville that General Hooker, "by adopting vigorous measures stopped the almost wholesale desertions, and infused new life and discipline in the Army."[33]

It was, then, a New Model army that entered on the Chancellorsville campaign. Joe Hooker did for the Army of the Potomac after Fredericksburg what George McClellan had done for it after Second Bull Run — each in his own way made the army strong enough and self-confident enough to endure the terrible tests to come. Nevertheless, Hooker's battle, at Chancellorsville, was an undeniable defeat. By May 6, 1863, the Army of the Potomac was in retreat back to the camps it had left in such high hopes ten days earlier.

Following the army's previous battle, at Fredericksburg, Ambrose Burnside had taken responsibility for the defeat upon his own shoulders. Joe Hooker did not do that. Nor did he lay blame for the defeat on the supposed superiority in force of the enemy and on a lack of support by an uncaring administration in Washington, as General McClellan had done after the Seven Days. Instead, Hooker let it be known that the real architects of the defeat were three of his corps commanders: Otis Howard, who let his Eleventh Corps be victimized by Stonewall Jackson; John Sedgwick, who repeatedly mishandled command of the army's left wing; and George Stoneman of the cavalry, who utterly failed to carry out his assignment to cut Lee's communications. (Hooker could properly have added the Third Corps' Dan Sickles to this list, except that Sickles was his protégé.) At this attack on several of its own, the army's high command took offense and closed ranks against the general commanding.

In startling fashion, a new generals' revolt arose almost immediately after the army returned to its Falmouth camps. A prime reason behind this uprising was Hooker's lack of any constituency among his lieutenants. Of the army's eight corps commanders, only three — Sickles, Howard, and Stoneman — could be said to owe their positions to Hooker. And after his condemnation of Howard and Stoneman for their failings in the campaign, only Dan Sickles had any reason to still register loyalty to the general commanding. Furthermore, Hooker in his ambition had set an unfortunate precedent with his noisy litany of complaints against McClellan and Burnside. It would be much remarked afterward that Joe Hooker had sown the wind for the whirlwind that would consume him.

The army's high command was unanimous in laying blame for

the defeat squarely and solely at Hooker's feet. Other factors, including any high command failings, were passed over. Chancellorsville, these generals decided, was a battle that *should* have been won, and *ought* to have been won. John Gibbon concluded that Hooker had "shown a complete want of *backbone* at the wrong moment. . . ." George Meade told his wife that "General Hooker has disappointed all his friends by failing to show his fighting qualities at the pinch." This, he added, had shaken confidence in the general, "particularly among the superior officers." Meade did detect one thing in Hooker's favor just then, however — there were no intriguers among his lieutenants. There were, in short, no Joe Hookers after his job.[34]

Henry Slocum and Darius Couch would act as ringleaders of this latest generals' revolt, although initially at least they seem not to have acted in concert. Slocum had advanced up the command ladder under Franklin, and then been given the Twelfth Corps after Antietam. At Chancellorsville, where he led the right wing of the army to open the campaign, Slocum's disenchantment with Hooker's generalship blossomed into lasting personal antipathy. Couch was a West Point classmate and disciple of McClellan's, and like McClellan he was exceedingly careful and cautious. He was the most senior of the corps commanders, and as such had been anointed by Hooker as his second-in-command. However, any loyalty Couch felt he owed a superior seems to have been directed toward General McClellan and his return.

Lincoln visited the army at Falmouth soon after the battle in company with General Halleck. Halleck met with the corps commanders in council, where there was expressed (in the words of Couch) "great dissatisfaction among the higher officers at the management at Chancellorsville." It was Slocum's thought to secure majority agreement among the corps commanders for a petition to the president calling for Hooker's replacement by their agreed-upon choice — General Meade.

To that end, Slocum, Couch, and John Sedgwick, all senior to Meade, sent that general assurances they would be pleased to serve under his command. The pivotal figure in the scheme was Meade, but he rejected Slocum's pleadings. He insisted he would not participate in any such movement against the general commanding. He went on to say, however, that if Mr. Lincoln should ask for his vote in formal council, he would vote for Hooker's replacement. Although more fair-minded than most of his fellows, Meade seems to have felt that Hooker would not be able to command effectively lacking the confidence of his lieutenants. Still, he believed, change must be initiated from the top, not from below. Without Meade in his camp, Slocum backed away from presenting his petition to the president.

Couch made his own approach to Meade at this time. "I declined to join Couch in a representation to the President . . . ," Meade told his wife. Just what that "representation" was to be is not clear, but like Slocum, Couch concluded not to approach Lincoln that day without some alliance with Meade. Two days later, Couch made formal application through channels to the president "to be relieved from a command in this army." When the application crossed Hooker's desk, Couch wrote, "Gen. Hooker seemed astounded and returned it."[35]

Frustrated in this effort at direct action, the conspirators went to work behind the scenes. Word of their attempted coup got back to Washington. General Heintzelman was visited by a general just up from Falmouth, and recorded in his diary the "great dissatisfaction" within the officer corps: "A corps commander wished the others to join him & see Mr. Lincoln when he was down there & state the opinion they had, but they would not join him." Andrew Curtin, the influential governor of Pennsylvania, paid a visit to the army and brought word back to the White House that Hooker had lost his lieutenants' confidence. He mentioned particularly Meade and John Reynolds of the First Corps in this regard. The press was enlisted in the usual manner — leaked stories that pointed up incompetence by General Hooker in the late battle. Some officers took the unusual step of persuading *New York Tribune* correspondent George Smalley to go to Meade and tell him that the army, or at least the officer corps, fully supported him for the post of commander of the Army of the Potomac.[36]

To the president, the critical aspect of army command was the support (or lack of it) by the subordinate generals. This had been a major factor in his decision to replace Burnside, and it was becoming a paramount factor in the case of Hooker. On May 14, a week after his return from Falmouth, Lincoln warned Hooker of dissension in his officer ranks. "I must tell you," the president wrote, "that I have some painful intimations that some of your corps and division commanders are not giving you their entire confidence. This would be ruinous, if true, and you should therefore, first of all, ascertain the real facts beyond all possibility of doubt."

Hooker went up to Washington to discuss the matter. He said he had no idea who the disaffected might be, nor did he suspect anyone. Surely that may be doubted. In any event, Hooker suggested that the president himself "ascertain their feelings." His lieutenants were free to visit the White House, he later testified, and "I would request them to call on him, and he could then learn their views for his own information." In reporting this curious arrangement to the Joint Committee on the Conduct of the War, Hooker said that "from time to time" most of the corps commanders did indeed go to Washington, but that he "never learned the result of their interviews with the President."[37]

Initially Lincoln intended to stay with Hooker, not wanting to be seen as changing generals after every battle, but the expressed discontent of the officer corps was sending a powerful message. Soundings were taken for Hooker's replacement. Winfield Scott Hancock, a divisional commander under Couch, wrote his wife that he had been approached, but assured her that he would not accept should the command be offered. "I do not belong to that class of generals whom the Republicans care to bolster up," he explained. When the subject of commanding was mentioned to John Sedgwick, he proclaimed Meade as the only choice. On May 22 Darius Couch went to the president with his resignation. Asked about taking the command — he was, after all, the most senior of

Hooker's lieutenants — he begged off and urged Meade for the post. Couch was put in charge of the Pennsylvania militia, and much to the Potomac army's benefit, Win Hancock took over the Second Corps.[38]

Another White House visitor, on June 2, was John Reynolds, who had heard through a third party that he was being considered for the army command. Earlier in the year, Reynolds had written home of his disgust at the way the Potomac army was managed: "If we do not get someone who can command an army without consulting Stanton and Halleck in Washington, I do not know what will become of this army." Apparently he stated his terms in just that fashion, knowing it would rule him out of consideration. As he would tell Colonel Wainwright, he "was unwilling to take Burnside's and Hooker's leavings." Reynolds went on to speak "very freely" about Hooker, and to urge the president to appoint Meade in Hooker's place.[39]

With the notable exception of Hooker's loyal friend Dan Sickles, the other generals who visited the White House in this period were no doubt as candid with their advice as were Couch and Reynolds. Secretary of the Treasury Chase, Hooker's strongest ally in the Cabinet, warned him that it was a mistake to let his corps commanders come to Washington "to tell their several stories." Each one, Chase observed, knows "how much better everything else would have been done, if his counsel or his ideas had been followed." Hooker, with all his experience in intrigue, apparently realized it was better that the dissidents be forced to take their stand in the open. Interestingly, there seems to have been no concern during this second revolt of the generals about what had so worried General Newton during *his* White House visit — that criticism of the general commanding would be considered manifestly improper conduct for an officer.[40]

Joe Hooker's relief from command on the eve of Gettysburg would come in a contretemps with General-in-Chief Halleck, but it was the generals' revolt that set the stage for it. With virtually no support from his chief lieutenants, most of whom had instead announced their loyalty to their own candidate, George Meade,

Hooker was pushed into a precarious position. This lack of soldierly support was a matter of grave concern to the president. It appears that by abruptly forcing Hooker to take direction from Halleck, between whom there was great mutual distrust, Lincoln was anticipating a showdown — and in Meade he had ready a successor who would command unquestioned loyalty.

This generals' revolt, unlike the earlier one that brought down Burnside, produced fewer consequences. Indeed, Couch's departure served to strengthen the Army of the Potomac, bringing to the fore in his place a true fighting general in Win Hancock. Couch would mobilize Pennsylvania militia during the Gettysburg campaign, and afterward lead a division in the western theater. Following Gettysburg, Slocum went west with the Twelfth Corps, where he managed to avoid having to serve under Hooker. He would finish his war service under Sherman.

Meade's accession to the command brought to an end the long-running revolt of the generals. The man the dissidents had sworn allegiance to now headed the Army of the Potomac, and they had little excuse for complaint. Furthermore, when U. S. Grant was named general-in-chief in 1864 and elected to travel on campaign with the Potomac army, he went unquestioned as a figure of command. The dissident generals had challenged the system and set a bad precedent during lesser regimes, but their example would not be repeated. To be sure, there would be times when Meade's removal was debated, but not because of intrigues fomented by his lieutenants. As Colonel Wainwright wrote when Meade's accession was announced, "At our own headquarters where Meade is known, the apppointment was very favourably received."[41]

NOTES

1. L. A. Whitley to James Gordon Bennett, Sept. 24, 1862, Bennett Papers, Library of Congress.

2. See McClellan to S.L.M. Barlow, July 15, 23, 30, McClellan to William H. Aspinwall, July 19, 1862, George B. McClellan, *The Civil War Papers of George B. McClellan: Selected Correspondence, 1860–1865*, ed. Stephen W. Sears (New

York: Ticknor & Fields, 1989), 360–61, 369–70, 376–77, 365–66; and Fitz John Porter to Manton Marble, July 1862, Marble Papers, Library of Congress.

3. Nathaniel Paige clipping, n.d., John Hay Papers, Illinois State Historical Library; *Washington Capitol*, Mar. 21, 1880.

4. Gideon Welles, *The Diary of Gideon Welles*, ed. Howard K. Beale (New York: Norton, 1960), vol. 1, 146; "Record of Dismissal of John J. Key," Abraham Lincoln, *The Collected Works of Abraham Lincoln*, ed. Roy P. Basler (New Brunswick, N.J.: Rutgers University Press, 1953–55), vol. 5, 442–43; John Hay, *Inside Lincoln's White House: The Complete Civil War Diary of John Hay*, eds. Michael Burlingame and John R. Turner Ettlinger (Carbondale: Southern Illinois University Press, 1997), 41, 232.

5. T. J. Barnett to S.L.M. Barlow, Sept. 23, Barlow Papers, Huntington Library; Montgomery Blair to McClellan, Sept. 27, 1862, McClellan Papers, Library of Congress.

6. General Orders No. 163, *Official Records* 19:2, 395; *New York Tribune*, Oct. 9, 1862.

7. *New York Times*, Nov. 12, 1862.

8. Hooker to James W. Nesmith, n.d., Oregon Historical Society; Hooker testimony, *Report of the Joint Committee on the Conduct of the War*, vol. 1 (1863), 578; Salmon P. Chase, *The Salmon P. Chase Papers*, ed. John Niven (Kent, Ohio: Kent State University Press, 1993), vol. 1, 396–97.

9. Walter H. Hebert, *Fighting Joe Hooker* (Indianapolis: Bobbs-Merrill, 1944), 150; *New York Express*, Oct. 22, 1862; Barnett to Barlow, Oct. 27, 1862, Barlow Papers; George G. Meade, *The Life and Letters of General George Gordon Meade* (New York: Scribner's, 1913), vol. 1, 318, 332; Welles, *Diary*, vol. 1, 229.

10. Burnside to Halleck, Dec. 17, 1862, *OR* 21, 66–67; Samuel P. Heintzelman diary, Jan. 11, 1863, Heintzelman Papers, Library of Congress.

11. William F. Smith, *Autobiography of Major General William F. Smith, 1861–1864*, ed. Herbert M. Schiller (Dayton: Morningside, 1990), 39, 59.

12. Franklin and Smith to Lincoln, Dec. 20, 1862, *OR* 21, 868–70.

13. McClellan memoirs draft, McClellan Papers; Smith, *Autobiography*, 58; Gouverneur K. Warren to brother, Dec. 18, 1862, Warren Papers, New York State Library.

14. Lincoln to Franklin and Smith, Dec. 22, 1862, Lincoln, *Collected Works*, vol. 6, 15; Franklin to Lincoln, Dec. 26, 1862, Stanton Papers, Library of Congress.

15. Stephen W. Sears, *George B. McClellan: The Young Napoleon* (New York: Ticknor & Fields, 1988), 329.

16. Franklin, Cochrane testimony, *Report of Joint Committee*, vol. 1 (1863), 712, 742; William F. Smith in *Magazine of American History* (Feb. 1886), 197.

17. Newton, Cochrane testimony, *Report of Joint Committee*, vol. 1 (1863), 731–33, 742–43.

18. Lincoln to Burnside, Burnside to Lincoln, Dec. 30, 1862, *OR* 21, 900.

19. Burnside testimony, *Report of Joint Committee*, vol. 1 (1863), 717–18.

20. Burnside to Lincoln, Jan. 1, 5, 1863, *OR* 21, 941–42, 944–45; Burnside memorandum, May 24, 1863, RG 94, U.S. Generals' Reports, National Ar-

chives; Burnside testimony, *Report of Joint Committee,* vol. 1 (1863), 718.

21. Lincoln to Halleck, Halleck to Stanton, Jan. 1, 1863, *OR* 21, 940–41.

22. Meade, *Life and Letters,* vol. 1, 344; Burnside General Orders No. 8 (unissued), Jan. 23, 1863, *OR* 21, 998.

23. Heintzelman diary, Jan. 5, 12, 1863, Heintzelman Papers.

24. Hooker testimony, *Report of Joint Committee,* vol. 1 (1863), 665–66, 670; Zachariah Chandler to wife, Jan. 26, 1863, Chandler Papers, Library of Congress; Hooker to Stanton, Feb. 25, 1864, *OR* 32:2, 468.

25. *New York Times,* Jan. 13, 1863.

26. Edward H. Taylor to "Bill," Jan. 25, 1863, Michigan Historical Collections, Bentley Historical Library, University of Michigan.

27. Henry W. Raymond, ed., "Excerpts from the Journal of Henry J. Raymond," *Scribner's Monthly* (Jan. 1880), 421–22.

28. Charles S. Wainwright, *A Diary of Battle: The Personal Journals of Colonel Charles S. Wainwright, 1861–1865,* ed. Allan Nevins (New York: Harcourt, Brace & World, 1962), 157–58, 159.

29. General Orders No. 8 (unissued), Jan. 23, 1863, *OR* 21, 998–99.

30. Raymond, "Raymond Journal" (Mar. 1880), 703–4; Burnside testimony, *Report of Joint Committee,* vol. 1 (1863), 720; Burnside to Lincoln, Jan. 23, 1863, *OR* 21, 998.

31. Burnside testimony, *Report of Joint Committee,* vol. 1 (1863), 720; Carl Schurz to Lincoln, Jan. 24, 1863, Lincoln Papers, Library of Congress; Raymond, "Raymond Journal" (Mar. 1880), 705. See "The Court-Martial of Fitz John Porter" elsewhere in this collection.

32. Burnside testimony, *Report of Joint Committee,* vol. 1 (1863), 720–22; Hooker to Samuel P. Bates, June 29, 1878, Bates Collection, Pennsylvania Historical and Museum Commission, Pennsylvania State Archives. The account of the command change by Charles F. Benjamin in *Battles and Leaders of the Civil War,* vol. 3, 239–40, is largely fictional.

33. Lincoln to Hooker, Jan. 26, 1863, Lincoln, *Collected Works,* vol. 6, 78–79; Darius Couch memoir, Old Colony Historical Society.

34. John Gibbon to McClellan, May 18, 1863, McClellan Papers; Meade, *Life and Letters,* vol. 1, 372, 373.

35. Couch memoir, Old Colony Historical Society; Alexander S. Webb to brother, May 1863, Webb Papers, Yale University Library; Meade, *Life and Letters,* vol. 1, 373, 379.

36. Heintzelman diary, May 13, 1863, Heintzelman Papers; Meade, *Life and Letters,* vol. 1, 374; George W. Smalley, *Anglo-American Memories* (New York: Putnam's, 1911), 158–59.

37. Lincoln to Hooker, May 14, 1863, *OR* 25:2, 479; Hooker testimony, *Report of Joint Committee,* vol. 1 (1865), 151.

38. David M. Jordan, *Winfield Scott Hancock: A Soldier's Life* (Bloomington: Indiana University Press, 1988), 75; Meade, *Life and Letters,* vol. 2, 6; Francis A. Walker, *History of the Second Army Corps* (New York: Scribner's, 1887), 254.

39. Oliver J. Keller, "Soldier General of the Army: John Fulton Reynolds," *Civil*

War History (June 1958), 123–25; Wainwright, *Diary of Battle*, 229; Meade, *Life and Letters*, vol. 1, 385.

40. *New York Herald*, May 16, 1863; Chase to Hooker, May 23, 1863, Hebert, *Fighting Joe Hooker*, 229.

41. Wainwright, *Diary of Battle*, 227.

[7]

In Defense of Fighting Joe

Major General Joseph Hooker

MAJOR GENERAL JOSEPH HOOKER has long received a uniformly bad press from Civil War historians. "Fighting Joe" invariably lags toward the bottom of any ranking of the commanders of the Army of the Potomac, clumped together with John Pope and Ambrose Burnside. The old whispers that he was drunk at Chancellorsville, his one battle as army commander, are whispered anew. Alternatively, if it is allowed that in fact he was sober at Chancellorsville, it is said his fault was going teetotal upon assuming his new responsibilities; better for the army had he downed a few whiskeys when the fighting began in the Virginia Wilderness. As T. Harry Williams put it, "The sudden shutting off of his familiar stimulant was bad for Hooker. He depended on whiskey to brace his courage."[1]

But the historians' primary charge against Joe Hooker is that, drunk or sober, when he was confronted by Robert E. Lee at Chancellorsville he lost his nerve and thereby lost the battle. James McPherson describes the scene metaphorically: "Like a rabbit mesmerized by the gray fox, Hooker was frozen into immobility. . . ." These authorities point to firm documentation for their case: an admission of his loss of nerve by Hooker himself. In their acclaimed studies, Shelby Foote, Bruce Catton, and Kenneth P. Williams all quote the general's confession. Hooker's biographer Walter Hebert adopts the confession as a chapter title — "Hooker

Loses Confidence in Hooker." A profile of Hooker in *American Heritage* trumpets, "He was close to winning the Civil War when he suffered an almost incredible failure of nerve." In a kind of final sanctification, Hooker's words are given voice in Ken Burns's 1990 television epic, "The Civil War."[2]

Is it any wonder, then, that Fighting Joe Hooker's military reputation has fallen into such low repute? What could be worse than an army commander losing his nerve in the midst of a battle? In fact, there *is* something worse — that general confessing his failing. For the historian seeking to document how the Union lost the Battle of Chancellorsville, here is the clear and simple answer, in the clear and simple words of the commanding general himself. And so in the books and the articles and the biographical studies — and on television — Joe Hooker has become fixed forever, as if in amber, as the general who lost his nerve.

It was not always thus. The revelation of Hooker's confession came nearly half a century after the occasion for it, in May of 1863, and not all that many of his wartime comrades were still alive then to hear of it. Joe Hooker was always tremendously popular with his men — a popularity the equal of McClellan's — and he was widely known and admired as the general who fed his troops as well as he led them. When he assumed command of the Army of the Potomac, in January 1863, Hooker was regarded, and deservedly, as the fightingest general in that army. On the Peninsula, in the Seven Days, at Second Bull Run and Antietam and Fredericksburg, he had proved himself a leader who showed no fear of going in with his men — he was wounded at Antietam — and who revealed no lack of decision in the heat of the fighting. Nor did the Chancellorsville defeat drive Hooker off the Civil War stage. In the Chattanooga campaign that fall he seized Lookout Mountain in spectacular fashion, and on the road to Atlanta the following spring his Twentieth Corps did more hard fighting for Sherman than any other outfit.[3]

Hooker remained popular and admired and respected after the war. Although crippled by strokes suffered in 1865 and 1867, he was active in veterans' affairs and visited the old battlefields and closely followed the early efforts at compiling histories of the war. He died, just shy of his sixty-fifth birthday, in 1879. A quarter century later, on Boston's Beacon Hill, an equestrian statue of Joseph Hooker, native son of Massachusetts, was unveiled with appropriate ceremony. Naysayers did not interrupt the proceedings.

Theodore A. Dodge, a fledgling historian of the war, was made uncomfortably aware of the admiration in which Hooker was held after he delivered a lecture on the Battle of Chancellorsville to a Boston audience in 1885. On that occasion, Dodge found not a few faults with Hooker's generalship at Chancellorsville — although he did not accuse him of drunkenness or of losing his nerve. Not long afterward, at a reunion of veterans of the Third Corps, Hooker's old outfit, Dodge found himself the object — indeed the victim — of an angry resolution: "Loyalty to the memory of our beloved commander, Major-Gen. Joseph Hooker, makes it a duty, on this occasion, to protest against unjust and uncalled-for criticisms on his military record as commander of the Army of the Potomac." In the words of poor Dodge, who was in attendance, "the bulk of the time devoted to talking on this occasion was used in denunciation of the wretch, in other words, myself," who had had the temerity to find fault with Fighting Joe.[4]

This is not to say that military historians of the late nineteenth century tiptoed around the subject of Chancellorsville. Theodore Dodge's attack was the sharpest delivered against Hooker, but it was certainly not the only one. After all, there was no gainsaying that he had been soundly defeated, despite having a two-to-one manpower edge over Lee, and that Jackson's surprise attack — Stonewall's last march — had victimized him in dramatic fashion. As general commanding, responsibility for the defeat was undeniably his. Therefore, undeniably, Hooker had been outgeneraled by Lee — in which category, of course, Hooker had plenty of company. Chancellorsville was General Lee's fifth campaign in less than a year, a brief span indeed to have taken the measure of four Union army commanders.

Although not recognized at the time — and not recognized by

latter-day historians either — Joe Hooker managed to have his say in the nineteenth-century debate over his generalship at Chancellorsville. He did so in an indirect way. Hooker wrote little after the war — there was no memoir, for example — and not a great deal during the war. Although he claimed that his report on Antietam (as printed in the *Official Records*) was written within two months of the battle, it was in fact only written fifteen years later. He filed no reports for Second Bull Run or Fredericksburg — and none for Chancellorsville. As to Chancellorsville, he liked to point out that his extended testimony before the Joint Committee on the Conduct of the War, in 1865, was to all intents and purposes his official report of the battle. Since his testimony, in today's parlance, was a "prepared statement," thirty-nine pages long, we can grant him his point.[5]

Hooker opened his second Chancellorsville campaign in 1876 with a letter to a Pennsylvania professor named Samuel Penniman Bates, who the year before had published a history of the Battle of Gettysburg. He "rejoiced to learn," said Hooker, that Professor Bates was "at present engaged in writing a history of the campaign of Chancellorsville," and he felt "extremely anxious that its narrative should be made up *impartially* to all concerned *and truthfully* as it concerns history." At the time, the only published study of Chancellorsville was the view from the Confederate side, by Jedediah Hotchkiss and William Allan, a book that Hooker volunteered to correct in detail for Bates's benefit. The general explained that he had "some manuscripts in my possession which I should like to lay before you before your work is completed." These dealt in particular with "the part Gen. Howard and his command played in the battle. . . ." As Professor Bates was soon to discover, mention of the name Oliver Otis Howard, who had commanded the Eleventh Corps at Chancellorsville, invariably caused General Hooker to see red.[6]

This letter was the first of fifty-six that Hooker wrote Bates over the course of the next three years, the last one written just three weeks before Hooker's death. Bates had responded eagerly to

Hooker's overture, especially to his offer of documents. The *Official Records* volumes on Chancellorsville were a dozen years in the future, and so what the general was offering just then was a Civil War historian's dream come true. Having thus set the hook, the general reeled in his catch. He sent Bates long discourses defending his role in all the controverted points of the campaign. He traveled to the battlefield with him, a visit that Bates would later record for the readers of *Century* magazine's "Battles and Leaders of the Civil War" series. He read and carefully critiqued each of Bates's chapters as he finished them, making sure, among other things, that the professor was clear on Joe Hooker's acerbic views of such of his battlefield lieutenants as the Eleventh Corps' Otis Howard, the Sixth Corps' John Sedgwick, and the cavalry's George Stoneman.

While modern-day reviewers have characterized Bates's writing as turgid and discursive, his book is acknowledged to be "not uninformed." In point of fact, it offers the only clue we have to Joe Hooker's thinking and his decisions at several crucial points in the fighting. Hooker did not live to see the book into print — it was not published until 1882 — but he seems to have been satisfied that his view of the Chancellorsville struggle would be represented. "So much *twaddle* has been written about this battle," he complained in one of his last letters to Bates, but he remained hopeful: "A day of reckoning however is close at hand, and that is all that I want." Perhaps at last Fighting Joe Hooker's day of reckoning is upon us, but the path from then to now has been long and very rocky.[7]

What in due course would send Joe Hooker's military reputation plummeting was nothing more sinister than a footnote in John Bigelow, Jr.'s *The Campaign of Chancellorsville.* Bigelow (as it has come to simply be known) fits the description of a weighty tome. Published in a limited edition of 1,000 copies by Yale University Press in 1910, it is an oversized, imposing volume containing 528 pages, 47 maps and plans, and the draping of Authority. The footnote, giving Major E. P. Halstead as source, appears in Bigelow's concluding chapter, titled "Comments," where he is describing what he terms "Hooker's irresolution in this campaign"; clearly Bigelow intended it to document that irresolution. The footnote relates an incident that took place "a couple of months" after Chancellorsville, during the march toward Gettysburg. The Army of the Potomac had just crossed the Potomac in pursuit of Lee, and army commander Hooker was riding with Abner Doubleday, who led a division in the First Corps, when Doubleday turned to him and asked, "Hooker, what was the matter with you at Chancellorsville? Some say you were injured by a shell, and others that you were drunk; now tell us what it was." Hooker answered, frankly and good-naturedly: "Doubleday, I was not hurt by a shell, and I was not drunk. For once I lost confidence in Hooker, and that is all there is to it."[8]

Since 1910, it is safe to say, every author (with one exception) writing about Chancellorsville, or about Joe Hooker, or about the change of command in the Army of the Potomac just before Gettysburg, or indeed writing any general military account of the period, or any study of the Union high command, has quoted or paraphrased or cited this exchange. These authors all appear to have done so without a second thought, so imposing is Bigelow's reputation.

Give it a second thought, however, and even on the face of it there is an odor to this incident. For example, Hooker is said to have replied that, no, he was not injured by a shell at Chancellorsville. Yet in fact he was quite seriously injured when a wooden pillar of the Chancellor house, against which he was leaning, was hit by a Confederate solid shot. In the weeks since the battle he had often spoken of this injury as a factor in his defeat, and for him now to deny it ever happened is not credible. His confession is even less credible. Joe Hooker, it is true, was likely to say all manner of surprising and outrageous things — but never in disparagement of himself. Quite the contrary. He had made sure it was widely known in these weeks that it was his lieutenants who had failed at Chancellorsville; he might have to accept the ultimate responsibility, but it was they who were really to blame for the lost campaign. For Joe Hooker to admit to a subordinate (and within hearing of that subordinate's aide hovering nearby) that he had lost his confidence, his nerve, in the midst of battle is just not believable.

Look closely at the retailer of this tale, E. P. Halstead, and it all quickly comes unraveled. Halstead had served on Doubleday's wartime staff, and in 1903 — forty years after the alleged event — he included this conversation between Hooker and Doubleday in a letter describing the First Corps' role at Chancellorsville. Bigelow acquired the letter as research for his book. When the movements of Hooker's headquarters and of the First Corps' headquarters are tracked for this period, it is clear that they were dozens of miles apart, with never an opportunity for the two generals to meet like this. Indeed, Hooker and Doubleday were never near enough to meet at *any* time on the march north from the Rappahannock and before Hooker left the army command. For good measure, the rest of Halstead's letter is a grossly inaccurate account of the First Corps' actions at Chancellorsville.[9]

Halstead's tale is not all that uncommon for Civil War historiography of the turn of the century — an elderly staff officer with at best a clouded recollection of some long-ago campfire speculation, or with at worst an urge to create a role for himself — in this case, a footnote — in the history of this war of the past. Of course the two principals were dead and unavailable to confirm or deny. Civil War bookshelves, alas, are crowded with memoirs and recollections of events that never happened, retailed by old Yanks and old Johnnies seeking a little sliver of notice in what had been for them the greatest experience of their lives.

With this slanderous cliché discounted, where does it leave us in evaluating Joe Hooker's generalship? It is useful to look first at what in the nineteenth century was termed the qualities for moral leadership. This was more than morality per se; it meant the whole of a man's character for leading in war. It needs to be understood, in this connection, that Joseph Hooker came into the Civil War, at least in the eyes of certain of his contemporaries, as something less than a gentleman. The antebellum army was a species of petty aristocracy, putting a high premium on social conformity, and with his rough edges Joe Hooker was no model of conformity.

His biographer Walter Hebert explains that during his posting in California in the 1850s "Idleness led Hooker along the usual path to the devil's workshop." He played cards for money, he drank, and he pursued female companionship in the manner of a middle-aged bachelor in the Victorian era — that is, he paid for his pleasure. It seems that civilian society was more tolerant of these habits than the military, and Hooker's raffish California reputation preceded him into the Civil War. General McClellan would write that in 1861 he gave a briefing on Hooker to Mr. Lincoln: "I told him that in the Mexican War Hooker was looked upon as a good soldier but an unreliable man, & that his course in California had been such as to forfeit the respect of his comrades — that he was then a common drunkard & gambler."[10]

It is true enough that Hooker enjoyed a game of cards played for money, but that he was a common drunkard is another matter. There is good evidence that the reputation of a drinker that attached to Joe Hooker was more perceived than real. John Hay, Lincoln's secretary, made a perceptive comment on the subject. In his diary Hay described dining one evening in Washington with a group that included the general. "Hooker drank very little," he wrote, "not more than the rest who were all abstemious, yet what little he drank made his cheek hot and red & his eye brighter. I can easily understand how the stories of his drunkenness have grown, if so little affects him as I have seen."

This would explain the contradictions in the contemporary evidence — Hooker *appearing* to have drunk to excess when in reality he drank no more, and probably less, than the average general and was in no way impaired in the process. It also belies the imputation, made first by the vindictive General Darius Couch, that Hooker was an alcoholic who found his courage in a bottle and lost it if he stopped drinking. There are too many adamant and wholly reliable eyewitnesses to Hooker's sobriety — among them General George Meade, artilleryman Charles Wainwright, and intelligence chief George Sharpe — for anyone today to believe otherwise. Joe Hooker did not abuse alcohol, nor was he dependent on it.[11]

Nevertheless, the undercurrent of tales about Hooker's drinking, originating from his California days, persisted all the way through his war service, apparently unquenchable. Some who saw him lying comatose after his injury at Chancellorsville, for example, spread the gossip that he was dead drunk. Following the battle, cavalryman George Armstrong Custer made sure his old commander, General McClellan, knew what was behind the report of Hooker's wounding by a shell. "If anything," Custer wrote, ". . . prevented him from succeeding, it was a wound he received from a projectile which requires a cork to be drawn before it is serviceable." Congressional investigators visiting the army could find no basis for such charges. The *New York Tribune* put its best correspondent, George Smalley, on the story. "I asked everybody likely to know," Smalley reported, "and not one witness could testify to having seen General Hooker the worse for whiskey." But the gossip was too deeply rooted to disappear.[12]

Another dimension of the general's moral character acted on the gossips like pure catnip. On January 31, 1863, soon after Hooker took command of the Army of the Potomac, artillerist Charles Wainwright entered in his diary, "I am asked on all sides here if he drinks. Though thrown in very close contact with him through six months, I never saw him when I thought him the worse for liquor." Then he added, "Indeed, I should say that his failing was more in the way of women than whiskey." Blue-blooded Charles Francis Adams, Jr., grandson and great-grandson of presidents, is often quoted on this latter failing of Hooker's. During that winter of 1862–63, sniffed Captain Adams, "the headquarters of the Army of the Potomac was a place to which no self-respecting man liked to go, and no decent woman could go. It was a combination of barroom and brothel." During this period in Washington, it was said, the general's carriage might be found of an evening drawn up outside one or another of the city's better-known brothels; indeed, a section of Washington's Second Ward thickly packed with brothels was known — and continued to be known for many years afterward — as Hooker's Division.[13]

In contrast with the tales of Hooker's drunkenness, there seems to be little doubt that the general patronized prostitutes, although Adams's contention that Army of the Potomac headquarters was little better than a brothel must be taken at a large discount. At age forty-eight and unmarried when he took command of the army, Joe Hooker apparently followed the practice of many bachelors of elevated station in the Victorian age, and he made no particular secret of it. The one myth in this connection is that the slang term for a prostitute derived from his name. In fact "hooker" long predated the Civil War, originating probably from streetwalkers "hooking" or snaring their clients.[14] This did not prevent insiders in Washington from winking and snickering at the nice conjunction between the general's name and the general's proclivity. The broad-minded dismissed the matter with a shrug. Hooker's enemies regarded it as evidence of his moral unfitness for high command.

One other burden Joe Hooker brought with him from his days in California was a mutually embittering relationship with Henry W. Halleck. For the general-in-chief of all the North's armies and the general commanding the largest of those armies to be at loggerheads was an awkward situation, to say the least; certainly it was one more burden President Lincoln had to bear. Halleck was characteristically guarded on the subject, saying only that Hooker was aware "that I know some things about his character and conduct in California, and, fearing that I may use that information against him, he seeks to ward off its effect by making it appear that I am his personal enemy. . . ." Hooker, characteristically, was not at all guarded about their dispute. During their days together in California, he explained, Halleck joined a law firm specializing in land claims, and Hooker, trying to protect the interests of acquaintances, charged Halleck to his face with "schemes of avarice and plunder. . . . Indeed I indulged in still harsher language. . . ." Whatever the truth of the matter — and Hooker's explanation is the more convincing of the two — it sounds like something Joe Hooker would say, and in a loud voice. He insisted Halleck carried a grudge against him right into the war. It was Halleck, he said, who had persuaded Lincoln to award command of the Army of the Potomac to Burnside in November 1862 rather than to him.[15]

When, two and a half months later, after the Fredericksburg disaster, Lincoln came to replace Burnside with Hooker, this time the president took the decision alone, without consulting General Halleck; he recognized Halleck's predisposition. Hooker's sole condition for accepting the appointment was his insistence on an arm's-length relationship with the general-in-chief — neither the Army of the Potomac "nor its commander expected justice at his hands," Hooker told the president. On all substantive matters he would deal only with Lincoln, and so it was until the finish of the Chancellorsville campaign. Halleck complained that he was the last person in Washington to know what was going on with the Army of the Potomac.[16]

Until Hooker retreated back across the Rappahannock, ending his Chancellorsville adventure, generally he was allowed to operate the Potomac army with a free hand. He could ignore the general-in-chief with impunity. Now, however, as Lee's army shifted northward and became an invading force, Mr. Lincoln began drawing in the reins on his army commander. The divide between Hooker and Halleck became an important factor in the growing crisis. "It was no use for me to make a request," Hooker said, "as that of itself would be sufficient cause for General Halleck to refuse it." The president sought to smooth the path between the two with a letter to Hooker marked "private." "If you and he would use the same frankness to one another, and to me, that I use to both of you," Lincoln wrote, "there would be no difficulty. I need and must have the professional skill of both, and yet these suspicions tend to deprive me of both. . . . Now, all I ask is that you will be in such mood that we can get into our action the best cordial judgment of yourself and General Halleck. . . ."[17]

It was to no avail, of course. Halleck, having regained the upper hand over his stubbornly independent subordinate, was not about to surrender it again. Neither he nor Hooker would blink, and in due course they clashed, disastrously for Hooker, over the garrison at Harper's Ferry. Hooker wanted the garrison for his army, Halleck refused him, Hooker filed his resignation in protest. It was accepted and Joe Hooker was gone — gone forever — from the army he had become so much a part of. Hooker noted bitterly that his successor, General Meade, was allowed to do as he wished with the Harper's Ferry garrison. In his valedictory to the Joint Committee on the Conduct of the War, Hooker leveled a broadside at Henry Halleck. "If the general-in-chief had been in the rebel interest," he testified, "it would have been impossible for him . . . to have added to the embarrassment he caused me from the moment I took command of the army of the Potomac to the time I surrendered it."[18]

For historians persuaded by Bigelow's footnote that Joe Hooker had lost his nerve at Chancellorsville, it was but a short step to the conclusion that he welcomed the chance to relinquish army command in the face of the new test looming ahead. General Hooker, wrote T. Harry Williams, "was looking for an excuse to get rid of his command. He was afraid of Lee." But once the Bigelow footnote is deleted, as it were, the matter takes on a different cast.

It is acknowledged that Hooker's march north from the Rappahannock was carried out with considerable skill. It was Hooker who dispatched cavalry to the town of Gettysburg as the most likely point of concentration for the Confederates, and his moves shadowing Lee seem to have been taken with considerable confidence. This in spite of the fact that he was in constant friction with the general-in-chief, and was also the recipient of a warning from Mr. Lincoln: "I must tell you that I have some painful intimations that some of your corps and division commanders are not giving you their entire confidence." Indeed, it seems that the real purpose behind Hooker's resignation was merely to precipitate a showdown with Halleck. Joe Hooker's comment on the change of command, although written later, appears to be a true reflection of his feelings in that summer of 1863. The "wavering and vacillating" of some of his lieutenants did bother him, he admitted. "However," he wrote, "this would have been a source of no regret, could I have commanded, *as I wished to,* at Gettysburg, but the fates were against me."[19]

In contrast with the McClellan era, Lincoln's relationship with Hooker as army commander had been comfortable and open. The president was remarkably candid with his general when appointing him to the command, and Hooker responded with full reports of his intentions and with details of his plans. He also respected, and acted on, the president's suggestions. Whatever Joe Hooker's failings — and Lincoln was very much aware of them — this man would fight. He might be rash, he might intrigue for promotion, he might be suspect in his personal habits, but on his record he would fight. After Antietam, when McClellan was dragging his feet and Lincoln was casting about for a general to replace him, the president had observed to a visitor, "Now there's Joe Hooker — he can fight — I think that point is pretty well established — but whether he can 'keep tavern' for a large army is not so sure."[20]

It was the president's experience that fighting generals were in short supply, and at first, after Chancellorsville, Lincoln was willing to give Hooker the benefit of the doubt. He was not disposed, he said, to throw away a gun just because it misfired once. In any case, it would look bad to the country if the administration continued to relieve its generals after each battle. What finally changed the president's mind, as much as anything else, was the outspoken complaints against General Hooker by the Potomac army's high command. It had not sat well with these corps commanders when Hooker blamed some of their own — specifically Howard, Sedgwick, and Stoneman — for the Chancellorsville defeat. A generals' revolt had orchestrated Burnside's overthrow after Fredericksburg; now, after Chancellorsville, the same fate befell Joe Hooker, ironically one of the originators of high-command discontent in this army.

When Lincoln warned Hooker about his dissident generals, he observed that the effect of such a revolt on the army would be "ruinous, if true." With a showdown battle sure to be fought any day, somewhere in Maryland or Pennsylvania, it was vital that there be harmony among the generals who had to direct the fighting. The dissidents made it clear to Lincoln that General Meade was their choice; Hooker had commended Meade as his best corps commander. With John Reynolds having taken himself out of contention for the high command, Meade's appointment was made without debate. Joe Hooker would have no second chance against Robert E. Lee; the fates, as he said, were against him.[21]

Amidst all the controversy that has swirled about this larger-than-life figure, all the gossip and debate about his moral character, it has been all too easy to overlook certain unique qualities of Joe Hooker's generalship. The first of these is how well Hooker was prepared for army command when compared with most of his fellow officers in the antebellum army. The primary training ground for the Civil War general had been the Mexican War. Much has been written of Lee's scouting missions on the march to Mexico City, of Jackson fighting his guns at Chapultepec, of McClellan's bravery under fire, and other such exploits. Yet beyond the indelible experience of serving under enemy fire, the tactical lessons of Mexico were mostly those of the smoothbore era. The age of rifled armaments — Springfields and Enfields and Parrott cannon — ushered in by the Civil War was something new under the sun for the American soldier.

What could be gained from the war with Mexico, however, was the experience of military administration — literally how to run a command, and how to do it efficiently. In this Joe Hooker's Mexican War experience was unexcelled. He served as chief of staff to no fewer than five generals. None was a professional; each relied on Major Hooker to run his command for him. This involved, in addition, leading troops in combat often enough to earn him three brevets for gallantry. When Joe Hooker met Lincoln for the first time, after First Bull Run, he blurted out, "I was at Bull Run the other day, Mr. President, and it is no vanity in me to say that I am a damned sight better general than any you had on that field." He may have spoken brashly, but he had the credentials to back up his brashness. And he did back it up.[22]

There is something refreshing about such candor, and indeed there is something refreshing about Joe Hooker. By all accounts, he was open and warm and disarmingly sincere in his personal relationships. "A gallant and chivalrous soldier," General Alpheus Williams said of him, "and most agreeable. . . ." To be sure, Hooker talked far too much and too indiscreetly and with too much brag, but what he said, upon examination, often sounds suspiciously like truth. His boast to Mr. Lincoln that he was a damned sight better general than any the Union had at First Bull Run is an example. Look at some of the Union names on that battlefield — McDowell, Heintzelman, Keyes, Hunter — and one is inclined to agree. When he observed that Ambrose Burnside had a brain the size of a hickory nut, he may not have been far off the mark. Hooker liked to boast, before Chancellorsville, that he had the finest army on the planet, and considering the sorry state of the army that he inherited from Burnside, and how he had restored it to life, there was truth there, too. In the midst of the Chancellorsville fight he issued an address to his army, saying, "our enemy must either ingloriously fly, or come out from behind his defenses and give us battle on our own ground, where certain destruction awaits him." This prediction would be much derided, yet at the time of its issue it was an exactly accurate statement of the case — and, if the truth be acknowledged, "certain destruction" ought to have been Lee's fate.[23]

Joe Hooker was outspoken enough to wear his ambition on his sleeve. He sincerely believed that he was a better general than George McClellan (and he was), and that his fighting record rated him the command in McClellan's place. He had no doubt at all that he was a better general than Ambrose Burnside (and without a doubt he was), and he unblushingly campaigned for Burnside's spot. The Army of the Potomac, rooted and grown to maturity in Washington, was the most politicized of Civil War armies, which fact Hooker understood perfectly; to get ahead in that army, one had to have friends in high places. It was necessary and vital that he work at that. General Halleck, head of the army, was his enemy and the roadblock to his advancement, but Hooker hoped to neutralize Halleck by cultivating members of Congress and the two Cabinet members he regarded as the most influential: Secretary of War Stanton and Secretary of the Treasury Chase. Others might call this intrigue; Hooker called it pragmatism.

The one friend in high places who understood Hooker best was, of course, Abraham Lincoln. Lincoln's famous letter of January 26, 1863, handed to Hooker along with his appointment as Army of the Potomac commander, weighed the general's assets and liabilities in blunt but kindly fashion. After fifteen months of frustration trying to reach and reason with General McClellan, Mr. Lincoln, the commander-in-chief, was determined that this general understand exactly what was expected of him. The letter's candor also owed much to the Lincoln-Hooker arrangement to shunt Halleck to the sideline in the forthcoming campaign; if Hooker insisted on dealing only with the president, it was best that he be clear on where he stood with the president. Hooker calmly accepted Lincoln's criticism that "you have taken counsel of your ambition" in undercutting Burnside, "in which you did a great wrong to the country . . . ," for he believed that accusation had been spread by Burnside himself as vengeance for losing the army command. Hooker was quoted as saying, "That is just such a letter as a father might write to his son," and it "ought to be printed in letters of gold." He was careful to preserve the letter, arranging for its publication in Professor Bates's book on Chancellorsville and in the *Official Records.*[24]

Hooker took hold of the army command as if he had been born to it, and Lincoln had every reason to be pleased with his new general; it appeared that Hooker could after all "keep tavern" for a large army. Joe Hooker's talents as a military executive, talents honed in the Mexican War, seem to have come as a complete surprise to his contemporaries. In just two months he turned the Army of the Potomac around, to universal amazement. He cut the number of deserters on the rolls from more than 25,000 to under 2,000. He introduced much-needed reforms in the daily running of the army, and saw to it that the men were well fed and well clad and well housed. This resulted in an enormous leap in morale. At the time of Hooker's appointment, Captain Henry Livermore Abbott, a proper Bostonian, dismissed the new commander as "nothing more than a smart, driving, plucky Yankee, inordinately vain & . . . entirely unscrupulous." Six weeks later Abbott was writing, "I must give Hooker the credit of saying that this step is the very best for the army that could be taken. . . ." The *New York Times* editorialized that the Army of the Potomac "is about as much Hookerized as it was at one time McClellanized."

These administrative changes and reforms were so solidly grounded that in the aftermath of the Chancellorsville defeat, in May 1863, there was nothing like the virtual collapse of the army that had followed Burnside's defeat at Fredericksburg the previous December. A Massachusetts soldier summed it up by insisting, "The morale of the Army of the Potomac was better in June than it had been in January," and he recalled "nothing of that spirit of insubordination and despondency. . . ." To Joe Hooker's lasting credit, if he led the Potomac army to defeat at Chancellorsville, he left it strong enough to survive and win at Gettysburg. In that sense he might be better remembered as "Administrative Joe" than as "Fighting Joe."[25]

A second aspect of Hooker's generalship — one largely unappreciated by historians — was his dedicated effort to finding a new way to fight once he was in command and got his army to the battlefield. Throughout his fighting record, from Williamsburg on the Peninsula under McClellan to Fredericksburg under Burnside, Joe Hooker had been in the forefront of frontal attacks. At Williamsburg his division suffered almost 1,600 casualties in an unsupported frontal attack. In the Seven Days he defended against the enemy's frontal attacks. At Second Bull Run he led a frontal attack, on Pope's orders and under protest, and pronounced it "a useless slaughter." At Antietam he lost a third of his corps in a head-to-head slugging match with Stonewall Jackson. At Fredericksburg, in a fury at Burnside's tactics, he assaulted Marye's Heights, "lost as many men as my orders required me to lose," and suspended the attack. It was obvious that the rifled musket and the rifled cannon had made storming tactics tragically costly. There had to be, Joe Hooker thought, a better way.[26]

The particular problem Hooker faced in the Chancellorsville campaign was to mount an aggressive offensive yet not throw his army against the entrenched enemy as Burnside had done — and, in fact, against an enemy far better entrenched in April than it had been at Fredericksburg in December. All Hooker's planning, all his maneuvering at Chancellorsville, was designed, first, to force Lee out of his entrenchments and, second, to press on Lee the choice of either attacking the Federals or giving up the Rappahannock line and falling back on Richmond. And after three days of brilliant maneuvering, Hooker achieved exactly that position.

Then the familiar story, with everything going sour for Fighting Joe. There was more than ample justification for each of the charges he leveled against his lieutenants. Howard, Sedgwick, and Stoneman in particular performed dismally on this battlefield. There were flukish failures of communications. Hooker made important tactical errors. Yet in spite of all these various failings and missteps, the battle was very winnable for the Union during that furious Sunday morning of fighting on May 3 — until the moment that General Hooker was hurled unconscious to the front-porch floor of the Chancellor house from the blow of a Confederate solid shot from one of Porter Alexander's rifled pieces firing from Hazel Grove.

Without Hooker's loss-of-nerve confession to explain his Chancellorsville defeat, this battlefront injury assumes major importance. It was 9:00 A.M. when Hooker went down. For three hours that morning he had been managing the contest like the Fighting Joe of past battles — personally posting his infantry and his guns, rushing reinforcements to threatened points, riding his lines to encourage his troops. He was in his element. Whatever else had gone wrong, one thing had gone right and exactly according to Hooker's original plan — it was the Confederates who were being forced to use storming tactics on this battlefield.

The night before, after Jackson's surprise flank attack on the Eleventh Corps, Hooker briefed Gouverneur Warren on how he planned to meet the enemy's renewed assault on May 3: "Genl. Hooker," Warren explained, "made his dispositions accordingly and intends to flank and destroy Jackson."[27] That remained his aim during the May 3 fighting — let the enemy fully commit his forces in attack, then counter with a flank assault on the Confederate left using his reserves. On the porch of the Chancellor house Hooker was too far forward for safety — Alexander had learned from prisoners that the house was Hooker's headquarters, and took it under fire deliberately — but it offered a commanding view of the field, and Joe Hooker was always a general who led from the front.

The morning had been an unrelenting struggle of attack and counterattack, tilting first to the Confederates, then to the Federals. At 9 o'clock the tilt was Confederate, but to achieve that, Jeb Stuart — who had replaced the wounded Jackson in command of that wing of the Rebel army — had committed his last reserves. Hooker's reserves were still ample, and at the moment he was hit he was being handed a call for reinforcements to meet Stuart's charge. The solid shot hit the wooden porch pillar, split it lengthwise, and (in Hooker's words) hurled half of it "violently against me . . . which struck me in an erect position from my head to my feet." He lay unconscious for between thirty and forty minutes. At first it was assumed he had been killed. When he was found to be breathing, Dr. Jonathan Letterman, his medical director, expressed doubt that he would revive. When at last Hooker regained consciousness and tried to mount his horse to show himself and reassure the troops, he collapsed and vomited. In a daze, he was carried to the rear. "The blow which the General received seems to have knocked all the sense out of him," a staff man told his family. "For the remainder of the day he was wandering, and was unable to get any ideas into his head. . . ." General Abner Doubleday wrote that Hooker "suffered great pain and was in a comatose condition for most of the time. His mind was not clear, and they had to wake him up to communicate with him."[28]

These are the classic symptoms of severe concussion. For the rest of the day the commanding general drifted in and out of awareness; he probably suffered periods of amnesia. The question here is why Darius Couch, the senior general on the field, did not immediately take the command. The answer lies in the absence of Dan Butterfield from field headquarters. Butterfield, Hooker's chief of staff, was directing the army's left wing around Fredericksburg. In his place temporarily on the other wing, with Hooker at the Chancellor house, was James Van Alen. Brigadier General Van Alen was a Sunday soldier, a wealthy New York political appointee of no particular skills whom Halleck had recently palmed off on Hooker's headquarters. Van Alen had no idea what to do in this crisis, and apparently no one told him. Dr. Letterman, who was authority for the fact that Hooker was incapable of command and ought to be replaced, seems to have been reluctant to take any action without a decisive chief of staff to lead the way. General Couch was eventually called to the scene, but by then Hooker had regained consciousness and, superficially at least, appeared to be uninjured, and (as Couch put it) "I went about my own business."[29]

Hooker collapsed soon afterward, and it was at least half an hour before he was in a rational enough period to call Couch back again. In the more than an hour since Hooker was struck down, the battle had reached its crisis and then slid rapidly into the Confederates' hands. During that time, every call to headquarters for reinforcements from Union commanders on the firing lines had been met by silence. The high command was struck mute. Even so, there might still have been a chance for victory — Reynolds's

First Corps and Meade's Fifth had hardly been engaged all that morning — but it would not be risked. Meade pleaded the case, but Hooker refused him.

Instead he turned command over to Couch, with orders to pull back to a new line to protect the army's Rappahannock crossings. What little of his mental faculties Hooker could collect seemed now to be focused narrowly on one object — to save the army. His plan appeared to be in a shambles. His reasoning was clouded. Over the next days his mind began to clear, but even then he could think of nothing more than inviting an attack by Lee against his fortified lines. Then, after yet another communications failure, Sedgwick and the Sixth Corps retreated across the Rappahannock prematurely, and Hooker was done. He recrossed the river with the rest of the army. Joe Hooker's grand campaign, begun with such high hopes, ended in a cliché — not with a bang but with a whimper.

It was less than two months later that Potomac army commander Hooker met the same fate as his four predecessors. The question in Washington now became what to do with him. In contrast with the earlier four, Mr. Lincoln was active in supporting a fighting role for Fighting Joe Hooker. "I have not thrown Gen. Hooker away," he told Meade, and attempted to promote a corps command for Hooker in the Army of the Potomac. Meade managed to evade this possibility. "It would be very difficult for Hooker to be quiet under me or anyone else," Meade remarked in a private letter, and there was certainly truth to that. It is hard to imagine the irrepressible Joe Hooker meekly playing the subordinate in the army he once commanded.[30]

The solution was found when it was decided to send reinforcements to Rosecrans in the western theater in the form of the Eleventh and Twelfth Corps from the Army of the Potomac. These two corps had never been at home in the Potomac army — especially the Eleventh Corps, with unhappy experiences at both Chancellorsville and Gettysburg — and the army was glad to see them gone. And this offered the answer to the Joe Hooker problem — let him command the two orphaned corps. By early October of 1863 Hooker was established with his new command at Stevenson, Alabama.

The command structure in the West was soon reshaped, and Hooker found himself increasingly an outcast. Grant, put in overall command in the western theater, seemed to resent Fighting Joe being forced on him from Washington and hoped to be rid of him. General Grant, it was reported to Secretary of War Stanton, felt Hooker's "presence here is replete with both trouble and danger." Hooker's strong showing in taking Lookout Mountain during the Chattanooga campaign in November did not persuade Grant, who in his recollections was dismissive of Hooker's so-called "Battle Above the Clouds." "It is all poetry," Grant said contemptuously. Hooker said defiantly, "I find I am regarded with a great deal of jealousy by those filling high places here," but he believed that his soldiership, as he called it, would carry him through: "I have never yet seen the time that there was no place for a man willing to fight."[31]

In the spring of 1864, now under Sherman, Hooker marched on Atlanta in command of his two corps, consolidated as the newly formed Twentieth Corps. He could take no comfort from having to report to William Tecumseh Sherman. Sherman, who had served with Hooker in the California days, wrote even before Chancellorsville: "I know Hooker well and tremble to think of his handling 100,000 men in the presence of Lee."[32] Presumably Sherman thought Chancellorsville confirmed his prediction. Like Grant, Sherman felt he had to tolerate Hooker because he was the president's choice. In any event, Hooker directed his corps effectively all during the advance to Atlanta's outskirts. Indeed, the Twentieth Corps did most of the fighting on this march and suffered by far the most casualties — more than 5,000. These achievements only intensified Sherman's efforts to be rid of Fighting Joe.

His opportunity came suddenly in the battle for Atlanta. General James B. McPherson, commanding the Army of the Tennessee, was killed in action. Logic dictated that John A. Logan, who succeeded McPherson during the fighting as senior officer on the field, be named permanent commander of the Army of the Tennessee. Certainly Logan was qualified and had earned the position. Sherman would say that he rejected Logan as army commander because he was not a West Pointer, but there likely was a very different motive in the choice he did make. In naming Oliver Otis Howard as head of the Army of the Tennessee, Sherman surely knew how Joe Hooker would react.

Of all the corps commanders under Sherman, Hooker had the most seniority and the most experience — experience in, among other things, commanding an army. Hooker believed he was entitled to McPherson's command. To give it to Otis Howard, his former subordinate, the man he believed above all others was responsible for the Chancellorsville defeat, was an insult on Sherman's part, and a carefully calculated insult at that. Hooker's resignation was prompt. "Justice and self-respect alike require my removal from an army in which rank and service are ignored," he explained.[33]

So ended Fighting Joe Hooker's service in the Civil War. How might he be summed up? Of two things we can be sure — he was not a drunk, and he never lost his nerve in battle. Once these canards are out of the way, it is possible to paint him in more realistic colors. In that essential role of an officer — to take care of his men — he was paramount. No general on either side was better at that than Joe Hooker. No general in the Army of the Potomac had a better combat record. In every battle in which he was engaged — except one — his performance has to be rated at least "creditable" and at best "excellent." He was rough-edged and not much of a gentleman, and he talked far too much and far too loudly. He did not bother to disguise his ambition, and he did not suffer fools gladly.

As to the battle for which he will always be remembered, Joe Hooker is entitled to be heard. "You may like to know my opinion of the battle of Chancellorsville," he wrote Professor Bates. "I won greater success on many fields in the war, but nowhere did I deserve it half so much. . . ." Sitting in judgment after Chancellorsville, Mr. Lincoln said, "I have not thrown Gen. Hooker away." Nor should the historians of this war.[34]

NOTES

1. T. Harry Williams, *Lincoln and His Generals* (New York: Knopf, 1952), 239. The most recent charge that Hooker was drunk at Chancellorsville is in Ernest B. Furgurson, *Chancellorsville 1863: The Souls of the Brave* (New York: Knopf, 1992), 285–87. Pope's command of the Army of the Potomac at Second Bull Run was unofficial but manifest.

2. James M. McPherson, *Battle Cry of Freedom: The Civil War Era* (New York: Oxford University Press, 1988), 645; Shelby Foote, *The Civil War: A Narrative* (New York: Random House, 1963), vol. 2, 315; Bruce Catton, *Glory Road: The Bloody Route from Fredericksburg to Gettysburg* (New York: Doubleday, 1952), 230; Kenneth P. Williams, *Lincoln Finds a General: A Military Study of the Civil War* (New York: Macmillan, 1949), vol. 2, 604; Walter H. Hebert, *Fighting Joe Hooker* (Indianapolis: Bobbs-Merrill, 1944), chap. 14; Gene Smith, "The Destruction of Fighting Joe Hooker," *American Heritage* (Oct. 1993), 3; Ken Burns, "The Civil War" (PBS, 1990), episode four.

3. Albert Castel, *Decision in the West: The Atlanta Campaign of 1864* (Lawrence: University Press of Kansas, 1992), 291.

4. Theodore A. Dodge, Lowell Lecture: "The Battle of Chancellorsville," *Southern Historical Society Papers,* vol. 14, 276–92; Dodge, *The Campaign of Chancellorsville* (Boston: Ticknor & Fields, 2nd ed., 1886), 266–67.

5. Hooker testimony, *Report of the Joint Committee on the Conduct of the War,* vol. 1 (1865), 111–49.

6. Hooker to Bates, Feb. 16, 1876, Samuel P. Bates Collection, Pennsylvania Historical and Museum Commission, Pennsylvania State Archives; Jedediah Hotchkiss and William Allan, *The Battle-Fields of Virginia: Chancellorsville* (New York: Van Nostrand, 1867).

7. Samuel P. Bates, "Hooker's Comments on Chancellorsville," *Battles and Leaders of the Civil War* (New York: Century, 1887–88), vol. 3, 215–23; Samuel P. Bates, *The Battle of Chancellorsville* (Meadville, Pa., 1882); Allan Nevins et al., *Civil War Books: A Critical Bibliography* (Baton Rouge: Louisiana State University Press, 1967), vol. 1, 23; Hooker to Bates, Sept. 22, 1879, Bates Collection.

8. John Bigelow, Jr., *The Campaign of Chancellorsville: A Strategic and Tactical Study* (New Haven: Yale University Press, 1910), 477–78n.

9. E. P. Halstead, Apr. 19, 1903, Bigelow Papers, Library of Congress.

10. Hebert, *Fighting Joe Hooker,* 38; George B. McClellan memoirs draft, McClellan Papers, Library of Congress.

11. John Hay, *Inside Lincoln's White House: The Complete Civil War Diary of*

John Hay, eds. Michael Burlingame and John R. Turner Ettlinger (Carbondale: Southern Illinois University Press, 1997), 80; Darius Couch in *Battles and Leaders,* vol. 3, 170; George G. Meade, *Life and Letters of George Gordon Meade* (New York: Scribner's, 1913), vol. 1, 365; Charles S. Wainwright, *A Diary of Battle: The Personal Journals of Colonel Charles S. Wainwright, 1861–1865,* ed. Allan Nevins (New York: Harcourt, Brace & World, 1963), 202, 214; George H. Sharpe memorandum, Joseph Hooker Papers, Huntington Library.

12. Robert G. Carter, *Four Brothers in Blue* (Washington: Gibson Press, 1913), 270–72; George A. Custer to McClellan, May 6, 1863, McClellan Papers; George W. Smalley, *Anglo-American Memories* (New York: Putnam's, 1911), 158.

13. Wainwright, *Diary of Battle,* 162; Charles Francis Adams, Jr., *Charles Francis Adams, 1835–1916: An Autobiography* (Boston: Houghton Mifflin, 1916), 161; E. N. Gilpin, Apr. 7, 1911, Bigelow Papers; Margaret Leech, *Reveille in Washington, 1860–1865* (New York: Harper & Brothers, 1941), 264.

14. *The American Heritage Dictionary,* 3rd ed., 869.

15. Halleck to Sherman, Sept. 16, 1864, William T. Sherman, *Memoirs* (Library of America ed., 1990), 590; Hooker to Bates, June 28, 1878, Bates Collection.

16. Hooker testimony, *Report of Joint Committee,* vol. 1 (1865), 175, 112; Halleck to Stanton, May 18, 1863, *Official Records* 25:2, 506.

17. Hooker testimony, *Report of Joint Committee,* vol. 1 (1865), 175; Lincoln to Hooker, June 16, 1863, Abraham Lincoln, *The Collected Works of Abraham Lincoln,* ed. Roy P. Basler (New Brunswick, N.J.: Rutgers University Press, 1953), vol. 6, 281.

18. Hooker testimony, *Report of Joint Committee,* vol. 1 (1865), 175.

19. Williams, *Lincoln and His Generals,* 259; *OR* 27:3, 349; Lincoln to Hooker, May 14, 1863, *OR* 25:2, 479; Hooker to Bates, Oct. 5, 1878, Bates Collection.

20. T. Lyle Dickey, Oct. 20, 1876, Michael Burlingame, ed., *An Oral History of Abraham Lincoln: John G. Nicolay's Interviews and Essays* (Carbondale: Southern Illinois University Press, 1996), 50.

21. Meade, *Life and Letters,* vol. 1, 385; Lincoln to Hooker, May 14, 1863, *OR* 25:2, 479. See "The Revolt of the Generals" elsewhere in this collection.

22. Hebert, *Fighting Joe Hooker,* 25–33, 49.

23. Alpheus S. Williams, *From the Cannon's Mouth: The Civil War Letters of General Alpheus S. Williams,* ed. Milo M. Quaife (Detroit: Wayne State University Press, 1958), 265; Hooker to Bates, Jan. 3, 1878, Bates Collection; Hooker address, Apr. 30, 1863, *OR* 25:1, 171.

24. Lincoln to Hooker, Jan. 26, 1863, Lincoln, *Collected Works,* vol. 6, 78–79; Hooker to Bates, May 29, 1878, Bates Collection; Anson G. Henry, Apr. 12, 1863, Illinois State Historical Library.

25. Henry L. Abbott, *Fallen Leaves: The Civil War Letters of Major Henry Livermore Abbott,* ed. Robert Garth Scott (Kent, Ohio: Kent State University Press, 1991), 165, 170; *New York Times,* Mar. 1, 1863; Andrew E. Ford, *The Story of the Fifteenth Massachusetts Volunteer Infantry* (Clinton, Mass., 1898), 253.

26. Hooker testimony, *Report of Joint Committee,* vol. 1 (1865), 668.

27. Gouverneur K. Warren to Daniel Butterfield, May 3, 1863, Hooker Papers.

28. Hooker memorandum, Mar. 21, 1877, courtesy Abraham Lincoln Book Shop; Jonathan Letterman, *Medical Recollections of the Army of the Potomac* (New York: Appleton, 1866), 137; William Candler, May 7, 1863, in Bigelow, *Chancellorsville,* 363n; Abner Doubleday memorandum, Doubleday Papers, New-York Historical Society.

29. Darius Couch in *Battles and Leaders,* vol. 3, 167.

30. Lincoln to Meade, July 27, 1863, Lincoln, *Collected Works,* vol. 6, 350; Meade, *Life and Letters,* vol. 2, 142.

31. Charles A. Dana to Stanton, Oct. 29, 1863, *OR* 31:1, 73; John Russell Young, *Around the World with General Grant* (New York: American News Co., 1879), vol. 2, 306; Hooker to Stanton, Feb. 25, 1864, *OR* 32:2, 469; Hooker letter, quoted in Castel, *Decision in the West,* 97.

32. M. A. De Wolfe Howe, ed., *Home Letters of General Sherman* (New York: Scribner's, 1909), 250.

33. Hooker to George H. Thomas, July 27, 1864, *OR* 38:5, 273.

34. Hooker to Bates, Apr. 2, 1877, Bates Collection; Lincoln to Meade, July 27, 1863, Lincoln, *Collected Works,* vol. 6, 350.

[8]

Dan Sickles, Political General

Major General Daniel E. Sickles

HIS BIOGRAPHER, surveying a long and raucous lifetime, styled him "Sickles the Incredible." Even to describe only his checkered career in the Army of the Potomac with that appellation is entirely fitting. Daniel Edgar Sickles came into the army with an incredible résumé indeed, and in two years' service he easily lived up to the reputation that had preceded him.[1]

Surprisingly, for an army that from first to last was so highly politicized, the Army of the Potomac was spared the most extravagant examples of that peculiar species *political general.* To be sure, it suffered painful consequences from the misadventures of political generals on neighboring battlefields — the blunderings of John Charles Frémont and Nathaniel Banks in the Shenandoah Valley in 1862, the missed opportunities by Ben Butler with the Army of the James in 1864 — but there were those of this calling within its own ranks who on balance actually made positive contributions. Franz Sigel, for example, surely rallied enough German Americans to the Union cause to offset any failings during his short stay with the Potomac army. His countryman Carl Schurz, who then took up Sigel's rallying call, turned out to be far less responsible for the hapless fighting record of the largely German-American Eleventh Corps at Chancellorsville and Gettysburg than was Oliver Otis Howard, the West Pointer and professional soldier who commanded the corps. Still, there was endless muttering among the old guard in the high command over generals who owed their stars to their politics.

Of the political generals who did achieve notice in the Army of the Potomac, Sickles was the most prominent and probably the most warlike — or at least to his contemporaries it must have appeared that way. He was a master at blowing his own horn. His way was to go to the attack off the field as well as on it, and in either case to take no prisoners. Those who got on the wrong side of Dan Sickles usually lived to regret it — most notably General George Gordon Meade.

During his formative years, Sickles had acquired some of the most rough-and-tumble political schooling in nineteenth-century America by apprenticing himself to New York's Tammany Hall. An ambitious, sharp-minded lawyer who was admitted to the bar in 1843, Sickles grasped politics as the shortest route to fame and the eventful life he craved. He clambered up the city's Democratic party ladder, on the way collecting allies and enemies with utter disregard for the consequences, attending the typically unruly Tammany meetings armed with bowie knife and pistol. He pursued his legal career in the same unfettered fashion. The New York diarist George Templeton Strong, himself a lawyer, described Sickles as "one of the bigger bubbles in the scum of the profession, swollen and windy, and puffed out with fetid gas." Few ever expressed a neutral opinion about Dan Sickles.[2]

His first step outside Tammany was election to the New York state assembly in 1847, at age twenty-eight. Sickles's style of living was high and highly irreverent, and he scandalized fellow legislators by taking with him to Albany as his very visible live-in companion a prostitute named Fanny White. Shrugging off a vote of censure, he gained renown for his debating and parliamentary skills. In national Democratic politics Sickles allied himself with the successful candidacy of Franklin Pierce, and was rewarded, following a lucrative stint as New York City's corporation counsel, with the position of secretary of legation in London. Thus he tied his fortunes to the next up-and-coming Democratic presidential hopeful,

James Buchanan, minister to Great Britain. Sickles in the meantime had taken as his wife Teresa Bagioli, who as a bride of sixteen was exactly half his age. When he sailed for London as Buchanan's secretary, he left Teresa behind and with child. Traveling with him instead was his faithful companion Fanny White.

During his time in Albany Sickles had been briefly connected with the state militia, taking the rank of major. This mere glimpse of the martial life comprised the sum total of his pre–Civil War military experience. Characteristically, during his London stay he improved himself to colonel for its greater social cachet. In 1855 he returned home and went back to Albany as state senator. The next year, attaching himself to Buchanan's electoral coattails, he was off to Washington as congressman from New York's Third District. Dan Sickles was immediately and happily at home in the swirl and turmoil of Washington politics. As sectional discord increased, he took up the cause of New York's commercial interests by opposing any coercion of the South. Indeed, from the House floor he warned that New York City might well consider seceding, to become a free city and "open wide her gates to the civilization and commerce of the world." That commerce, he strongly implied, would pertain to the states below the Mason-Dixon Line, whatever their national affiliation.[3] Such statements were most welcome to Southern fire-eaters. Ten days later South Carolina seceded.

During the time he was making such belligerent declarations, Congressman Sickles found himself saddled with the role of social pariah. The Southern diarist Mary Chesnut, viewing him from the House gallery, entered in her journal, "I saw Mr. Sickles sitting alone on the benches of the House of Representatives. He was as left to himself as if he had smallpox."[4] This veritable quarantine sprang from his recent actions and conduct that had shocked the country to the depths of its Victorian soul.

On February 27, 1859, in Lafayette Square a block from the White House, in broad daylight, Daniel Sickles had shot and killed Philip Barton Key, Washington's district attorney and the son of the author of "The Star-Spangled Banner." "Is the damned scoundrel dead yet?" Sickles inquired as he peered over his smoking pistol. Young Key, it developed, had been Teresa Bagioli Sickles's lover, a fact the congressman said he had just discovered. Sickles's subsequent trial for murder was the lurid sensation of the day. His eight-man legal team was headed by Edwin M. Stanton, who not only proceeded to play the expected "unwritten law" defense card, but then proposed the novel theory of temporary insanity to palliate the killing. The prosecution did not choose to offer a sampling from the quite ample evidence of Sickles's own extramarital affairs. Upon the verdict of acquittal, Stanton called for three cheers from the courtroom.

At this point, Dan Sickles might have rested on his laurels as a defender (albeit a rather dangerous one) of family values, but such a predictable and conservative course would not have been typical of him. Instead, he took the tarnished Teresa back to his bed and board. All the better people had already assigned the appropriate scarlet letter to the fallen woman, and they were shocked into paroxysms of moral outrage when Sickles apparently forgave her transgression. Washington society banished him to Coventry. The hard-shelled Sickles was not particularly bothered by this. He seems to have cared, in his fashion, for poor, cast-out Teresa, although continuing on with his own usual adulterous habits.[5]

The political damage, however, was enough to persuade him not to stand for reelection in 1860. The sectional crisis that winter served at least Dan Sickles well, and soon he came charging back into the political spotlight — now as a vehement patriot. Once again, in his fashion, he took a heartfelt decision. His onetime Southern allies, he cried, had turned to arms at such places as Fort Pickens, Florida, and to the threat of arms in Charleston Harbor, in order to gain their way with secession. "It will never do, sir, for them to protest against coercion," he told the House in January 1861, "and, at the same moment, seize all the arms and arsenals and forts and navy-yards and ships. . . . When sovereign states by their own deliberate acts, make war, they must not cry peace." In February, when president-elect Lincoln arrived in Washington for his inauguration, Dan Sickles was the first House Democrat to welcome him at a congressional reception. Mr. Lincoln did not forget the gesture.[6]

The firing on Fort Sumter found ex-congressman Sickles back in New York, once again a private citizen. Soon afterward, over drinks with his cronies at the bar at Delmonico's, the subject of raising a regiment came up. It was just the sort of challenge the impulsive Sickles relished. He had, after all, no matter how briefly, served as major in the New York militia. Others, he knew, were recruiting volunteers without even that fragment of experience. Almost overnight, using flag-waving oratory, organizational skills, and promissory notes, he had his regiment, the 70th New York volunteers, well in hand. From Albany came authorization to recruit a brigade. Within a month of Sumter that too was in hand. The newspapers, in applauding these efforts, nicely burnished his tarnished reputation. Sickles christened his command the Excelsior Brigade, taking the name from the state seal. A brigade, he knew, was customarily commanded by a brigadier general.

Abruptly party politics reared its head. New York's Governor Edwin D. Morgan, a Republican, discovered that this Democrat from Tammany Hall was getting too far out ahead in the state's race to supply manpower to the endangered Union. It was publicly most embarrassing. Morgan telegraphed Sickles to disband the Excelsior Brigade except for the one original regiment. A regiment, Sickles knew, was customarily commanded by a mere colonel. He hurried to Washington to lay his problem before Mr. Lincoln. Acutely aware of the need to rally Democratic support for the impending conflict, Lincoln sent Sickles back to New York with the temporary rank of brigadier general and a promise that somehow, some way, the Excelsior Brigade would be accepted into federal service. And after several further twists and turns, it was. Brigadier General Daniel Sickles led his brigade to the seat of war at Washington. Marching to Brady's Gallery for the obligatory portrait, General Sickles assumed a belligerent standing pose, arms folded, guardsman's mustache bristling, hard eyes glaring.[7]

The Excelsiors were assigned to Joseph Hooker's division and posted to lower Maryland. Over the course of time, Joe Hooker would come to regard Dan Sickles as his protégé, but it was not so in the beginning. Hooker displayed an old regular's mistrust of any general who had risen by political means. "In my official intercourse with veteran politicians suddenly raised to high military rank," he announced sardonically, "I have found it necessary to observe their correspondence with special circumspection." There was also the matter of Sickles's still very notorious reputation. Charles Wainwright of Hooker's staff noted in his diary that he was introduced to Sickles one day at headquarters, "but fortunately he did not offer to shake hands." On another occasion, Hooker insisted that in his absence he dared not leave his division under Sickles, "with whom I would expect to have it dishonored in less than 12 hours after leaving." Sickles was always a quick study, however, and he displayed much industry in managing his brigade, and in addition began exercising his talents for making himself agreeable and convivial with his superior. He took encouragement about the security of his position when Edwin M. Stanton, his savior in the Key murder trial, was appointed the new secretary of war. Sickles was prompt to name his brigade's Maryland posting Camp Stanton.[8]

Sickles's political warfare was not over, however. On March 17, 1862, the Senate, under Republican control and having listened to the sour-grapes complaints of Governor Morgan, refused to confirm Sickles's appointment as brigadier general. While Sickles geared up for renewed action in that sector, the Excelsior Brigade sailed off without him for the Virginia Peninsula and General McClellan's grand campaign against Richmond.

In his fight for rank, Sickles had an influential ally in Secretary of War Stanton. The president, too, drummed up support for a renomination effort. In the capital Sickles pulled his strings and buttonholed key members of the Senate, and was heartened by strong editorial support from New York's largest papers, James Gordon Bennett's *Herald* and Horace Greeley's *Tribune*. Greeley initiated a petition campaign. The power of the press was something Dan Sickles could appreciate, and he was learning how to cultivate that power. All these efforts paid off. Stanton's War Department once again proposed his name for brigadier general, Mr. Lincoln sent it to the Senate, and this time, on May 13, Sickles was approved — by a vote of 19 to 18.[9]

Sickles hurried to the Peninsula to resume his command, but his squabble over rank had rendered him too late to share in his brigade's baptism of fire. At Williamsburg on May 5 the Excelsiors were severely mauled, the four of its five regiments present losing a total of 772 men. During the balance of the Peninsula campaign Sickles had little opportunity to display any command mettle. At Seven Pines his brigade saw only reserve and skirmishing duty. On the first of the Seven Days, at Oak Grove, he was given his one chance to shine. The Excelsior Brigade formed one-half the striking force in McClellan's assault, the sole Federal offensive action in the week-long struggle. Sickles's part of the advance soon fell behind, however, leaving his neighboring brigade to absorb the heaviest of the enemy fire. When Sickles finally did engage, one of his regiments broke under a sudden counterattack and retreated pell-mell in what Sickles admitted was "disgraceful confusion." Eventually his front was stabilized, but at the end of the day the Excelsior Brigade and its chastised commander had very little to show as compensation for 136 casualties.[10]

In the concluding battles of the Seven Days, at Glendale and Malvern Hill, Sickles was in reserve or in support, with few chances to sharpen or even to display his command skills. Nevertheless, throughout the campaign he had impressed at least Joe Hooker, his division commander, with the good care he took of his men and with his combative spirit. Although seldom called, Dan Sickles seemed always ready for a fight.

While the Army of the Potomac languished at Harrison's Landing on the James during the hot summer weeks, Sickles hurried off to Washington to see Secretary Stanton about an extended leave. It was essential, he explained, that he recruit for his much-depleted brigade. In the rest of the army during this time leaves were hard to come by, but not for Dan Sickles, political general. "The General has a way of getting what he wants," one of his men observed. Sickles had a second, unstated reason for needing to go home. His supporters in the Third District were sounding him out to run for his old seat in the House. In his brigadier general's uniform and with a sheaf of complimentary newspaper clippings in his hand, they said, he would be unbeatable.

A practiced political campaigner, Sickles as his first priority took to the stump to attract not voters but rather volunteers for the Excelsior Brigade. He trumpeted the war effort and, in largely Democratic New York City, his support for the president. "I did not vote for him," he admitted, "but I will fight under his orders, and I will trust him everywhere. . . . In God's name, let the State of New York have it to say hereafter that she furnished her quota to the army without conscription — without resorting to a draft!" Whatever else he was, Dan Sickles was a no-holds-barred War Democrat. He organized rallies in upstate New York too, recruiting and calling for support of the Union cause. "The General himself," said a fellow speaker, "was in excellent wind and held out for a good hour and a half."[11]

He managed to find time for straight politicking as well, but in the end decided not to seek his old House seat. The army looked to be the faster route to prestige and distinction than the Congress. In any case, he saw his duty to be with his men in the field. Yet all this recruiting and speechmaking and mending of political fences had consumed weeks and then months, and by the time he finished all these tasks and rejoined the Army of the Potomac, it had gone on to fight two more major battles — at Second Bull Run and Antietam — without him. This generated considerable resentment in the officer corps. By report, said Colonel Wainwright, Sickles was going to be promoted commander of his division, "although he has always managed to be absent when it was hotly engaged." General Sickles, wrote another officer in his corps, "has got credit for doing a great deal more fighting than he has ever done. New York correspondents have cracked him up where the credit for fighting was justly due to other brigades and regiments. But so it is."[12]

However that may have been, Sickles's lack of battlefield experience proved no hindrance at all to his climb up the chain of command. Returning from his long absence, he took over Hooker's old division after Hooker moved up to corps command. This marked him for a corresponding advancement in rank. At the Battle of Fredericksburg his division was in reserve, and he again saw no action. Afterward one of his staff made note of the general's hurried departure for Washington. "I suspect that he is working for his *Major Generalship,* and doubtless he will get it," the man wrote. "He is one of those industrious, indefatigable, unconquerable men, that never leave a stone unturned when their mind is once 'set'; and such men usually accomplish whatever they undertake." It was an accurate prediction. When Dan Sickles returned to the army at Falmouth in January 1863, he wore the two stars of a major general.[13]

His march into the higher ranks went one step further when Joe Hooker took over command of the Potomac army from Burnside on January 26. High-command changes followed rapidly. After unifying the cavalry under George Stoneman, former head of the Third Corps, Hooker followed the usual practice of promoting one of that corps' divisional commanders to the spot vacated by Stoneman. In this instance there were two, Sickles and David B. Birney. Neither was a professional soldier. Birney, a lawyer by trade and without political-party experience, had gone to war as colonel of a Pennsylvania regiment. His outspoken antislavery stance (he was the son of the noted antislavery crusader James G. Birney) gave him considerable political influence nonetheless. He also had substantial combat experience, certainly more so than Sickles. Yet Dan Sickles became Hooker's choice for the Third Corps. For the second time in its history (the first was Daniel Butterfield at Fredericksburg), the Army of the Potomac had a political general at the head of one of its corps.

Clearly the choice was not based primarily on soldierly merit. However combative Sickles acted, his experience in actual battlefield command was limited to a single afternoon's fighting at Oak Grove on the Peninsula, and he did not do well on that occasion. Apparently he had assuaged Hooker's initial doubts about him at least in part by his convivial sociability — Joe Hooker bearing a reputation, like Sickles, that preceded him. It is very probable that had his competition for the corps post been a professional soldier rather than David Birney, Sickles would have remained division commander. But in this choice between amateur soldiers, it appears that Joe Hooker simply chose the one he liked the best. In so doing, he was pushing Dan Sickles beyond the limits of his command abilities.

The army's old guard was not pleased by the promotion, although that is not to say they would necessarily have applauded Birney in the post either. Gouverneur Warren described Sickles as "morally debased, and of no military experience." George Meade, one of the most level-headed of the army's generals, thought Sickles and Butterfield, another nonprofessional who was now Hooker's chief of staff, had altogether too much influence on the new army commander. The danger Hooker ran, Meade told his wife, "is of subjecting himself to bad influences, such as Dan Butterfield and Dan Sickles, who, being intellectually more clever than Hooker, and leading him to believe they are very influential, will obtain an injurious ascendancy over him and insensibly affect his conduct." Meade was here delivering the professional soldier's classic verdict against the political general. He was also signaling his initial stance in his long, bitter, and painful feud with Dan Sickles.[14]

Corps commander Sickles took to his new eminence as if he had been born to it — indeed, as if it were his due. Third Corps headquarters became easily the most sociable place in the army, where liquor flowed freely and high spirits abounded. Sickles hosted his gatherings with the practiced, sumptuous hand of the Tammany politician that he was. He had one of his "festivals" catered by

Delmonico in person. When a Third Corps captain elected to hold his wedding in camp, Sickles seized on the occasion for a grand celebration. "Then succeeded a ball, given by General Sickles at his headquarters," wrote Colonel Regis de Trobriand, "where, as usual, there was feasting to the heart's content." In these weeks there was gossip, too, that General Sickles was living fully up to his notorious reputation. When Captain Charles Francis Adams, Jr., penned his oft-quoted remark that Army of the Potomac headquarters that winter "was a combination bar-room and brothel," Dan Sickles was one of the offenders Adams specifically named as a "blemished character" responsible for the offenses.[15]

It was in the spring campaign of 1863, at Chancellorsville, that Sickles had his first test as corps commander, and his first-ever meaningful test in field command. He revealed great pugnacity but little vision — a combination perhaps tolerable in a brigade or even a division commander, but unfortunate and potentially dangerous in a corps commander.

On May 2, the day of Stonewall Jackson's celebrated flank march around Hooker's army massed at Chancellorsville, Sickles was in command in the one sector from which a telling assault on the Confederates' march route might have been launched. When Jackson's column was sighted that morning as it crossed one of the few openings in the encircling forest, Sickles leaped to the conclusion that the enemy army must be in full retreat from the battlefield. Yet, somehow, he was never able to marshal a meaningful attack (or, he thought, a pursuit), although drawing in substantial reinforcements from neighboring corps. Repeatedly he was checked by the Rebel artillery, and then he became entangled with troops General Lee threw in his path to distract him. Despite being within the view of the Federals for some five hours while crossing the forest opening, Jackson's column made good its escape without damage. All Sickles had to show for his frustrating day's efforts was a single Confederate regiment left as rear guard. That Jackson might be embarked on a surprise offensive flanking movement entirely eluded his understanding.

That night, after Jackson's devastating flank attack had routed the Eleventh Corps holding the Federal right, Sickles found himself, after the disappointments of the day, only tenuously connected with the rest of the army. With his usual impulsiveness, he determined on a night march to regain his old lines. He set off without reconnaissance, without knowing where either friend or foe might be in the darkness, and without fully informing the rest of the army that he was coming. When Sickles's stumbling column brushed against the pickets of both armies, the result was chaos. Everyone within range opened fire with rifle and cannon. "We were fired on from all sides; from the front, from the right, from the left, and even from the rear . . . ," Regis de Trobriand wrote. Finally they fell back to their starting point, licking their wounds. Although an accurate count was never made, Sickles's casualties must have exceeded 500, with many of those caused by friendly fire. "Whoever took part in the fizzle in the woods on the night of the 2nd of May," one of his men wrote sourly, "will remember it as long as they live."[16]

In the savage and relentless struggle on May 3, the decisive day of the campaign, Sickles was awkward getting his corps back within the army's lines as ordered, losing four guns in the process. Thereafter, fighting defensively, he was at his pugnacious best. Jauntily he went right into the front lines to direct fire. "Sickles goes by in his turn at a walk, with a smiling air, smoking a cigar," de Trobriand remembered. " 'Everything is going well,' said he, in loud voice, intending to be heard." While the results of the day would go against the Union, it was not for want of effort on the part of Dan Sickles. One of his brigade commanders unaccountably took his troops to the rear in the midst of the fighting, and a furious Sickles had the man court-martialed and cashiered. In the final accounting, the Third Corps was found to have suffered 4,124 casualties in the campaign, second only to the much larger Sixth Corps.[17]

Dan Sickles's final posture at Chancellorsville was a curious one, in light of the future controversy regarding staying or retreating at Gettysburg, soon to be narrated. With his army driven from

Chancellorsville and backed up against the Rappahannock, Joe Hooker called five of his corps commanders together to discuss their course. Should they resume the fight, he asked, or should they recross the river and end the campaign? Surprisingly, the combative Sickles counseled retreat. Playing now the part of political general, he insisted that the decision should be essentially a political one. He thought the prospects for victory "doubtful" and the consequences of defeat grave for the Northern war effort — Washington would be endangered; the country would be demoralized. "The uncertainties are against us," he said. He was one of two corps commanders (the other was Darius Couch) who advised retreat; the other three favored staying and fighting. Hooker, however, had already decided on ending the campaign, and on May 6 the army started back across the Rappahannock bridges.[18]

In the Northern press, at least, Sickles would be generously praised for his role at Chancellorsville. *Harper's Weekly* included his portrait in its pictorial coverage of the campaign. Sickles had made persistent efforts to cultivate James Gordon Bennett's *New York Herald,* the country's largest newspaper, which now made him a hero of the lost battle. Bennett, who was famous for going to extremes, even went so far as to issue an editorial call for Dan Sickles to replace Joe Hooker as head of the Army of the Potomac. Such puffery did not sit well with such soldiers as Alpheus Williams, who had witnessed more of the fighting at Chancellorsville than any other Union general. Afterward he complained to his daughter, "matters are not settled by merit but by impudence and brass and well paid reporters. A 'Sickles' would beat Napoleon in winning glory not earned. He is a hero without an heroic deed! Literally made by scribblers." The war, Williams said, warming to his subject, "is carried on exclusively to make heroes of charlatans and braggarts!"[19]

There was a second curious footnote to the Chancellorsville campaign. General Meade, who at the corps commanders' council had outspokenly advocated staying and fighting, heard Hooker later claim that in fact Meade was one of those who had favored withdrawal. An angry Meade polled the other corps commanders for their recollections of his position at the council. Sickles's response was a lawyerly brief that contradicted the other responses and surely left George Meade seething. It was true that Meade had initially called for attacking the enemy, said Sickles. However, he went on, "At the close of the discussion, my impression was that your original preferences appeared to have been surrendered to the clear conviction of the commanding general of the necessity which dictated his return to the north bank of the Rappahannock. . . ."

Since no official written record was kept at the council, Sickles felt no discomfort over his devious response, and proceeded to leak the correspondence to editor Bennett of the *Herald.* Sickles's motive in all this, no doubt, was to register his loyalty to his mentor, Joe Hooker, who just then was suffering many slings and arrows for giving up the recent campaign. This was a safe enough position to take so long as Hooker was in command of the army, but just a month after sending this letter, Dan Sickles found himself serving in an Army of the Potomac commanded by General Meade.[20]

Much high-command intrigue preceded this change of command. In the bitter aftermath of Chancellorsville, the old guard among the corps commanders, the regulars, lined up decisively behind Meade as their choice to displace Hooker. They saw the failure of the late campaign as essentially the result of a failure of character, with the trio of Hooker, Butterfield, and Sickles utterly lacking in redeeming character traits. The ringleaders in this generals' intrigue were Couch and Slocum; those two, and John Sedgwick, had seniority over Meade but assured that general that they were willing to serve under him. Reynolds and Howard, though not as active in this effort, were certainly in favor of it. Hooker's only supporter among the corps commanders was Sickles. Typically, he was not shy about expressing his opinion to those who counted. "The President has been closeted for two hours today with Gen. Sickles," reported the *Herald*'s Washington correspondent on May 15. General Hooker's removal from the command, Sickles would later say, was "a misfortune to the army."[21]

In late June, as the theater of war shifted northward, across the Potomac, Dan Sickles was once again in the role of outsider, this time among the army's corps commanders. His rise to his lofty place, it was generally agreed, was due to his political influence with the president and the secretary of war and his friendship with the late general commanding. Sickles's experience of command, on the other hand, was recognized by his knowing brothers-in-arms as skimpy. There might not be reservations about his courage under fire, after Chancellorsville, but questions persisted about his generalship. Already he had antagonized the new general commanding, who was clearly not comfortable having a political general as head of the Third Corps. As the army moved into Pennsylvania in pursuit of Lee, Sickles received two sharply worded rebukes from Meade for failing to march his command as prescribed. Sickles could hardly help but realize that he was being put on notice.[22]

For Sickles, July 1, the first day of Gettysburg, was marked by confusion and conflicting orders. On the march that day, he had to pick and choose between an order from Meade to hold his command at Emmitsburg, and a call from Reynolds to come fast as reinforcement for the hard-pressed forces at Gettysburg. Leaving two of his six brigades at Emmitsburg — giving at least a nod to Meade's order — Sickles elected the soldierly course of heeding Reynolds's plea from the battlefield. On the way, he disregarded a second dispatch from Meade, to secure Emmitsburg, as an order out-of-date and overtaken by events. By these decisions, marching to the sound of the guns, he felt he was exercising the discretion usually accorded a corps commander in a fluid situation. And on July 1, at least, there was no question raised over any disobedience of the orders of the general commanding.[23]

The advance of the Third Corps did not reach Gettysburg until evening on July 1, too late to affect the fighting that day. It was 9 o'clock on the morning of July 2 before Sickles had his six brigades reunited and taking position alongside the rest of the army on Cemetery Ridge. General Meade had reached the field about midnight, and at first light he rode the Federal positions to survey the ground on which he had elected to fight. The most immediate threat seemed to be on the right, and there he focused most of his personal attention. Hancock's Second Corps — Hancock had recently replaced the departed Couch — was posted to hold the center. Sickles was ordered to extend Hancock's line southward along Cemetery Ridge to the Round Tops on the far left. Until the late-arriving Sixth Corps could reach the scene, the army's sole reserve, behind the main lines, was the Fifth Corps. This left the Third Corps, and the Third Corps alone, to hold the army's left.

Having thus positioned his forces to meet an expected attack that day, General Meade took the usual precaution of drawing up a plan for an orderly withdrawal in the event the battle went against him. This marked Meade as a thoroughgoing professional soldier. For Dan Sickles, as it proved, the paper would be prime ammunition in a long-running battle of words.[24]

It was about 7 o'clock that morning when Meade had his first inkling of a problem with General Sickles. Captain George Meade, headquarters aide-de-camp, reported back to his father that in checking on the Third Corps he discovered that it was not yet in the position designated; Sickles was said to be unsure where he was supposed to be. General Meade sent Captain Meade back to the general holding the left with a reiteration of the earlier order — the Third Corps should be on Hancock's left and along Cemetery Ridge, and it should be positioned there promptly. This was said, his son remembered, "in his quick, sharp way when annoyed."[25]

It was about 11 o'clock when Sickles himself appeared at headquarters. He repeated his puzzlement over the position he was to hold; for the third time that morning, this time by Meade himself, the posting was repeated to him. He did get Meade's leave to take Henry Hunt, chief of artillery, back with him to help post the Third Corps guns. In a final request, Sickles asked the general commanding if he was authorized to post his command in the manner he judged most suitable. Meade replied, as he later testified, "Certainly, within the limits of the general instructions I have given you; any ground within those limits you choose to occupy I leave to you." In the light of events, Dan Sickles either did not listen carefully to what Meade told him, or (to put the best face on it) in his inexperience he failed to grasp how little was the discretion allowed in these specific orders. This was not the fluid situation of July 1.

Upon returning to his command, Sickles took General Hunt with him some 1,500 yards out in front of the Cemetery Ridge line Meade had assigned the Third Corps. Ahead on rising ground there was a peach orchard — *the* Peach Orchard, it would soon become — which Sickles insisted was the better position for his troops. Hunt explained that whatever its advantages might be, the Third Corps did not have men enough to cover this extended ground. Furthermore, advancing his corps to the area of the Peach Orchard would leave him in a highly vulnerable salient; worse, he would be distant from any connection with the Second Corps on his right and without any secure anchor at Little Round Top on his left. Thus the explanation of a trained military mind — which made little or no impression on the decidedly untrained mind of Daniel Sickles. Instead, he tried to persuade Hunt to authorize his movement to the new position. Only the general commanding had that authority, said Hunt.[26]

As a battlefield tactician, the impulsive Sickles revealed himself that day to be like the chess neophyte who sees a promising opening move but fails to see ahead to the further moves in consequence. Soon afterward, when a reconnaissance beyond the Peach Orchard ran into Confederate troops, Sickles determined that he must make his opening move without delay — and without seeking authorization from headquarters. He marched the entire Third Corps off Cemetery Ridge and out ahead into a bulging salient that reached beyond the Peach Orchard ridge to the Emmitsburg Road. Puzzled observers in the neighboring Second Corps, seeing Sickles's brigades taking position three-quarters of a mile ahead of the main line, wondered if somehow they had missed the signal for an advance.[27]

It was the army's chief engineer, Gouverneur Warren, who

brought report of Sickles's startling venture to headquarters. The news arrived there just before Sickles himself rode up, in answer to an earlier summons. Amidst a group of general officers and staff, Meade confronted his errant lieutenant in cold anger. George Gordon Meade was a man of fearsome temper — his staff styled him the "Old Snapping Turtle" — which all too often was under imperfect control. "I never saw General Meade so angry if I may so call it," wrote an officer who witnessed the scene. "He ordered General Sickles to retire his line to the position he had been instructed to take. This was done in a few sharp words."[28]

Meade called for his horse and followed Sickles back to the scene of what was looking more and more like a crime. At the Peach Orchard, before his entourage, he continued his sharp scolding. After listening as Sickles explained his dispositions and argued that he had acted within his instructions, Meade sternly pointed back to Cemetery Ridge and said, "General Sickles, this is neutral ground, our guns command it, as well as the enemy's. The very reason you cannot hold it applies to them." Sickles asked if he should return to his starting point, and Meade told him he might try, and warned, "You cannot hold this position, but the enemy will not let you get away without a fight. . . ." Just then Confederate artillery opened on the Peach Orchard, signaling an attack. Should he still go back, asked Sickles. "I wish to God you could," Meade replied, "but the enemy won't let you!" The Third Corps would have to fight where it was.[29]

These bristling encounters, which to Sickles were not only humiliating rebukes but, worse, very public ones, would set him on an unswerving course toward bitter controversy with Meade. Dan Sickles, as he had demonstrated repeatedly, never forgave nor forgot what he regarded as a challenge to his honor. He had murdered the man who made a cuckold of him. Now he would do his best to ruin the general who had cast a stain on what he liked to think of as his military honor.

At the moment, however, battle overrode all such considerations. James Longstreet's assault tore into the vulnerable and overextended Third Corps and wrecked it; casualties would exceed 30 percent. What was left of Sickles's forces fled back to their original position on Cemetery Ridge, and many did not stop there. At length, reinforcements from the Second and Fifth Corps, and Henry Hunt's massed guns, were able to patch together a new line which by nightfall finally — and narrowly — held off Longstreet's attacking divisions. At the center of this savage fire Dan Sickles had coolly stood his ground and by example tried to hold his men to their work. Then a Confederate cannon shot smashed into his right leg and mangled it. He made sure the command was turned over to David Birney, and then, to reassure the troops, clamped a long cigar in his mouth as the stretcher bearers carried him from the field. For Dan Sickles this was his exit from the battle and — as it proved — the war as well.[30]

That evening surgeons amputated his leg above the knee, and by July 5 he was back in Washington and being cared for at a private home on F Street. His first visitor that day was President Lincoln. Sickles knew by report that the battle at Gettysburg had ended in Union victory, but he knew also that his Third Corps was a ruin and with it perhaps his reputation. While by no means was his recovery from the amputation yet assured, he seized this first opportunity to defend his military honor. "He certainly got his side of the story of Gettysburg into the President's mind," James Rusling of the general's staff recalled. A few days later, the wounded hero of Gettysburg — as the *Herald* among other papers had already proclaimed him — received a personal note from Mr. Lincoln. "I understand you are troubled with some report that the 3rd. Corps has sustained a disaster, or repulse," the president wrote. ". . . I have heard of no such disaster or repulse. I add that I do not believe there has been any such." In the war of words, Sickles had gained the first point.[31]

To be sure, General Meade was not yet aware of any war of words. In his official report on Gettysburg, dated October 1, Meade's comment on Sickles's unauthorized venture into the Peach Orchard was a good deal milder than what he had had to say on the subject on the afternoon of July 2. Now, three months later, he merely noted that General Sickles had "not fully apprehended the instructions in regard to the position to be occupied. . . ." Sickles was hardly mollified by the phrase "not fully apprehended." Then the report of General-in-Chief Halleck lent new weight to his grievance. By Halleck's reckoning, the Peach Orchard incident was caused by nothing less than General Sickles "misinterpreting his orders. . . ." With his extensive Washington contacts, there is little doubt that the recuperating Sickles was promptly apprised of both reports. He would have heard, too, the whispered story making the rounds (on the authority of General Warren, a legitimate hero of Gettysburg) that corps commander Sickles would have been court-martialed for his July 2 action had he not been maimed in the subsequent fighting.[32]

The catalog of George Meade's sins, so far as Dan Sickles was concerned, was made complete on October 18. On that date, hobbling about laboriously on his crutches, Sickles visited the Third Corps and was greeted uproariously. When he spoke earnestly to Meade about resuming his command, however, he was told that his present condition precluded him from actively campaigning in the field. This was said with all proper solicitude, yet Meade was careful to pledge nothing promising on the subject. Although keeping his own counsel, it seems that Meade was now determined that Sickles have no further command in this army.

Two days later, Sickles was back in Washington and retailing his peculiar history of the Battle of Gettysburg at the White House. With the president that day was Navy Secretary Gideon Welles, who recorded in his diary Sickles's assertion that it was he who was actually entitled to much credit for the decision to fight on the Gettysburg line, while Meade "was for abandoning the position and falling back." Welles added the caveat "Allowance must always be made for Sickles." Still, a pattern was clearly emerging. Dan Sickles was accelerating his campaign to poison the mind of the commander-in-chief against the general commanding the Union's principal army, and Sickles had no intention of letting the facts of the matter get in the way. His motive had become twofold. In addition to reviving his military reputation at the expense of the man he believed had blackened it, Sickles realized that the only way to regain command of the Third Corps was to rid himself of the army commander who decided such matters.[33]

In February 1864 Congress's busybody Joint Committee on the Conduct of the War held hearings on Gettysburg and invited Sickles to be its first witness. He was delighted to comply, and his crutches and pinned-up pants leg made his battlefield tale compelling. Sickles wanted his listeners to understand that the men in the ranks had been demoralized by the replacement of Joe Hooker with Meade. He painted the general commanding as weak and indecisive throughout the campaign. He himself, he testified, had been without orders on July 2, so he had acted on his own responsibility to deprive the enemy of the crucial Peach Orchard position. With knowledge of Meade's precautionary withdrawal plan, he startled the committee by asserting, "I was satisfied, from the information which I received, that it was intended to retreat from Gettysburg." All in all, according to heroic Dan Sickles, Gettysburg was a battle won not by General Meade but in spite of him.[34]

Generals Abner Doubleday and Albion Howe, and later Daniel Butterfield, all nursing grievances of their own against Meade, testified to the same effect. All this sent Senators Benjamin Wade and Zachariah Chandler, spokesmen for the committee, to the White House with the demand that Meade be replaced as head of the Army of the Potomac. Lincoln gave the two senators no satisfaction, but word of the plotting against Meade was soon all over the capital. "When I reached Washington," Meade wrote his wife, "I was greatly surprised to find the whole town talking of certain grave charges of Generals Sickles and Doubleday, that had been made against me in their testimony before the Committee on the Conduct of the War."

Meade, summoned to testify by Chairman Wade on March 5, gave a careful, lengthy account of his management of the Gettysburg campaign and battle. While in sharp contrast with the numerous fictions Sickles had narrated, Meade's testimony did not include a condemnation of his lieutenant. "I am of the opinion that General Sickles did what he thought was for the best," he said, "but I differed from him in judgment. And I maintain that subsequent events proved that my judgment was correct, and his judgment was wrong." He hoped that would settle the matter, he told Mrs. Meade, but he still feared the evil results of "spreading over the country certain mysterious whisperings of dreadful deficiencies on my part. . . ." A few days later, after seeing a harsh attack on him in the *New York Tribune* — an attack drawn largely from Sickles's committee testimony — he decided his fears were justified.[35]

Meade was encouraged by the response to a second round of testimony on Gettysburg that he delivered to the Wade committee, and also by a vote of confidence he received from General Grant, who had just come from the western theater to take the post of general-in-chief. Meade offered to vacate his command of the Army of the Potomac so Grant might install a general of his own choice. "This he declined in a complimentary speech," Meade told his wife with quiet satisfaction. He was of the opinion that "Sickles had overreached himself," but as he soon discovered, that disaffected general had only just begun to fight. The day after Meade's second committee appearance, the *New York Herald* published a long letter, signed "Historicus," that in effect reprised Sickles's testimony to the Wade committee, along with numerous additional slurs against Meade's generalship before, during, and after Gettysburg.[36]

To this point, Sickles's assault on Meade had circulated largely by word of mouth and through brief, scattered newspaper accounts leaked from the Wade committee. The attack of Historicus, however, was very detailed and very calculated and very public, delivered in the newspaper with the largest circulation in the nation. Aggrieved by its virulence, Meade demanded an investigation by the president and the War Department. Historicus, he said, had gained access "not only to official documents but to confidential papers that were never issued to the army, much less made public."

Then he added, "I cannot resist the belief that this letter was either written or dictated by Maj. Gen. D. E. Sickles."[37]

Meade was right on target in pointing his finger at Sickles, but surely not as the actual author of the Historicus letter. However much brass Dan Sickles displayed, he would hardly have risked being unmasked as Historicus; that would immediately destroy the letter's credibility. Dictating the letter's contents was closer to the mark. Historicus was without any doubt someone on Sickles's staff — and almost without any doubt Major Henry E. Tremain. Somewhat later in the Meade-Sickles controversy, Major Tremain would write another newspaper letter of attack in very much the same style, although on this occasion signing himself "Eye Witness." Eye Witness asserted that General Meade had refused to make an attack on another battlefield, this one Chancellorsville, at a critical point in the fighting there on May 3. This charge by Eye Witness was as much a fabrication as the earlier charges by Historicus had been. Henry Tremain, like Dan Sickles standing in his shadow and pulling his strings, was not one to let facts get in the way of shocking accusations.[38]

Mr. Lincoln responded that while it was natural that Meade should feel "some sensibility on the subject," he did not think the general's honor demanded a court of inquiry: "The country knows that, at all events, you have done good service," and Meade should not be diverted by an investigation from "trying to do more." General Halleck had sage advice for Meade in the case of political general Sickles. Do not challenge him personally or in a public forum, he advised. Sickles "would there be perfectly at home" in any controversy, and "with his facilities for controlling or giving color to the New York press" he would make short work of Meade. Best to simply ignore his tormentor, said Halleck; and like the president he predicted that the army commander's military reputation would suffer no irreparable damage. With some reluctance — he was, he said, less philosophical than was Halleck about the impact of such slanders on the public mind — General Meade took the high road and remained silent.[39]

Several of his comrades-in-arms refused to be silent, however, and they filled the columns of the *Herald* with letters contradicting Historicus and defending Meade (and themselves) for actions taken at Gettysburg. This inspired Historicus to respond with a second letter to the *Herald.* This one, written in lawyerly rebuttal form, was clearly intended as a summation of the case for the jury of public opinion; Major Tremain, like Sickles, was by trade a lawyer.

By this time, too, Sickles had a fresh bone to pick with Meade. As part of a major reorganization undertaken on the eve of the spring 1864 campaign, the Army of the Potomac was reduced from five corps to three. One of the discontinued corps was the Third, Dan Sickles's old command. While this reorganization had no connection with the Meade-Sickles controversy, it at least relieved Meade of a potentially awkward situation should Sickles somehow get himself declared physically fit for field duty. As for Sickles, his sole chance now for a corps command of any kind with the Potomac army would have to come at the behest of a new general commanding. Sickles had Historicus close his summation with a blunt assertion: If, in light of everything now known of the matter, the government permitted General Meade to remain at his post, it would represent "a singular indifference to public opinion."[40]

On April 1, in response to insidious implications in Butterfield's testimony, promptly leaked to the press, Meade appeared before the Wade committee for a third time. This had become necessary, he told General Gibbon, because of Dan Butterfield's "hellish ingenuity to rob me of my reputation." Before the committee Meade roundly denounced Butterfield's contention that the contingency plan he was instructed to draw up on July 2 was in fact an order for the army to retreat from its Gettysburg lines — an order only forestalled by the Confederate attack. This "retreat order" had become the cornerstone of Sickles's whole construction against Meade. "I utterly deny, under the full solemnity and sanctity of my oath . . . ," said Meade, "ever having intended or thought, for one instant, to withdraw that army. . . ."

A parade of authentic fighting generals — Warren, Hancock,

Hunt, Gibbon — went before the Wade committee to testify to Meade's unswerving determination to stand and fight at Gettysburg. The most telling blow to the retreat-order tale was delivered by John Gibbon. He testified that on July 2 Butterfield had asked him to look over the contingency plan and check the location of the various routes mentioned, and Gibbon asked him point-blank if General Meade intended "to leave this position." No, said Butterfield; the plan had been drafted only "in case it should be necessary to leave."[41]

The Meade-Sickles controversy faded out of the newspapers and congressional hearing rooms as the new campaign opened in Virginia. Neither Grant nor the administration made any move to displace Meade, who would still be in command of the Army of the Potomac at Appomattox. Sickles, meantime, did not gain a troop command again. Nor did he ever budge an inch from his unique and highly fictionalized version of what happened at Gettysburg on those hot July days. Dan Sickles would live well into the next century, unrepentant, fulminating to the end against the generalship of George Meade. As for Meade, he was forced to spend his last years — he died in 1872, at age fifty-seven — defending himself against this raffish political general who was remorseless in his efforts to tarnish the fame of the victor of Gettysburg.

Dan Sickles's dashing wartime reputation as a general, as Alpheus Williams explained, was very much the invention of newspaper scribblers. Certainly courageous enough when the fighting began — on those few occasions when he was present — Sickles reached the limit of his command skills when leading the Excelsior Brigade. Whatever the measure of his political contribution to the Union cause as one of the most visible War Democrats holding high command, it was largely overridden by his discreditable record as a corps commander. The bill for Sickles's blundering at Chancellorsville was paid by his men. At Gettysburg the bill was higher and the consequences graver.

The contemporary judgment of Frank Haskell, the perceptive soldier-historian of Gettysburg, was unsparing: "I know, and have heard, of no bad conduct or blundering, on the part of any officer, save that of Sickles, on the 2nd of July; and that so gross, and came so near being the cause of irreparable disaster, that I cannot discuss it with moderation." Haskell prayed that the wounded Sickles would never be returned to high command, "where his incapacity, or something worse, may be fruitless destruction to thousands again."[42] General Meade apparently shared that view, and saw to it that Sickles did not again command in his army. The resulting cost to Meade in personal obloquy was high, for Dan Sickles was vengeful beyond compare, yet the ultimate winner in the Meade-Sickles controversy proved in the end to be the Army of the Potomac.

NOTES

1. W. A. Swanberg's *Sickles the Incredible* (New York: Scribner's, 1956) is the standard biography, eclipsing Edgcumb Pinchon, *Dan Sickles: Hero of Gettysburg and "Yankee King of Spain"* (New York: Doubleday, Doran, 1945).

2. Swanberg, *Sickles*, 82–83; George Templeton Strong, *The Diary of George Templeton Strong*, eds. Allan Nevins and Milton Halsey Thomas (New York: Macmillan, 1952), vol. 1, 77–78.

3. Sickles speech in House of Representatives, Dec. 10, 1860, in Swanberg, *Sickles*, 109.

4. Mary Boykin Chesnut, *A Diary from Dixie*, ed. Ben Ames Williams (Boston: Houghton Mifflin, 1949), 247.

5. Swanberg, *Sickles*, 54, 64, 66; Thomas J. Fleming, "A Husband's Revenge," *American Heritage* (April 1967), 65–75. Sickles's reconciliation with his wife was only sporadically successful. She would die in 1867, age thirty-one.

6. Sickles speech in House of Representatives, Jan. 16, 1861, in Swanberg, *Sickles*, 111; Pinchon, *Dan Sickles*, 150–51.

7. Swanberg, *Sickles*, 118.

8. Joseph Hooker to Seth Williams, Nov. 1, 1861, *Official Records* 5, 637; Charles S. Wainwright, *A Diary of Battle: The Personal Journals of Colonel Charles S. Wainwright, 1861–1865*, ed. Allan Nevins (New York: Harcourt, Brace & World, 1962), 17; Hooker to James W. Nesmith, Dec. 26, 1861, Hooker Papers, Oregon Historical Society.

9. Swanberg, *Sickles*, 143–46.

10. Stephen W. Sears, *To the Gates of Richmond: The Peninsula Campaign* (New York: Ticknor & Fields, 1992), 184–89; Sickles report, *OR* 11:1, 450; 11:2, 37–38.

11. *New York Tribune*, Aug. 7, 1862; Swanberg, *Sickles*, 159.

12. Wainwright, *Diary of Battle*, 93; Robert McAllister, *The Civil War Letters of General Robert McAllister*, ed. James I. Robertson, Jr. (New Brunswick, N.J.: Rutgers University Press, 1965), 212.

13. James F. Rusling, *Men and Things I Saw in Civil War Days* (New York: Methodist Book Concern, 1914), 292.

14. Gouverneur Warren to brother, Apr. 17, 1863, Warren Papers, New York State Library; George G. Meade, *The Life and Letters of General George Gordon Meade* (New York: Scribner's, 1913), vol. 1, 351.

15. Princess Felix Salm-Salm, *Ten Years of My Life* (London: R. Bentley, 1876), 41; Regis de Trobriand, *Four Years with the Army of the Potomac* (Boston: Ticknor, 1889), 425–26; Charles Francis Adams, Jr., *Charles Francis Adams, 1835–1916: An Autobiography* (Boston: Houghton Mifflin, 1916), 161.

16. Stephen W. Sears, *Chancellorsville* (Boston: Houghton Mifflin, 1996), 254–57, 300–302.

17. De Trobriand, *With the Army of the Potomac*, 460; Sears, *Chancellorsville*, 492. The sentenced brigadier, Joseph Revere, was allowed by Lincoln to resign.

18. Warren memorandum, [May 1863], *OR* 25:1, 512.

19. *New York Herald*, May 8, 1863; Alpheus S. Williams, *From the Cannon's Mouth: The Civil War Letters of General Alpheus S. Williams*, ed. Milo M. Quaife (Detroit: Wayne State University Press, 1959), 203.

20. Sickles to Meade, May 26, 1863, *OR* 25:1, 510–11; Swanberg, *Sickles*, 195–96.

21. Sears, *Chancellorsville*, 435–36; *New York Herald*, May 16, 1863; Sickles testimony, *Report of the Joint Committee on the Conduct of the War*, vol. 1 (1865), 302.

22. Seth Williams to Sickles, June 29, 30, 1863, *OR* 27:3, 399, 420.

23. The most detailed account of Sickles and Meade at Gettysburg is Richard A. Sauers, *A Caspian Sea of Ink: The Meade-Sickles Controversy* (Baltimore: Butternut and Blue, 1989); for Sickles's July 1 march, see 20–22.

24. John Gibbon, *Personal Recollections of the Civil War* (New York: Putnam's, 1928), 139.

25. George Meade, *With Meade at Gettysburg* (Philadelphia: Winston, 1930), 101–2.

26. Henry J. Hunt in *Battles and Leaders of the Civil War* (New York: Century, 1887–88), vol. 3, 301–2.

27. Sauers, *Meade-Sickles Controversy*, 36.

28. William H. Paine, May 22, 1886, Meade Papers, Historical Society of Pennsylvania.

29. James C. Biddle, Aug. 8, 1880, Meade Papers; Isaac R. Pennypacker, "Military Historians and History," *Pennsylvania Magazine of History and Biography* (53), 40. The events of July 2 are detailed in Harry W. Pfanz, *Gettysburg: The Second Day* (Chapel Hill: University of North Carolina Press, 1987).

30. *OR* 27:1, 178; Swanberg, *Sickles*, 217.

31. *Washington Chronicle*, July 6, 1863; Rusling, *Men and Things*, 14; Lincoln to Sickles, July 10, 1863, Abraham Lincoln, *The Collected Works of Abraham*

Lincoln, ed. Roy P. Basler, Supplement (Westport, Ct.: Greenwood Press, 1974), 193.

32. Meade, Halleck reports, *OR* 27:1, 116, 16; John Chipman Gray and John Codman Ropes, *War Letters, 1862–1865* (Boston: Houghton Mifflin, 1927), 256.

33. Sickles testimony, *Report of Joint Committee,* vol. 1 (1865), 304; Gideon Welles, *Diary of Gideon Welles,* ed. Howard K. Beale (New York: Norton, 1960), vol. 1, 472–73.

34. Sickles testimony, *Report of Joint Committee,* vol. 1 (1865), 297–304.

35. *Report of Joint Committee,* vol. 1 (1865), xix, Meade testimony, 332–33; Meade, *Life and Letters,* vol. 2, 169, 176; *New York Tribune,* Mar. 8, 1864.

36. Meade, *Life and Letters,* vol. 2, 177–78; Historicus, *New York Herald,* Mar. 12, 1864, in Meade, *Life and Letters,* vol. 2, 323–31, and also in *OR* 27:1, 128–36.

37. Meade to E. D. Townsend, Mar. 15, 1864, *OR* 27:1, 127–28.

38. Eye Witness, *New York Times,* June 3, 1867, in Henry E. Tremain, *Two Days of War: A Gettysburg Narrative and Other Excursions* (New York: Bonnell, Silver and Bowers, 1905), 355–73. Tremain admits authorship on p. 373.

39. Lincoln to Meade, Mar. 29, 1864, Lincoln, *Collected Works,* vol. 7, 273; Halleck to Meade, Mar. 20, 1864, *OR* 27:1, 137–38.

40. Historicus, *New York Herald,* Apr. 4, 1864, in Meade, *Life and Letters,* vol. 2, 337–40. The letters by Meade's supporters are summarized in Sauers, *Meade-Sickles Controversy,* 51–53.

41. Gibbon, *Personal Recollections,* 187; Meade, Gibbon testimony, *Report of Joint Committee,* vol. 1 (1865), 436, 442.

42. Frank L. Byrne and Andrew T. Weaver, eds., *Haskell of Gettysburg: His Life and Civil War Papers* (Kent, Ohio: Kent State University Press, 1989), 184.

[9]

Raid on Richmond

Colonel Ulric Dahlgren

Brigadier General
Judson Kilpatrick

In casting about for a silver lining in the clouded story of Chancellorsville, the Northern press was quick to characterize Stoneman's raid as a dashing achievement. The *Washington Evening Star,* under the dateline May 9, 1863, styled it the "late brilliant cavalry raid." The *Evening Bulletin* of Philadelphia led off its coverage by announcing, "The expeditions sent out by General Hooker under General Stoneman seem generally to have been very successful. That commanded by Colonel Kilpatrick went . . . almost to Richmond. . . ." In typical press fashion, the *Bulletin* went on to indulge in a bit of speculation: "There were hours when, from what we hear, any one of them might have captured Richmond, bagged the whole administration, and set the Union prisoners free, for the city was wholly undefended."[1]

General Hooker, having just led the Army of the Potomac away in retreat from the dismal Chancellorsville battlefield, had a very different view of Stoneman's raid. Hooker cared nothing for how near Colonel Kilpatrick's contingent might have come to the Confederate capital. He cared only about how far Stoneman and his troopers had strayed from their assigned task of destroying General Lee's railroad lifeline. That failure, said Joe Hooker, was a prime cause of the Chancellorsville defeat. However that might be, there was one particular aspect of the Stoneman raid that captured President Lincoln's attention.

He had talked that morning with a newly exchanged officer "just from Richmond," the president telegraphed Hooker, and the man had a story worth listening to. "He says there was not a sound pair of legs in Richmond, and that our men, had they known it, could have safely gone in and burnt every thing & brought us Jeff Davis."[2] The prospect of a force of Union raiders carrying off the president of the Confederate States of America was dazzling, and not something Mr. Lincoln would soon forget.

In this Civil War, the administrations in both Washington and Richmond, and their generals, made frequent public obeisance to the so-called rules of civilized warfare. Violations, especially in the case of noncombatants, were publicized and condemned, and sometimes violators were punished. The assassination of the enemy's leaders, it was agreed, was beyond the pale. On the other hand, the capture of public officials of high rank, even by subterfuge, was considered to fall within the rules. Thus for President Lincoln to entertain thoughts of spiriting Jefferson Davis out of Richmond, and to mention that possibility to the commander of his principal army, was nothing extraordinary.

Some months later, during the winter of 1863–64, as the armies of Meade and Lee faced one another across the Rapidan in northern Virginia, the matter came up again in connection with a new issue agitating the Lincoln administration. Although the war seemed to have turned in the Union's favor following Gettysburg and Vicksburg and Chattanooga, no end to it was yet in sight. Among the growing multitude of sufferers, as the war dragged on, were said to be the Federal officers and men imprisoned in the Confederate capital. It was reported that the straitened Confederacy did not or could not properly care for those it had captured. Exchanged prisoners came back from Richmond with harrowing stories of hunger, overcrowding, and disease, especially at Belle Isle, where enlisted men were held, and at Libby Prison, where officers were confined. "In the three hospitals for Union soldiers in Richmond," a paroled surgeon wrote in December 1863 of sufferers from Belle Isle and Libby, "total mortality is averaging 50 per day or 1,500 a month. . . ." The cause of many of these deaths, the *Washington Evening Star* explained, was "starvation and exposure."[3]

This prisoner question pressed on President Lincoln, and he was open to any suggestions as to how it might be resolved. It was recalled how near Stoneman's raiders had come to Richmond the previous May, and how lightly defended the place was said to have been. The *Philadelphia Evening Bulletin* was not the only paper at the time to point out how easily the prisoners could have been rescued — and high officials of the Rebel administration captured in the bargain. Indeed, on that occasion Mr. Lincoln had grasped the point even before the press had.

The first solution proposed to the president came not from Meade's Army of the Potomac but rather from the fertile mind of Major General Benjamin Butler, in command of Federal forces at the tip of the Virginia Peninsula. General Butler's woeful lack of military ability never deterred him from pursuing the main chance. His idea was to make a sudden surprise dash on Richmond with a powerful cavalry force from Union-held Williamsburg, some forty-five miles southeast of the capital. As Butler spelled out the key points of the raid for his expedition commander, Isaac J. Wistar, there were three objectives: first, to liberate the prisoners; second, to destroy public buildings, arsenals, and the important Tredegar Iron Works; and third, to capture "some leaders of the rebellion." On January 20, 1864, Butler visited Washington and successfully sold his plan to Lincoln and Secretary of War Stanton.[4]

The objective of seizing "some leaders of the rebellion" was soon enough made more specific, and the capture of Jefferson Davis became an officially sanctioned part of the operation. Butler himself revealed to a visitor, who passed it on to Horace Greeley, editor of the *New York Tribune,* that one of the raiding parties would "first capture Davis. . . ." General Wistar wrote out his operational plan in close detail for his subordinates. Once Richmond was reached, the 2,200 cavalrymen were to break off into detachments with specific tasks. The prisoners at Libby and Belle Isle would be liberated. The city's main bridges and railroad depots would be burned. The Tredegar Iron Works "and numerous public buildings, factories and store-houses adjacent" would be destroyed. Finally, Major James Wheelan, leading 300 troopers of the 1st New York Mounted Rifles, would "turn to the right and capture Jeff. Davis" at the Confederate White House on Clay Street.[5]

Alas for General Butler, his best-laid plan was frustrated right at the start. It had been anticipated that Wistar's cavalry would encounter nothing more than a twenty-man Rebel picket at the Bottom's Bridge crossing of the Chickahominy, a dozen miles from Richmond. Instead, when they arrived at the crossing on February 7, they found the bridge planking taken up, the nearby fords blocked by felled trees, and several regiments of infantry with artillery well dug in. Wistar thought he might be able to force a crossing, at no little cost, but even then the rest of Richmond's defense force would be alerted and waiting for him. The critical element of surprise had been lost. After some ineffectual skirmishing, Wistar ordered his troopers back to their base.

Butler would lay blame for the fiasco on an escapee from the guardhouse who had deserted and revealed the details of the raid to the Rebels. It is to be wondered how a guardhouse inmate could learn so much about a secret plan, but in any event, somehow the scheme was compromised. That was little consolation to the Second Corps of the Army of the Potomac, which had been ordered to make a demonstration at Morton's Ford on the Rapidan to distract Lee from reacting to Butler's raid. The demonstration was bluntly repelled, suffering 261 casualties. The historian of the Second Corps would remark sarcastically that by report, Butler's loss in the operation was six forage caps.[6]

A successor was ready to step into Ben Butler's shoes. Officially, the war records are silent on the originator of this second raid on Richmond, but in retrospect his identity is clear enough: Brigadier General Judson Kilpatrick, commander of the Third Division, Cavalry Corps, Army of the Potomac. This was the same Kilpatrick, then a colonel, who had led his brigade to the very gates of

Richmond during Stoneman's raid nine months before. Now, over five days in February–March 1864, Judson Kilpatrick would attach his name to one of the more notorious operations of the Civil War.

Kilpatrick was the sort that attracted notoriety. He was twenty-eight and a West Pointer, of the small stature typical of cavalrymen, with a cold face and bold eyes and great bushy sideburns. He was a blatant womanizer and went out of his way to display flamboyance. Colonel Theodore Lyman, a shrewd observer at Meade's headquarters, termed him "the valiant Kilpatrick" and said it was hard to look at him without laughing.[7] Kilpatrick was generally considered a tough man in a fight, although his military judgments were frequently suspect. He was inordinately ambitious. His nickname was "Kill-cavalry," and was applied in reference to both the enemy's troopers and his own.

Kilpatrick's more or less partner in this enterprise, whose name would attach jointly to it, was similar to Kilpatrick only in his ambition for action. Ulric Dahlgren was twenty-one and a nonprofessional soldier. His father was Rear Admiral John Dahlgren, the navy's ranking expert on ordnance and just then commanding the South Atlantic Blockading Squadron. The admiral and the president were close friends, and it was Lincoln who had gotten Ulric a commission when he decided to give up his law and civil engineering studies to go to war. Young Dahlgren had served on the staff of Franz Sigel and then on the staffs of three heads of the Army of the Potomac — Burnside, Hooker, and Meade.

Dahlgren was tall and slim and blond and very dashing, and he invariably volunteered for every hazardous duty he could find. He craved adventure and glory, without regard for the cost. In the aftermath of Gettysburg he had wangled a place in a cavalry fight, where he was alongside Judson Kilpatrick, and was wounded severely enough to lose his right leg to amputation. He was getting about now on his wooden leg and looking for some interesting way to get back into the war. As recently as February 1 he had visited Mr. Lincoln at the White House. Although Colonel Dahlgren no doubt described his search for action, there is no indication that a raid on Richmond was discussed; at least he said nothing of it when writing his father that night about the visit.[8]

The first official document relating to the Kilpatrick-Dahlgren raid is an order dated February 11, 1864, for Kilpatrick to report to President Lincoln, "as requested by the latter." Surely the president had not bypassed the secretary of war and the general-in-chief and the Army of the Potomac's General Meade and then skipped on down the chain of command to pluck out a brigadier of cavalry for what proved to be a very special mission. The originator of the project had to be Kilpatrick himself. His overweening ambition would have given him no pause in skipping up through the chain of command and in some fashion importuning the commander-in-chief directly. Lincoln must have liked the idea well enough to invite Kilpatrick to the White House to explain it. On February 12 Kilpatrick met with the president and afterward separately with Secretary of War Stanton, to whom he spelled out in some detail his plan for a raid on Richmond.[9]

Kilpatrick is the sole source for just what he discussed with Lincoln and Stanton that day. By the cavalryman's account, the raid he proposed had three objectives: to "attempt the release of our prisoners at Richmond," to destroy the enemy's communications, and to distribute in Confederate territory copies of the president's recent proclamation of amnesty that sought to bring secessionists back into the fold. The latter objective, a political one, was hardly something Kilpatrick would have thought of; no doubt it was inserted by Lincoln. There was no mention in the written plan, as submitted by Kilpatrick on February 16, of capturing President Davis or members of his Cabinet.

In light of subsequent events, however, it is impossible to believe that topic did not come up in these discussions. Seizing Davis had been talked of in the White House and the War Department at least since the Stoneman raid. It had been a stated objective in the planning of Ben Butler's recent aborted raid, the plans of which were approved by Lincoln and Stanton. As the evidence would show, making the Confederate president a target was undeniably a part of the Kilpatrick-Dahlgren raid, and it defies belief that the idea of it came to the raiders only later and out of the blue.

Perhaps in their meeting Mr. Lincoln reprised for Kilpatrick his earlier remark to Joe Hooker about how easily he, Kilpatrick, might have "burnt every thing & brought us Jeff Davis" when last he was at the gates of Richmond. Certainly the Stoneman raid came up in these conversations, for Kilpatrick's experience in it was the cornerstone on which he built his whole proposal for directing a raid of his own on Richmond. It seems most likely that the cavalryman left his brief meeting with the president with two objectives clearly stated — to liberate the prisoners, and to distribute the amnesty proclamation — and perhaps with a third objective, or at least a hope, of bringing the Confederate president back with them should the raiders gain sufficient control of Richmond.

In all likelihood, it was during Kilpatrick's meeting with Secretary Stanton that Davis became a definite target. Stanton had earlier demonstrated his contempt for traditional "usages of war" by drafting a series of draconian orders for the treatment of Southern civilians which were issued over General John Pope's signature. To intrigue and conspire was second nature to Edwin Stanton. It is not hard to imagine the bellicose war secretary whispering ill of Jefferson Davis in the ear of the eager Kilpatrick — in the manner of King Henry II, famously speaking of Thomas à Becket, Archbishop of Canterbury, saying to his eager courtiers, "Will no one rid me of this man!" — and the ambitious, reckless Judson Kilpatrick thus believing his duty to be clear.[10]

However it happened, targeting Jefferson Davis now became, in the mind of General Kilpatrick, a thus-far-secret fourth objective of the raid. Next, the operation had to be fitted into place within the chain of command. Henry Halleck, who was in the process of being replaced as general-in-chief by U. S. Grant, was not consulted. Instead, Kilpatrick sent his plan for freeing the prisoners, destroying communications, and distributing the amnesty proclamation — prefaced by the smug announcement that it was already endorsed by president and secretary of war — to his superior, Alfred Pleasonton, head of the cavalry corps. Pleasonton passed it without comment up the line to General Meade. Meade fired it back, demanding to know if the cavalry chief thought it feasible. "Not feasible at this time" was Pleasonton's verdict. He saw no chance of Kilpatrick's achieving surprise, and added that the Confederates had forces positioned "for frustrating such an effort." As for distributing the president's amnesty proclamation, Pleasonton said he could arrange to do that with far less trouble, even in Richmond.

Apparently unimpressed by these arguments, and recognizing that his superiors, Lincoln and Stanton, were backing the operation, Meade gave it his official sanction. Kilpatrick was to take what numbers he needed from a pool of 4,000 troopers and a battery of artillery. The Army of the Potomac would initiate a major infantry-cavalry diversion beyond the Confederate left, allowing Kilpatrick to make his way around the enemy right and "on the shortest route" strike for Richmond "to effect an entrance into that city and liberate our prisoners. . . ." Meade concluded his approval by clarifying just how the plan had originated: "No detailed instructions are given you, since the plan of your operations has been proposed by yourself, with the sanction of the President and the Secretary of War. . . ." Privately, to his wife, Meade termed the operation "a desperate one," yet the plight of the prisoners "seems to demand running great risks for the chances of success." There is nothing to suggest that General Meade knew that Jefferson Davis would be a target of the raiders.[11]

Meade's sanction was issued February 27; the operation was scheduled to commence the next day. At some point well before that, Ulric Dahlgren had appeared unannounced at cavalry headquarters and won for himself a key role in the raid. Rumors of some sort of a big cavalry raid had been circulating widely through the army, and through Washington, since mid-February, and Dahlgren picked up on them. Theodore Lyman explained just how the rumor mill operated: "A secret expedition with us is got up like a picnic, with everybody blabbing and yelping. . . . Kilpatrick is sent for by the President; oh, ah! everybody knows it at once: he is a cavalry officer; it must be a raid. All Willard's chatters of it. Everybody devotes his entire energies to pumping the President and Kill-cavalry! Some confidential friend finds out a part, tells another confidential friend, swearing him to secrecy, etc., etc."[12] Despite the blabbing and yelping, however, the Kilpatrick-Dahlgren raid would not be forced to abort, like the Butler raid before it, because it was compromised before it even began. It appears that whatever notices of a Federal movement the Confederates managed to overhear were soon explained by Meade's diversionary effort to the west.

The adventurous Dahlgren seems to have simply talked his way into the operation, demonstrating that his recuperation was complete and that his wooden leg was no handicap on horseback. Kilpatrick no doubt knew of him and of his reputation for bold exploits — and no doubt knew also of the young colonel's influential friends in high places, notably in the White House. In assigning him, Pleasonton spoke of Dahlgren's "knowledge of the country and his well-known gallantry, intelligence, and energy." What is less clear is why Kilpatrick would entrust the youthful, inexperienced Dahlgren with so responsible a role in the raid. Indeed, this was to be Dahlgren's first time commanding more than a handful of troops.

The most likely explanation is that Kilpatrick thought he recognized in his new lieutenant a no-holds-barred mentality compatible with his own. Ulric Dahlgren was without professional military training or experience, and without any preconceived commitment to abide by the rules of civilized warfare — if indeed he was even aware of those rules. He saw only adventure and glory beckoning. Dahlgren would write exuberantly to his father, ". . . there is a grand raid to be made and I am to have a very important command. If successful it would be the grandest thing on record and if it fails many of us will 'go up' . . . but it is an undertaking that if I was not in it I should be ashamed to show my face again. . . ."[13]

The plan decided upon was for the raiders, some 3,500 strong, to cross the Rapidan on the evening of February 28 to the east of Lee's army — which meantime ought to be distracted by Meade's diversion to the west — and push almost due south toward Richmond. Beyond Spotsylvania Court House, the expedition would divide. Dahlgren, leading a 460-man detachment, was to loop off to the west to strike the James some twenty-five miles above Richmond. Dahlgren would cross the river there in order to come up on Richmond from the south, where it was believed to be lightly defended. With the main body, Kilpatrick would approach the capital from the north. On the morning of March 1, Dahlgren's force was to break into the city, release the prisoners, and carry them off down the Peninsula to General Butler's lines. They might be joined by Kilpatrick in the city or on its outskirts, depending on circumstances.[14]

Before they left the Confederate capital for the safety of the Peninsula, however, Kilpatrick and Dahlgren intended to carry out an additional and unofficial agenda of their own design — a scheme of arson, destruction, and assassination unlike anything that had gone before in this war.

Their scheme was spelled out in what came to be famously known as the Dahlgren papers. Dahlgren seems to have made this series of memoranda as compensation for his inexperience; for this "very important command" he chose to be exceedingly conscientious about being sure he remembered everything he was to do. From the papers' contents, it is clear that the occasion for the memoranda was a planning meeting with his superior, Kilpatrick, in order to coordinate the movements and objectives of the two columns. Writing on cavalry headquarters stationery, Dahlgren made notes on the itinerary and schedule of the operation, what tools of destruction were to be carried — oakum, turpentine, explosives — and drew up instructions for his own subordinate who would lead a party along the north bank of the James while he marched south of the river and into the city. In a pocket notebook Dahlgren made detailed notations of what needed to be done once the city was in their hands. Finally, among his papers there was an address he intended to deliver as inspiration to his men undertaking the expedition.

Scattered through these documents were notations of stark and brutal impact: The raiders, Dahlgren wrote, must exhort "the released prisoners to destroy & burn the hateful City & do not allow the Rebel leader Davis and his traitorous crew to escape." Once Richmond was occupied, "it must be destroyed and Jeff Davis and Cabinet killed." The prisoners were to be instructed "to gut the city. . . . Jeff. Davis and Cabinet must be killed on the spot."

The phrasing of Dahlgren's notes suggests that rather than the raiders, it was to be the released prisoners, presumably maddened by their cruel treatment, who would carry out the bloodiest of these deeds — exactly the sort of rationale, it may be surmised, that the devious Stanton could have planted in Kilpatrick's mind. However that might be, these murderous directions were not anything a twenty-one-year-old officer in his first responsible command had thought up by himself and intended to carry out on his own responsibility. They could only have been based on instructions from his immediate superior, Judson Kilpatrick — instructions that from the tone of the notes it is clear Dahlgren was willing to carry out without question or qualm.[15]

The Army of the Potomac's highly efficient Bureau of Military Information was brought into the operation. The B.M.I.'s second-in-command, John McEntee, and several of his men were assigned to go with the raiders, and the bureau's latest intelligence from its agent in Richmond helped secure approval for the operation. A mere thousand or two thousand Union cavalry approaching from the north, the B.M.I. spy predicted, "could land on the Pamunkey at dark and ride in unmolested and take Davis. Only a small picket at Mechanicsville." John Babcock, the very capable B.M.I. officer attached to Meade's headquarters, wrote Dahlgren, "I have found the man you want" to guide the party to the best crossing of the James. The guide was a black freedman named Martin Robinson, "well acquainted with the James River from Richmond up. . . . Question him five minutes, and you will find him the very man you want," Babcock promised.[16]

The operation opened on schedule early on February 28 with

General Meade's diversion. The Sixth Corps struck off westward toward Madison Court House, from which point George Armstrong Custer's cavalry command was to ride in the direction of Charlottesville. With the enemy thus distracted, the Kilpatrick-Dahlgren raiders trotted down to Ely's Ford on the evening of the twenty-eighth, swept up the unsuspecting Rebel picket guard there, and splashed across the river. "The moon threw its silvery light upon Rapidan waters when we forded it," wrote a poetic Union signalman, "and it seemed as if the Almighty Judge was looking silently upon our doings." But by dusk on February 29 the Almighty Judge seemed to be casting a cold eye on the raiders, and icy rain and sleet pelted down on them. Dahlgren and his 460 troopers made their way toward Fredericks Hall Station on the Virginia Central, while Kilpatrick's 3,000-man main body crossed the railroad at Beaver Dam Station farther to the east. Tearing up track and burning whatever supplies and rolling stock they found, they pushed on in their appointed courses. Although they cut every telegraph line they encountered, word of their coming sped ahead.[17]

By midmorning on March 1 Kilpatrick had reached the Brook Turnpike a half-dozen miles north of Richmond, and by 1:00 P.M. he was closing on the city's outer fortifications. According to the plan, Dahlgren should by now have broken into Richmond through its undefended southern portals. Kilpatrick opened fire with his light battery to signal his presence. The only response came from the enemy entrenchments, and it was a sharp one. What Kilpatrick described as a "considerable" force of infantry and artillery "effectually checked my advance." Something had gone very wrong. The Confederates confronting him were far more formidable than the elderly militiamen and government clerks he had expected to face. And there was no sign, no trace of Dahlgren. The bright prospect of a grand rush into the streets of the Rebel capital blinked out, and with it went Kilpatrick's resolution.

After skirmishing uncertainly and losing some sixty men, he fell back to the village of Mechanicsville and took stock. At length he seemed to regain his resolve and prepared to renew his assault on the city's defenses, only to find himself under sudden attack from the rear. By report it was cavalry from Lee's army under Wade Hampton, a name that Kilpatrick had learned to respect. There was a rush of confused fighting in the darkness, and then Kilpatrick abruptly gave up on the whole operation. "I abandoned all further ideas of releasing our prisoners" was how he put it in his report. Abandoned as well was his silent agenda of arson and assassination. His only resolve now was to escape to Butler's lines on the Peninsula without additional harm. He made, in the sour view of one of Dahlgren's men, "a rather precipitate and . . . demoralized run, with Hampton on his rear."[18]

Little had gone right for Judson Kilpatrick, and in the meanwhile Ulric Dahlgren had nothing better to show for *his* efforts. For Dahlgren the high point of his adventure had already been reached, at Sabot Hill, home of Confederate Secretary of War James Seddon on the James above Richmond. Sallie Bruce Seddon would recall the moment, drenching it with the scent of magnolias, some years afterward: the handsome young Yankee officer at her door, with wooden leg and crutches, introducing himself as Colonel Dahlgren. She inquires, Not by chance the son of Admiral John Dahlgren? — "Why, your father was an old beau of mine in my girlhood days. . . ." Then, in the drawing room, a toast, in fine blackberry wine in crystal goblets, to better times . . .[19]

Young Dahlgren's bearing soon enough turned from gallant to ruthless. The freedman Martin Robinson, the guide vouched for so strongly by the B.M.I.'s John Babcock, led Dahlgren's party as promised to the ford at Dover Mills on the James, where it was intended they cross. But the river here, swollen by an unusual volume of winter rain, was running too deep and too fast to ford. In his rage and frustration at what he took (with neither cause nor logic) to be treachery, Dahlgren had Robinson hanged from the nearest tree, supplying his own rein to speed the execution. As it happened, this would be the sole murder carried out under the expedition's murderous agenda.[20]

Unable now to approach Richmond from its lightly defended southern front, and encountering ever-more-destructive fire from the Confederate home guard as he neared the capital, Dahlgren abandoned his mission and devoted his flagging command efforts to escape. Soon the party broke into two segments. Captain John F. B. Mitchell, 2nd New York cavalry, took charge of the larger group and managed to join Kilpatrick in Butler's lines on the Peninsula without serious loss. Dahlgren, with perhaps a hundred men, attempted a wider swing north and east. They were pursued closely by Confederate cavalry and home guards, who laid an ambush for the desperate Yankees near the village of Stevensville some thirty miles northeast of Richmond.

Lieutenant James Pollard, 9th Virginia cavalry, reported the final act of the drama, played out at 10 o'clock on the night of March 2. "Col. Dahlgren who was in command and riding at the head of the column," wrote Pollard, "saw a man who at that moment moved his position, and ordered him to surrender: which drew a volley from our men and Col. Dahlgren fell dead, struck by several bullets." Of the balance of Dahlgren's command, only twenty-one would evade capture and make good their escape.[21]

General Kilpatrick in his report put the best face possible on the dismal outcome of the raid. The Virginia Central was heavily damaged, he claimed, with tracks torn up and depots and supplies burned. Along the James, Dahlgren's men had burned a number of gristmills and damaged the James River Canal. Several thousand of the president's amnesty proclamations were "scattered throughout the entire country." The cost of this, when it was toted up, came to 340 men killed, wounded, and captured — about one of every ten who set out on the raid — and more than 1,000 horses. No effort was made by either Kilpatrick or Dahlgren to carry out the primary, stated purpose of the raid — to liberate the Union prisoners. Acting to discourage further such raids, by the end of March the Confederates finished moving the last of the prisoners held at Belle Isle to a new prison in Georgia, a place called Andersonville.[22]

The Kilpatrick-Dahlgren raid seemed destined to go on the books as simply another failure of the Union's cavalry arm, and of its leadership. "Behold my prophecy in regard to Kill-cavalry's raid fulfilled," wrote Colonel Lyman. "I have heard many persons very indignant with him . . . that he is a frothy braggart, without brains and not over-stocked with desire to fall on the field; and that he gets all his reputation by newspapers and political influence."[23] The death of the dashing Ulric Dahlgren did generate a certain melancholy. Yet it was Dahlgren, having committed his ultimate blunder by failing to destroy his notes and planning papers before venturing into enemy territory, who now assured the raid of a lasting infamy.

In the aftermath of the Dahlgren ambush, thirteen-year-old William Littlepage, a member of a schoolboy company of Virginia home guards, had came upon the colonel's body lying in a roadside ditch. Young Littlepage rifled the dead man's pockets in hopes of finding a watch that he might give to his teacher, whose watch had recently been taken by a Yankee soldier. What he found instead was a cigar case containing documents, some folded papers, and a pocket notebook, which booty he took to his teacher, Edward Halbach. Incensed at the contents of the papers, Halbach started them up the chain of command, and soon they were in the hands of Jefferson Davis. By March 5 the Dahlgren papers were in print in the Richmond press, and the South was convulsed with loathing. These papers demonstrated, editorialized the *Richmond Sentinel*, "that Dahlgren's infamy did not begin or die with him, and that he was but the willing instrument for executing an atrocity which his superiors had carefully approved and sanctioned. Truly there is no depth of dishonor and villainy to which Lincoln and his agents are not capable of descending." Such sentiments were echoed throughout the Southern press. The Charleston diarist Mary Chesnut wrote of learning of Dahlgren's death "and the horrid tablets found in his pocket."[24]

For Varina Davis, First Lady of the Confederacy, as for many others, there was a deep sense of shock that the traditional "usages of war" had come to such a pass. She could recall the far-off days in Washington when "Commodore Dahlgren had brought the little fair-haired boy to show me how pretty he looked in his black velvet suit and Vandyke collar." Now, she wrote, "I could not reconcile the two Ulrics."[25]

General Braxton Bragg, military adviser to Mr. Davis, insisted to Secretary of War Seddon that the "fiendish and atrocious conduct of our enemies" fully justified the summary execution of those captured from the raiding parties. This was also the unanimous verdict of the newspapers. "They are murderers, incendiaries, outlaws, detected and arrested in the execution of their crimes," cried one editor. "They have forfeited the character of soldiers, and they should not be treated as such." Secretary Seddon agreed that Bragg's proposal had merit, but he was cautious enough to first ask General Lee for his opinion on the matter. Although he labeled the Yankee plot as evidenced by the Dahlgren papers "barbarous and inhuman," Lee pointed out that none of these acts had actually been carried out; all were intentions, not crimes. In any event, he thought executing prisoners of war a bad idea in principle, leading only to retaliation. With Robert E. Lee on their side, the Kilpatrick-Dahlgren prisoners could rest easy.[26]

Richmond was nevertheless determined to exploit the propaganda value of the Dahlgren papers. Photographs were made of the most incriminating documents and sent abroad to Confederate diplomat John Slidell. Slidell had a London lithographer reproduce Dahlgren's address to his men and dispatched copies to the capitals of Europe to demonstrate the true caliber of the enemy the Confederacy was facing. Surely, Slidell thought, this would ease the path for foreign intervention.[27]

The Northern press soon put the Dahlgren papers into print, picked up from Richmond newspapers passed through the lines. Some skepticism was expressed about their authenticity. A Philadelphia paper suspected Rebel forgery, reasoning that a captured President Davis would have been worth far more to the North as a hostage than a dead President Davis. Other papers, such as the

New York Times, ran the documents without comment. Still others found nothing to condemn should Dahlgren's instructions be found to be authentic; admiration was expressed for the "spirit-stirring and patriotic appeal" of the gallant Dahlgren's words.[28]

On March 30, General Lee was instructed to send a set of the photographed documents under flag of truce to General Meade, along with a demand for an explanation. Were the "designs and instructions of Colonel Dahlgren," Lee sternly asked his opposite number, "authorized by the United States Government or by his superior officers," and did they have "the sanction and approval of those authorities"?[29]

Meade had already seen the Dahlgren papers as they had appeared in the Richmond press and been appalled both by their contents and by the implications to be drawn from them. He ordered Pleasonton, his cavalry chief, to initiate a "careful inquiry" into the Dahlgren matter. Pleasonton, scrambling to stay well away from the affair, called upon Kilpatrick to make every effort "to learn the truth of this matter." This, as it happened, was equivalent to ordering the fox to investigate losses in the henhouse. He had questioned the survivors of Dahlgren's party, Kilpatrick replied, and all denied knowledge of any address made to them by the colonel or any instructions "of the character alleged in the rebel journals." However, Kilpatrick added, before the raid Dahlgren had shown him that very address, except that it lacked the inflammatory passage about exhorting the prisoners to burn the hateful city and kill the traitor Davis and his Cabinet. "All this is false," said Kilpatrick indignantly.[30]

In his reply to General Lee, Meade wrote, "neither the United States Government, myself, nor General Kilpatrick authorized, sanctioned, or approved the burning of Richmond and the killing of Mr. Davis and cabinet, nor any other act not required by military necessity and in accordance with the usages of war." He enclosed a copy of Kilpatrick's statement of his investigation, although somewhat modified. The accusation of forgery was softened to an implication, and Kilpatrick added the disclaimer that he had issued no instructions to Dahlgren to pillage, burn, or kill, nor had he received any such instructions from his superiors. Kilpatrick thus left Ulric Dahlgren, forever silent in his grave, the sole suspect in the heinous crime.[31]

There the matter rested, so far as the two armies were concerned, but George Meade was not reconciled to its implications. "This is a pretty ugly piece of business," he confided to Mrs. Meade. His reply to General Lee, he said, "necessarily threw odium on Dahlgren," and Kilpatrick's letter impugned the authenticity of the Dahlgren papers. As to that, Meade went on, "I regret to say Kilpatrick's reputation, and collateral evidence in my possession, rather go against this theory. However, I was determined my skirts should be clear. . . ."

That collateral evidence was very likely the testimony of Captain John McEntee, the Bureau of Military Information officer on Meade's staff who had been with Dahlgren on the raid and had managed to evade capture. Marsena Patrick, the army's provost marshal, recorded in his diary a conversation with the newly returned McEntee. Captain McEntee had only contempt for Kilpatrick, wrote General Patrick, "and says he managed just as all cowards do. He further says, that he thinks the papers are correct that were found on Dahlgren, as they correspond with what D. told *him*. . . ."

Here, then, was a trustworthy witness to the fact that Dahlgren, if he did not actually deliver his inflammatory address to his men, had indeed had instructions to burn, pillage, and kill, and that he had not kept those instructions to himself. From that starting point, General Meade had no trouble divining Judson Kilpatrick's role in all this. Officially Meade would have to hew to the line that neither his army command nor his government had any hand in the nefarious scheme. But it was surely no coincidence that before the 1864 spring campaign opened, Judson Kilpatrick was relieved as a cavalry commander with the Army of the Potomac and sent to the western theater. Nor is it surprising that some months later Kill-cavalry would be made welcome by General

Sherman in his planning for the March to the Sea. "I know that Kilpatrick is a hell of a damned fool," said Sherman in his brutal way, but that was exactly the sort he wanted to help cut a destructive swath through Georgia.[32]

There would be a curious wartime denouement to the Dahlgren affair. One of the lithographed copies Slidell had made in London of Colonel Dahlgren's proposed address to his men was shown to Admiral Dahlgren, who immediately pounced on it as "a barefaced, atrocious forgery." His son's signature was misspelled! It appeared as "U. Dalhgren," with the *h* and the *l* transposed. A blunder such as that, the admiral insisted, in an argument more emotional than evidential, discredited everything the "miserable caitiffs" in Richmond had passed off as the Dahlgren papers. His son was vindicated, and an unstained hero after all. On August 8, 1864, the *New York Herald* was the first paper to publish this new sensation. To many Northerners it seemed persuasive. Southerners dismissed it out of hand.[33]

During the rest of the war, and for nearly fifteen years afterward, the authenticity of the Dahlgren papers continued to puzzle. Then, in 1879, ex–Confederate general Jubal Early solved the puzzle — and something over a century later, historian James O. Hall confirmed what Early had discovered. Dahlgren's address to his men had been written in ink on thin paper, and where Dahlgren's signature appeared at the bottom of the page, there was writing across the back of that page that showed through. The 1864 London lithographer had touched up this show-through in order to have clean copy to work from. Not being familiar with Dahlgren's name, he deciphered the signature as best he could, never realizing that the show-through from the back of the sheet had created a misspelling — which he perpetuated in the lithographed copies.[34]

The latter-day authentication of the Dahlgren papers, with their message of assassination and destruction, and the contemporaneous confirmation of that message by Dahlgren himself, as reported by Captain McEntee, effectively ends any doubts about the papers themselves. It is equally certain that Judson Kilpatrick was the leader, and Ulric Dahlgren the willing follower, in developing the murderous agenda for the raid on Richmond. Dahlgren's death left Kilpatrick free to write himself out of that partnership, and when General Meade pressed him, he did just that. It is nearly as certain that sentencing to death President Davis and his Cabinet was not an original thought with Kilpatrick. He was ignoble enough to attempt to carry out that sentence, but he was hardly courageous enough to act as executioner without some authorization.

The idea of a raid on Richmond to release the prisoners had President Lincoln's approval, and he certainly contemplated Jefferson Davis's capture, but there is neither evidence nor hint that he went any further in his brief meeting with Kilpatrick. That a captured Davis might not survive among the liberated prisoners may have occurred to Lincoln, of course, but nothing suggests he would have regarded that as anything but an operational risk. Surely the appeal in all this for Mr. Lincoln was holding the president of the Confederacy hostage for, say, the wholesale release of Union prisoners of war.

Both circumstance and logic point to Secretary of War Stanton as authorizer of the dark premise of the Kilpatrick-Dahlgren raid. He was on record as pressing for war without limits. Of Kilpatrick's superiors, only Stanton discussed the planning with him in any detail. The idea of liberating the maddened prisoners and exhorting them to carry out the death sentences and the pillaging was a masterstroke of rationalization and perfectly in character for the secretary of war.

Covering up his tracks was also perfectly in character. In November of 1865 Stanton called on Francis Lieber, who was in charge of the captured Confederate archives, for all the papers and documents found on Colonel Dahlgren's body. They were delivered to him on December 1 — and have not been seen since. "The suspicion lingers," writes historian Hall, "that Stanton consigned them to the fireplace in his office." The historical record today consists only of one badly faded set of the photographs made by the Confederates of Dahlgren's address and a page of his instructions for the raid, in the National Archives; lithographed copies of the address, made in Europe; and the transcriptions of the various documents printed in the Richmond newspapers in 1864. All the originals, delivered into Edwin Stanton's hands in 1865, are beyond recall.[35]

Militarily, the Kilpatrick-Dahlgren raid must be counted a total failure, costing more in men and animals than any damage it inflicted on the Confederate economy. Only the slightest of its objectives, the distribution of Lincoln's amnesty proclamation, was carried out. Yet from its collapse, at the gates of Richmond, would run a bloody trail toward Ford's Theatre in Washington. The Federals, by proposing to assassinate the Confederacy's president, set in motion a train of events leading to the assassination of their own president.

The wartime debate over whether the Dahlgren papers were forgeries was actually one-sided, carried on in the closing months of the war entirely in the North. Southerners, especially those in the highest councils in Richmond, did not doubt the bloody outcome had their capital been occupied by the Kilpatrick-Dahlgren raiders. They had the documents, and they knew they were authentic. There was further unanimity in Richmond about the lesson that ought to be drawn from all this. The evidence found on Colonel Dahlgren's body seemed a clear signal that Lincoln's minions intended waging the most heinous kind of warfare against the South. The effort had failed this time, it was true, but henceforth fire must be fought with fire. The *Richmond Sentinel* put the issue bluntly: "If the Confederate capital has been in the closest danger of massacre and conflagration; if the President and Cabinet have run a serious risk of being hanged at their own door, do we not owe it chiefly to the milk-and-water spirit in which this war has hitherto been conducted?"[36]

After March 1864 there was a rapid increase in clandestine activity designed to exploit the Copperhead antiwar faction in the

North. The Confederate secret service stepped up planning to effect the capture of Lincoln, in imitation of what the Federals had attempted in the aborted Butler raid. The site of the capture was to be the Soldiers' Home on the outskirts of Washington, where Lincoln often stayed in the summer months to escape the city's heat. Way stations were established between Washington and Richmond to shelter the kidnapping party during the expedition. Five months after the Kilpatrick-Dahlgren raid, an actor with Confederate sympathies, John Wilkes Booth, was recruited by the secret service to play a major role in this kidnapping scheme.

What was new about these covert Confederate efforts was their enhanced sense of motive. Now the South claimed it was simply playing by the North's deadly rules. It was easy to rationalize such efforts — and to rationalize increased support and resources for their ever-more-violent coloring — when everyone involved could point to the fact that the Federals under Kilpatrick and Dahlgren had shown no compunction about pillaging and burning Richmond and killing President Davis and his advisers. By 1865 the terrible logic of this course would come to dominate events. As if in direct imitation of the Dahlgren party, an officially sanctioned expedition set out from Richmond for Washington to blow up the White House and its occupants. Like the Dahlgren party, it was caught and captured. The intensely planned efforts to kidnap Lincoln failed as well. But Booth, one of the kidnapping plotters — whether acting alone or on orders from Richmond has never been determined — did not fail.[37]

There is no knowing, of course, whether Lincoln would have lived had the Kilpatrick-Dahlgren raid never taken place — or if Dahlgren had had sense enough to destroy his planning notes before he set out. But in either case, there would have been considerably less motive for carrying out the chain of events that led to Ford's Theatre. Surely these two nations at war would have been better off had Edwin Stanton, Judson Kilpatrick, and Ulric Dahlgren not elected to break the rules for what in that day passed for civilized warfare.

NOTES

1. *Washington Evening Star, Philadelphia Evening Bulletin,* May 9, 1863.

2. Lincoln to Joseph Hooker, May 8, 1863, Abraham Lincoln, *The Collected Works of Abraham Lincoln,* ed. Roy P. Basler (New Brunswick, N.J.: Rutgers University Press, 1953–55), vol. 6, 202–3.

3. Daniel Meeker in *Army and Navy Journal,* Dec. 5, 1863; *Washington Evening Star,* Nov. 4, 1863.

4. Butler to I. J. Wistar, Feb. 4, 1864, Benjamin Butler, *Private and Official Correspondence of Gen. Benjamin F. Butler* (Norwood, Mass.: Plimpton Press, 1917), vol. 3, 373–74. The proposed Butler raid is detailed in Joseph George, Jr., "'Black Flag Warfare': Lincoln and the Raids Against Richmond and Jefferson Davis," *Pennsylvania Magazine of History & Biography* (July 1991), 291–318.

5. James W. White to Horace Greeley, Feb. 9, 1864, Sidney H. Gay Papers, Columbia University; Wistar to S. P. Speer, Feb. 5, 1864, *Official Records* 33, 521–22.

6. Wistar, Butler reports, *OR* 33, 146–48, 143–44; Francis A. Walker, *History of the Second Army Corps* (New York: Scribner's, 1887), 396.

7. Theodore Lyman, *Meade's Headquarters, 1863–1865: Letters of Colonel Theodore Lyman from the Wilderness to Appomattox,* ed. George R. Agassiz (Boston: Atlantic Monthly Press, 1922), 76.

8. Lincoln to Stanton, June 6, 1862, Lincoln, *Collected Works,* vol. 5, 262; Ulric Dahlgren to John A. Dahlgren, Feb. 1, 1864, John A. Dahlgren Papers, Library of Congress.

9. Seth Williams to Alfred Pleasonton, Feb. 11, 1864, *OR* 33, 552; Stephen Z. Starr, *The Union Cavalry in the Civil War* (Baton Rouge: Louisiana State University Press, 1981), vol. 2, 58.

10. Judson Kilpatrick to Pleasonton, Feb. 16, 1864, *OR* 33, 172–73; Mark Grimsley, *The Hard Hand of War: Union Military Policy Toward Southern Civilians, 1861–1865* (Cambridge: Cambridge University Press, 1995), 86–88.

11. Andrew A. Humphreys to Pleasonton, Feb. 17, Pleasonton to Humphreys, Feb. 17, Humphreys to Kilpatrick, Feb. 27, 1864, *OR* 33, 173, 171–72, 173–74; George G. Meade, *The Life and Letters of General George Gordon Meade* (New York: Scribner's, 1913), vol. 2, 167–68.

12. Lyman, *Meade's Headquarters,* 77.

13. Pleasonton to Kilpatrick, Feb. 26, 1864, *OR* 33, 183; Ulric Dahlgren to John A. Dahlgren, Feb. 26, 1864, John A. Dahlgren Papers.

14. Kilpatrick report, *OR* 33, 183–87.

15. The Dahlgren papers are reproduced, from a variety of sources, in: Virgil Carrington Jones, *Eight Hours Before Richmond* (New York: Henry Holt, 1957), appendix; *Southern Historical Society Papers,* vol. 13, 540–44, 555–56; and *OR* 33, 178–79, 219–21. The papers, their history, and their authenticity are definitively examined in James O. Hall, "The Dahlgren Papers," *Civil War Times Illustrated* (Nov. 1983), 30–39.

16. Edwin C. Fishel, *The Secret War for the Union: The Untold Story of Military Intelligence in the Civil War* (Boston: Houghton Mifflin, 1996), 543, 556; John Babcock to Kilpatrick, n.d., *OR* 33, 221; Richard G. Crouch in *Southern Historical Society Papers*, vol. 34, 184.

17. Accounts of the raid may be found in: Jones, *Eight Hours Before Richmond;* Emory M. Thomas, "The Kilpatrick-Dahlgren Raid," *Civil War Times Illustrated* (Feb., Apr. 1978); Duane Schultz, *The Dahlgren Affair: Terror and Conspiracy in the Civil War* (New York: Norton, 1998); George, "'Black Flag Warfare'"; and Starr, *The Union Cavalry*, vol. 2.

18. Kilpatrick, Joseph Gloskoski reports, *OR* 33, 184–85, 189; Reuben R. Bartley in *Southern Historical Society Papers*, vol. 13, 519.

19. William Preston Cabell in *Southern Historical Society Papers*, vol. 34, 353–58.

20. John F. B. Mitchell report, *OR* 33, 195; Richard G. Crouch in *Southern Historical Society Papers*, vol. 34, 184; C. Vann Woodward, ed., *Mary Chesnut's Civil War* (New Haven: Yale University Press, 1981), 580.

21. Mitchell report, *OR* 33, 195–96; James Pollard manuscript, Western Reserve Historical Society.

22. Kilpatrick, F. C. Newhall reports, *OR* 33, 186–87, 188; Lonnie R. Speer, *Portals to Hell: Military Prisons of the Civil War* (Mechanicsburg, Pa.: Stackpole Books, 1997), 205.

23. Lyman, *Meade's Headquarters*, 79.

24. Edward W. Halbach in *Southern Historical Society Papers*, vol. 33, 547–49; *Richmond Sentinel*, March 5, 1864; Woodward, *Mary Chesnut's Civil War*, 578. Dahlgren's notebook, held back for a time by a Virginia cavalry officer, was not put into print until April 1.

25. Varina Howell Davis, *Jefferson Davis, Ex-President of the Confederate States of America: A Memoir by His Wife* (New York: Belford, 1890), vol. 2, 472.

26. Braxton Bragg to James Seddon, Mar. 4, Seddon to Lee, Mar. 5, Lee to Seddon, Mar. 6, 1864, *OR* 33, 217–18, 219, 222–23; *Richmond Sentinel*, Mar. 5, 1864.

27. Hall, "The Dahlgren Papers," 36.

28. George, "'Black Flag Warfare,'" 313–15.

29. S. Cooper to Lee, Mar. 30, Lee to Meade, Apr. 1, 1864, *OR* 33, 223, 178.

30. Humphreys to Pleasonton, Mar. 14, Pleasonton to Kilpatrick, Mar. 14, Kilpatrick to Pleasonton, Mar. 16, 1864, *OR* 33, 175–76.

31. Meade to Lee, Apr. 17, 1864, *OR* 33, 180.

32. Meade, *Life and Letters*, vol. 2, 190–91; Marsena R. Patrick, *Inside Lincoln's Army: The Diary of Marsena Rudolph Patrick, Provost Marshal General, Army of the Potomac*, ed. David S. Sparks (New York: Yoseloff, 1964), 347–48; James Harrison Wilson, *Under the Old Flag* (New York: Appleton, 1912), vol. 1, 372. It should be noted that during the time of the Dahlgren affair General Meade was also entangled in the Sickles-Gettysburg controversy. See "Dan Sickles, Political General" elsewhere in this collection.

33. Hall, "The Dahlgren Papers," 37.

34. Jubal Early in *Southern Historical Society Papers,* vol. 13, 559; Hall, "The Dahlgren Papers," 37–38.

35. Hall, "The Dahlgren Papers," 38–39.

36. *Richmond Sentinel,* Mar. 6, 1864.

37. These matters are fully examined in William A. Tidwell, James O. Hall, and David Winfred Gaddy, *Come Retribution: The Confederate Secret Service and the Assassination of Lincoln* (Jackson: University Press of Mississippi, 1988).

[10]

Gouverneur Kemble Warren and Little Phil

Major General Gouverneur K. Warren

IT IS DUSK on the victorious battleground. The dead and wounded define the smoking, muddy, trodden field. Dimly in the distance are the flashes and rumble of the last guns. Prisoners in ragged butternut are led away. Up to a group of mounted Union officers surveying their triumph, records an eyewitness, rides a lone general "with almost the agony of death upon his face." Singling out the senior commander, Philip H. Sheridan, the general asks him quietly if he will reconsider his order. "Reconsider, hell!" Sheridan barks. "I don't reconsider my decisions. Obey the order!" In the sudden stunned silence the general bows his head and turns his horse and rides off the darkening field.

Gouverneur Kemble Warren, major general, Army of the Potomac, is remembered for two things. First, of course, is his fame as a hero of Gettysburg. On Day Two of the battle, recognizing the critical importance of Little Round Top, Warren rushed troops to the site in the nick of time to hold it for the Union. Today General Warren, memorialized in bronze, stands guard in singular splendor on the heights of Little Round Top. Warren's second noteworthy Civil War moment is infamous. Virtually at war's end, in the act of directing his troops to a sweeping victory at Five Forks near Petersburg, he was relieved of his corps command and sent unceremoniously to the rear. Nothing like it had ever happened in the Army of the Potomac, and the shock of it would reverberate for the better part of two decades.

In 1865, before Five Forks, Gouverneur Warren was ostensibly an elite member of the Potomac army's high command. His number-two ranking in the West Point class of 1850 had allowed him to pick his branch of service, and he selected the exclusive company of the topographical engineers. At the outbreak of war he had followed the volunteer route to the colonelcy of the 5th New York, and on the way fought in the Army of the Potomac's first battle, at Big Bethel. Warren would take part in that army's every campaign thereafter but the last one, and be twice wounded. By the end of 1862 he was a brigadier and commanding a brigade in the Fifth Corps. He served Hooker at Chancellorsville and Meade at Gettysburg as the army's chief engineer, and his Gettysburg exploit helped earn him his second star and temporary command of the Second Corps. In the reorganization of the army for the Overland campaign in 1864, he was promoted to permanent head of one of the three corps, the Fifth. At the time, General-in-Chief Grant was heard to say that should anything happen to Meade, he would seriously consider Warren to command the Army of the Potomac. At Five Forks "Little Phil" Sheridan did not sack just any general.[1]

The Five Forks incident, abrupt as it appeared, was deeply rooted in past events on old battlefields. Warren had first displayed his distinctive notions of corps command at Mine Run back in November 1863. Throughout that post-Gettysburg period Meade and Lee had been maneuvering against each other without much result, and at last Meade believed he had found an opening along Mine Run, below the Rapidan. Careful plans were laid, with Warren's Second Corps scheduled to spearhead a pivotal turning movement. The appointed hour came and the army poised to leap forward at the sound of Warren's guns. Instead there was only silence. In due course a courier reached Meade's headquarters with a dispatch from General Warren. It announced that he had canceled the attack on his own initiative — the Confederates had reinforced the position to the point that an assault would be fruitless.

"We tried to take it all philosophically," wrote Theodore Lyman of Meade's staff, "but it was hard, very hard." Seething, Meade rode to Warren's command post and there ensued a tense, earnest conversation. Finally Meade nodded, and the army pulled back. He had to close the campaign empty-handed. Colonel Lyman was reminded of the old nursery rhyme: "The King of France went up the hill with forty thousand men; / The King of France came down the hill and ne'er went up again." While Meade came to accept that an attack in the changed circumstances would indeed have been hopeless, he found Warren's arbitrary, unilateral decision unsettling. Might better the corps commander have left so momentous a decision to the general commanding?[2]

Gouverneur Warren neither looked nor acted the part of a warrior general. He was slender and slight of build, and his dark complexion, piercing black eyes, and long straight black hair gave him, people thought, a little of the appearance of an Indian. In manner, however, he was more the fussy Yankee schoolmaster, cautious, fidgety over details, often mean-spirited with subordinates, insistent on doing everything himself so that it would be done properly. In this he was very much an echo of General McClellan, whom he admired extravagantly. Certainly Warren was a thoroughly professional soldier and more than brave enough under fire; he could and did command from the front line when he deemed it necessary. But his real interest was in the science of command. Warren believed that leading a corps gave him discretion and leeway in carrying out his duties — which often enough he performed with the smugness of the righteous. It developed that not everyone would be tolerant of either his manner or his philosophy of command — particularly not U. S. Grant.[3]

Preparing for the spring campaign of 1864, Meade put the Mine Run experience behind him in reorganizing the army's high command. He gave Warren the Fifth Corps, alongside the veterans Hancock (Second) and Sedgwick (Sixth). Looking over Meade's shoulder, Grant nodded in approval of Warren's promotion. Yet Warren's conduct in the opening battle of the campaign, in the

Wilderness, triggered second thoughts. Ordered to the attack, he (and his generals) found many grounds for delay in putting the Fifth Corps into action. In retrospect, their impulse to go slowly and to wait for proper support was probably the better course in this chaotic battle, but in the heat of the moment both Meade and Grant grew testy and impatient over the delays. "We are waiting for you," Meade told Warren grimly. With that, Warren attacked and was sharply repulsed.[4]

As the two armies rushed together into a deadly embrace at Spotsylvania Court House, Gouverneur Warren's tenure as corps commander very nearly came to an end. His slowness, his caution, his questioning — indeed his challenging — of orders got on everyone's nerves. It was during the initial frantic race toward Spotsylvania that he had his first brush with Phil Sheridan. In this Warren was more or less an innocent victim, caught in the middle of a feud between Sheridan and Meade. But Sheridan, with his short fuze and his long memory, would not forget this encounter with the Fifth Corps and its commander.

Sheridan had brought with him the reputation of a head-down fighter when he came east that spring to take command of the Army of the Potomac's cavalry corps. As an infantry general his commands had been in the thick of the fight on virtually every western battlefield. At Chattanooga he personally led his division in the spectacular, triumphant charge right up the face of Missionary Ridge, all under the observant eye of General Grant. Little Phil — so his soldiers christened him — was a bantam-sized Irishman, black-haired, black-eyed, bullet-headed. His command of profanity was extensive and his gentlemanly qualities were few. He was a skilled battlefield tactician who always led from the front, and he had scorn for any general who did it any other way. "I have never in my life taken a command into battle," Sheridan once said, "and had the slightest desire to come out alive unless I won."

From the first, Sheridan and Meade had clashed over the proper use of the cavalry in this campaign, and after the race for Spotsylvania ended ignominiously in a massive nighttime tangle of horsemen and foot soldiers, the two generals went at it toe to toe. Sheridan's language throughout, said an observer, "was highly spiced and conspicuously italicized with expletives," but when it came to temper, few were a match for George Meade. Their argument focused on which had had the right of way, infantry or cavalry, and in this instance the infantry happened to be Gouverneur Warren's Fifth Corps. At one point in his tirade, noted Colonel Lyman, Sheridan "went on to say that he could see nothing to oppose the advance of the 5th Corps; that the behavior of the infantry was disgraceful, etc., etc."[5]

In the desperate struggle for the Bloody Angle at Spotsylvania on May 12, Warren appeared to headquarters to be too slow putting in a supporting attack, and then not driving it home. The Rebels were too strongly posted to be moved, Warren insisted repeatedly; the tactics of attack were all wrong. "Warren seems reluctant to assault," an angry General Meade explained to Grant, and he added, "I have ordered him at all hazards to do so." If Meade's patience with his Fifth Corps commander was wearing thin, Grant's had worn through. His dispatch to Meade in reply was curt: "If Warren fails to attack promptly, send Humphreys to command his corps, and relieve him."[6]

In the end, as at Mine Run, Meade acknowledged that the enemy's position before Warren was indeed too strong — a fact demonstrated forcibly enough when the delayed Fifth Corps assault was repelled — and he decided not to relieve his general. Still, he said sharply, Warren had "no right to delay executing his orders under any circumstances. . . ." This was a "serious embarrassment," but he hoped in future Warren would "overcome the difficulty."

At the heart of the matter was a grim reality: General Lee seemed able to frustrate every Union move in the campaign. Everywhere they turned, it seemed, the Yankee troops encountered Rebels in good number manning sturdy field fortifications. A corps commander like Gouverneur Warren, facing this reality on the battle line day after day, could see no merit to orders from a distant headquarters to launch yet another frontal assault. Meade, and more importantly, Grant, believed that only if their orders were carried out instantaneously and forcefully, before the enemy was set and dug in, could they achieve the breakthrough they sought. Warren's manner of ignoring or questioning his orders, and his cautious, time-consuming, McClellan-like preparations were bound to generate friction with his two superiors. Even before the Bloody Angle, Meade had confessed to Colonel Lyman how bitterly disappointed he was becoming with these habits: "I told Warren today that he lost his nerve, at which he professed to be very indignant."[7]

As the Potomac army pressed on toward Richmond, it did not appear that General Warren was progressing at overcoming his difficulty. In the approach to Cold Harbor, Grant believed Warren did not move quickly enough to take advantage of an opportunity to catch some of Lee's forces outside their ever-present entrenchments, and "his chagrin was extreme" at the missed chance.

During the first thrust at Petersburg following the crossing of the James, it was Meade's turn to be chagrined. Warren (along with several fellow generals, to be sure) fumbled away the chance to seize the momentarily undefended Petersburg defenses. On June 18, for example, a critical Fifth Corps attack scheduled for noon did not commence until late afternoon, giving the enemy time to reinforce and hold a new line. The consequence, said Meade, was "a serious misfortune," and he determined to sack Warren right then. His patience was exhausted, he explained to Grant; there was a "defect" in General Warren that he would not or could not correct — "he cannot execute an order without modifying it. . . . Such a defect strikes at the root of all military subordination, and it is entirely out of the question that I can command this army if each corps commander is to exercise a similar independence of action." Although Meade in a carefully reasoned letter formally requested Grant "to relieve from duty with the Army, Maj. Genl. G. K. Warren," he must have thought better of it after he cooled down; it was not at all clear whom to put in Warren's place. The army was hurting for capable generals. It was reported to Washington that "Grant thinks the difficulty between Meade and Warren has been settled without the extreme remedy which Meade proposed last week."[8]

For his part, Warren had become discouraged and almost demoralized by the murderous casualties and what he regarded as the senseless frontal assaults of the campaign. "For thirty days now," he confessed to Colonel Lyman, "it has been one funeral procession past me; and it is too much!" He had little respect for Grant, who, he was sure, was far more responsible than Meade for the army's trials. "The popular idea of General Grant is, I believe, very wrong . . . ," Warren told his wife from the trenches at Petersburg. "To sit unconcerned on a log, away from the battlefield, whittling — to be a man on horseback or smoking a cigar — seems to exhaust the admiration of the country; and if this is really just, then Nero fiddling over burning Rome is sublime."[9]

Warren had his good days and his bad days during the protracted siege of Petersburg. Even on the good days, General Grant remained a critic. Leading a successful raid against the Weldon Railroad in August 1864, Warren reported that he had beaten back a Confederate counterattack. "Whipped it easily," he announced pridefully. Grant's comment was tart: "it seems to me that when the enemy comes out of his works and attacks and is repulsed he ought to be followed vigorously to the last minute with every man."[10]

By spring 1865, as Grant massed forces for the new campaign, Gouverneur Warren ranked as the Potomac army's senior corps commander, having survived both the battlefields and his detractors in high places. John Sedgwick was gone, killed at Spotsylvania. Win Hancock was gone too, assigned to a departmental command. Horatio Wright had replaced Sedgwick in command of the Sixth Corps, and Andrew Humphreys now led the Second. John Parke succeeded Ambrose Burnside as head of the Ninth Corps. E.O.C. Ord had the Army of the James.

As he worked out his plans for what no doubt would be the

climax of the war, General-in-Chief Grant quietly took to himself the direct management of at least the opening of the operation. Consequently, although Warren could not know it, his fate, should he have a role in the movement, rested not in Meade's hands but in Grant's. At that moment, just what was the general-in-chief's view of the commander of the Fifth Corps? More than once in the past year's campaigning, Grant had explicitly taken note of Warren's deliberateness of movement and of his reluctance to engage the enemy on other than his own terms. At Spotsylvania he had given Meade leave to replace Warren right in the midst of the fighting. At Petersburg he surely would have confirmed Meade in a decision to sack the Fifth Corps commander.

Although written with the benefit of hindsight, Grant's opinion of Warren as expressed in his *Memoirs* contains elements that are on the record well before the events of Five Forks on April 1, 1865. After praising Warren as a man of fine intelligence, great earnestness, and quick perceptions, Grant entered his disclaimer: "But I had before discovered a defect which was beyond his control, that was very prejudicial to his usefulness. . . . He could see every danger at a glance before he had encountered it. He would not only make preparations to meet the danger which might occur, but he would inform his commanding officer what others should do while he was executing his move." In a postwar interview, Grant was more explicit. When given an order, he said of General Warren, "instead of obeying — and know that the power which was guiding him would guide the others — he would hesitate and inquire and want to debate." When events put Gouverneur Warren at the Five Forks crossroads on April 1, then, it would seem that his fate there was foreordained.[11]

As Grant first perceived the operation that would reach a climax at Five Forks, it was to be primarily a show for Phil Sheridan and his cavalry corps. After his string of victories in the Shenandoah Valley, Sheridan had returned to the Petersburg front, the Northern press proclaimed, the newest hero of the war. It was said that he genuinely liked a fight, and was primed for one. Grant obliged him. As soon as the campaigning season arrived, Sheridan and his troopers were to embark on a massive raid beyond the western flank of the Confederates' Petersburg entrenchments so as to sever Lee's last rail lifelines, the South Side and Richmond & Danville railroads. That accomplished, Sheridan might return as he had come, or ride on to join Sherman's army, then in North Carolina confronting the remnants of Joe Johnston's Confederate forces.

Soon enough, however, Sheridan's orders would be rewritten — at least in part at the urging of Sheridan himself, who expressed no interest in leaving center stage just before the final curtain. Sheridan's new and even more significant objective was to turn Lee's western flank and knock him loose from his Petersburg lines — and the infantry of the Fifth Corps was to supply the muscle for it. "I feel now like ending the matter if it is possible to do so . . . ," Grant told the cavalry commander.[12]

Starting the night of Monday, March 27, the Federals began shifting forces for an advance westward from their Petersburg entrenchments. Sheridan's cavalry corps, 9,000 strong, swung off south and west through open country toward Dinwiddie Court House. From that point the first of Sheridan's original objectives, the South Side Railroad, was distant nine miles to the northwest — by way of Five Forks. Five Forks was simply an open space in the woods where roads from five directions came together, which fact alone made it of considerable military importance. It was also considerably important, just then, because it was a good four miles beyond the most westerly of General Lee's defenses. If Yankees in force seized Five Forks, Lee's right flank would be turned.

Lee was managing to track Sheridan's cavalry force, and as he had done so often in the year past, he promptly surmised his opponent's intent. He shifted his cavalry to the right flank to hold Five Forks, and determined to reinforce the troopers with the infantry of George Pickett's division. In so doing, he would be removing a sizable segment of the Army of Northern Virginia — some 5,500 cavalry and 5,000 infantry — from the protection of his formidable entrenchments. Thus one of Grant's goals was achieved without a shot being fired. Lee had no real choice in the matter. If he was to escape Petersburg with his army to join Joe Johnston in North Carolina — an inevitable course and probably a forlorn hope — his western flank must be secured. Lee's orders to Pickett were uncompromising: "Hold Five Forks at all hazards."[13]

As Grant's scheme was originally conceived, the role of the Federal infantry was merely to be a supporting one — not to attack but to fix the enemy in his lines in order to secure a free hand for Sheridan's cavalry. To do so, Warren's Fifth Corps, holding the left, was to sidestep farther to the left. Humphreys's Second Corps, next in line, would make a matching shift westward. To fill the resulting gap in the lines, a good part of Ord's Army of the James was marched all the way around from the right. These movements took the better part of two days. By nightfall on Wednesday, March 29, Sheridan and his troopers had reached Dinwiddie Court House, six miles south of Five Forks, after a slow and muddy march, and the whole operation was turned toward a new objective.

Thinking now a great deal more ambitiously of "ending the matter," General Grant canceled Sheridan's orders "to cut loose and go after the enemy's [rail]roads. . . ." Instead, in the morning he was to "push round the enemy if you can and get into his right rear." In a second dispatch, Grant further significantly enlarged Sheridan's mission: If in the latest circumstances the cavalryman believed there was a fair chance of turning the enemy's right, Grant said he would "detach the Fifth Corps, and place the whole under your command for the operation."[14]

By prior arrangement, Sheridan was receiving all his orders directly from the general-in-chief rather than through Meade's Army of the Potomac headquarters. Grant was very much aware of the hard feelings between Meade and Sheridan, and, in any case, for this crucial operation he seems to have wanted to be sure the general leading it was unfettered and unlimited, a risk-taking aggressor after his own heart. In these March days, with final victory at last within his sights, General Grant was haunted by the fear that Lee might yet elude his grasp and escape to join forces with Joe Johnston in North Carolina and prolong the conflict. All too often during the past year, Grant had seen the Potomac army's high command come up short in critical moments — and this could be the most critical moment of all. Furthermore, in these fast-changing circumstances it appeared that at some point General Meade's control of the Fifth Corps infantry might be forfeited to the cavalry commander, who in his turn reported only to the general-in-chief.[15]

During these opening days, the Federals' command structure for the Five Forks operation was a particularly awkward one. Sheridan and the cavalry dealt back and forth only with Grant. Warren and the Fifth Corps reported only to Meade. Warren's movements, and any dealings Warren had with Sheridan, were by Meade's orders, and for this operation Meade was acting under Grant's tactical as well as his strategic direction. Throughout, Grant and Meade maintained separate headquarters several miles apart, between which the working of the telegraph was sometimes erratic. This unwieldy system would remain in force right up until the last day's clash at Five Forks, and the virtually inevitable misunderstandings it generated would have their effect on events.

This was rough country to have to fight or march in, made all the worse when it began to rain late that Wednesday. The landscape was all lowlands, uniformly flat, with expanses of dripping second-growth woodland, tangled underbrush, and swamps and marshes, with few openings and with its streams and runs rapidly overflowing under pressure of the steady rainfall. The roads swam with mud. Veterans compared it to the Wilderness of benighted memory.

At Dinwiddie Court House on the twenty-ninth, Sheridan's troopers skirmished with no more than an enemy cavalry picket, but to the east that afternoon Fifth Corps infantry ran into a considerably brisker fight, one described by General Warren as "a sanguinary encounter." Warren's orders put his lead division, under

Charles Griffin, advancing up the Quaker Road toward its junction with the Boydton Plank Road to feel out the western end of the Confederates' fortified line. Two Rebel brigades came out aggressively to meet this incursion, for the Boydton Plank Road was an important supply route for Lee's army.

At the point of Griffin's advance was the brigade led by Joshua Lawrence Chamberlain, one of the heroes of Gettysburg whom General Warren had found to defend Little Round Top. Chamberlain had a stiff fight on his hands until the Yankee guns and reinforcements sent in by Griffin finally pushed the enemy back into his entrenchments. Each side lost something under 400 men, but the day's honors went to Warren. He had drawn out a sharp reaction from the Rebels, forced them to withdraw to their trenches, and now held one of their supply routes. That evening a note reached him from Meade's headquarters: "The major-general commanding directs me to congratulate you and Major-General Griffin upon your success to-day." For Gouverneur Warren this dispatch must have acted as a palliative, for during the day's march headquarters had prodded him to irritation for supposedly misunderstanding an order. Warren's corps artillerist, Charles Wainwright, said of his chief, "The devil within him seemed to be stirring all day."[16]

Wednesday's rain became Thursday's deluge. The countryside was a quagmire. The army's chief quartermaster termed it the worst day for moving wagon trains in his experience. Grant thought it "impossible for us to do much until it dries up a little," and he told Sheridan to picket Dinwiddie Court House and bring the rest of his troopers back to where they could regroup and obtain forage. Phil Sheridan was not ready to give up the advance so easily, and he rode back to Grant's headquarters to argue his case. To the staff there on his arrival he was all animation and enthusiasm. "I tell you, I'm ready to strike out to-morrow and go to smashing things!" he announced. He continued in the same vein in conversation with the general-in-chief and was apparently persuasive. "We will go on," Sheridan remembered Grant saying.

With that settled, Sheridan raised the matter of his infantry support. He wanted Horatio Wright's Sixth Corps, which had served him well through the Shenandoah Valley campaign. That would not be possible, Grant explained. Wright was posted back at the center of the lines opposite Petersburg, and it would require too much time and too much shifting to bring him up in time. The Fifth Corps was right at hand, a half-dozen miles to Sheridan's right, and was the logical choice for the operation. The two generals, in their respective memoirs, said nothing more of their conversation during this momentous conference, but once the subject of the Fifth Corps was raised, surely they discussed its commander — and surely Grant must have reminded Sheridan of what to watch out for when dealing with Gouverneur Warren.[17]

In the drenching rain on March 30 the two sides consolidated their positions and readied themselves to fight. Three brigades of Pickett's Virginians, along with two supporting brigades from Bushrod Johnson's division, dug in around the Five Forks crossroads, with the troopers under Fitzhugh Lee, nephew of the commanding general, taking station in advance to feel out Sheridan at Dinwiddie Court House. This mixed force of infantry and cavalry was operating in isolation, four miles to the west of Lee's main entrenchments. In those entrenchments, forming the Confederate right, Dick Anderson's corps confronted Warren's Fifth Corps.

As he went about his business that day, General Warren was in some perplexity. The operational orders from Grant, filtered with delays through Meade's headquarters, were at times conflicting about what he was supposed to do, and exactly where Sheridan was taking position on his left, and whether or not he was to be in contact with the cavalry. He reported in detail the difficulties he faced as he made his cautious deployment against the enemy's main line in front of him. At 4 o'clock that afternoon, exercising the prerogative of a corps commander, Warren decided to offer something positive of his own. Between where the Confederate entrenchments ended and Five Forks ran the White Oak Road, and Warren suggested that next morning he advance his corps to block that road, thus cutting the link between the two Confederate forces. Headquarters approved. However, at no time did Grant take Warren into his confidence concerning the revised scheme he and Sheridan were then working out for the Fifth Corps.[18]

Meanwhile, Sheridan was reporting that prisoners taken in skirmishing that day were identified as coming from Pickett's division; now it was clear that the enemy had infantry in force as well as cavalry in front of him. To Sheridan this spelled opportunity. The Confederates in some numbers had come out from behind their entrenchments. "I believe I could, with the Sixth Corps, turn the enemy's left [at Five Forks] or break through his lines," he told Grant, then added dismissively, "but I would not like the Fifth Corps to make such an attempt." Grant repeated that the Sixth Corps before Petersburg was posted too far away "for the operation by our left." Then, reflecting his own distrust of Warren, the general-in-chief offered Sheridan the more easily managed exchange of Humphreys's Second Corps for Warren's Fifth. The two corps, already mobilized for the operation, need only change places. At this point, however, Robert E. Lee stepped in, and events overtook any further discussion of Grant's intriguing proposal.[19]

Friday, March 31, would witness a decided check to Grant's and Sheridan's ambitions. Once again, as he had done so often before, General Lee set about breaking up a Federal offensive by seizing at least the local initiative. He rode out from Petersburg to supervise his spoiling attack in person. Sheridan and Warren, when they pushed forward on the thirty-first, would run into more than they had bargained for.

Warren's preparations for blocking White Oak Road were being rather leisurely carried out that morning. At the point of his proposed advance was the division of Romeyn Ayres. Although an earlier warning from Grant for Warren "to watch closely on his left flank" was lost in the command tangle at Meade's headquarters, Warren had been specifically ordered to reinforce Ayres and put him on guard, "as the enemy may attack him at daylight." Warren's second division, intended for that reinforcement and commanded by Samuel Crawford, was not yet posted close enough nor deployed for effective support. Warren's third division, under Charles Griffin, was three-quarters of a mile behind Crawford. While Ayres went forward to feel out the enemy positions, Warren found it "necessary" to remain at his headquarters a mile or so in the rear to deal with dispatches from army headquarters. What General Warren anticipated that morning was a slowly developing reconnaissance in force, moving his supporting troops forward in stages if needed. What he did not anticipate — or at least what he was not prepared for — was a surprise attack by the enemy.[20]

General Lee had managed to marshal four brigades to meet this Federal threat. He saw the enemy coming at him with its left carelessly "in the air," and as Ayres's troops approached the White Oak Road, yelling men in butternut came running straight at them out of the woods on their flank. Ayres's three brigades were each hit in turn, and one after another they broke and headed for the rear. Crawford's division of three brigades, unprepared for this sudden onrush of fugitives (General Crawford, wrote one of his men sarcastically, "was, as usual, unready"), collapsed in confusion and was borne back by the tide. "They broke and ran," a Virginian recalled, "we at their heels yelling like devils, and burning powder for all we were worth."

The crash of musketry brought General Warren galloping to the scene. His first act was to send off an aide to ask Humphreys's Second Corps on his right for help. Then he attempted to rally his routed troops by seizing the colors of one of the fleeing regiments and calling on them to stand against the enemy. This Sheridan-like gesture had some effect, but a final halt came only after the two beaten divisions rallied alongside Griffin's men, who were holding a firm defensive position behind flooded Gravelly Run.[21]

From that secure base and with Humphreys's support Warren organized a cautious countermove. This went slowly until General Lee, lacking any reinforcing troops, ordered a withdrawal from the advanced positions his men had gained. Reaching White Oak

Road, Warren with his careful engineer's eye made a personal reconnaissance of the Rebel entrenchments. "The examination showed me that the enemy's defenses were as complete and as well located as any I had ever been opposed to," he observed in his report. By late afternoon the Fifth Corps was content to be astride White Oak Road to the west of these entrenchments, which move it was believed would inhibit any effort by Anderson's corps to support Pickett at Five Forks. This after all was the original intent of Warren's March 31 advance, achieved finally at a cost of more than 1,800 casualties. Lee lost something less than half that number.

When the shooting stopped, General Warren, "white with rage" (as a war correspondent put it), rode up to Samuel Crawford, one of the routed divisional commanders, and without preamble "called him every vile name at his command." This abuse was delivered in the presence of dozens of officers and men while the humiliated Crawford sat his horse as "stolid as a block of marble." The corps artillerist, Charles Wainwright, termed such "awful fits of passion" as this a virtual disease with Warren. In this instance its effect on General Crawford was soon to become apparent.[22]

General Grant cast a cold eye on the conduct of events that day, and Warren earned yet another black mark in the general-in-chief's book of command. If it was true that Warren had checked the enemy, Grant asked Meade, "what is to prevent him from pitching in with his whole corps and attacking before giving him time to intrench or return in good order to his old intrenchments? I do not understand why Warren permitted his corps to be fought in detail. When Ayres was pushed forward he should have sent other troops to their support."

At an earlier day, Colonel Lyman of Meade's staff had remarked of General Warren that he "is not up to a corps command. . . . He cannot spread himself over three divisions. He cannot do it, and the result is partial and ill-concerted and dilatory movements." That analysis was made when Warren was still new to corps command, yet it might just as well have been applied to the fight that day for the White Oak Road. Gouverneur Warren, it appeared, had grown little as a commander during his year in charge of the Fifth army corps. Thus, at least, was General Grant's conclusion.[23]

That Friday Sheridan's cavalry corps came in for similar rough handling. With his infantry and Fitz Lee's cavalry, Pickett delivered a spoiling attack of his own. On each of the several roads leading from Dinwiddie to Five Forks, Sheridan's troopers were knocked back with driving force. Three of the Federal brigades had to scramble away well to the eastward to avoid being cut off. Against infantry the Yankee troopers had to fight dismounted, and in so doing they were at an immediate disadvantage. With every fourth man serving as a horse holder, their effective combat strength was promptly reduced 25 percent. In addition, having to get down off their mounts to do their fighting was not the usual thing for horse soldiers, and in general they did not stand up to foot soldiering quite as well as Pickett's tough veterans. "Scattered all over the fields before us are our men, now rapidly falling back," wrote a Yankee trooper coming up to reinforce a wavering line, ". . . & our Officers call to them to help to hold the enemy but not a man of them stops."[24]

Sheridan pushed every man he could find, including the regimental bands, into a last-ditch defensive line covering Dinwiddie Court House and let it be known that they were going back just that far and no farther. Brandishing his starred headquarters pennant, he galloped from one end of the battle line to the other, seeing and being seen, rallying everyone to his duty. No one in Union blue was better at this sort of thing than Phil Sheridan, and at dark, narrowly, the line held.

Afterward Sheridan told Colonel Horace Porter of Grant's staff, who was with him as an observer, that this had been one of the liveliest days in his experience. Go back to General Grant, Little Phil told Porter, and tell him off the record that it was the enemy's force, not his, that was in the real danger: "It is cut off from Lee's army, and not a man in it should ever be allowed to get back to Lee." At last the Rebel infantry was out from behind its fortifications, "and this is our chance to attack it." In his on-the-record dispatch to the general-in-chief, Sheridan reported the fighting on his front that day, and remarked in closing, "This force is too strong for us." But, he added, "I will hold on to Dinwiddie Court House until I am compelled to leave." That blunt assessment galvanized Grant into immediate action to rescue an operation seemingly gone sour.[25]

At 9 o'clock that night, acting on Grant's order, Meade directed Warren to pull back "at once" from his front on the White Oak Road and send one of his divisions to report to Sheridan at Dinwiddie. Then, at 10:15, Meade multiplied his demands: Warren was ordered with the balance of the Fifth Corps to march west promptly to strike the flank and rear of Pickett's force threatening the cavalry. In approving this new move, Grant wanted Meade to urge Warren "not to stop for anything." Half an hour after authorizing the sending of the entire Fifth Corps to rescue the cavalry, Grant notified Sheridan of these actions. "You will assume command of the whole force sent to operate with you," Grant told him. Then the general-in-chief promised — rashly, as it turned out — that these reinforcements "should reach you by 12 to-night."[26]

Later, during the long-running debate over Warren's sacking, much would be made of Grant's telling Sheridan that the Fifth Corps would be with him by midnight on March 31. At the time, however, there was no debate; it was obvious to anyone on the scene who read the dispatch that Grant had been misinformed about the situation. Nothing in Sheridan's actions that night suggests that he actually thought the Fifth Corps could pull up stakes where it was on the White Oak Road and march six miles on atrocious roads through the darkness to Dinwiddie in an hour and a half or so. (It is a puzzle why Grant might have thought so.) Sheridan's one communication that he sent directly to Warren, written at 3:00 A.M. on April 1, made no complaint about the Fifth Corps' not yet being at his side, and instead discussed his plans for action at dawn "if the enemy remain."[27]

In any event, whether or not Sheridan yet realized it, he was already rescued from his plight — and, ironically, by Gouverneur Warren. Before anyone at headquarters ordered it, Warren had taken it upon himself to send supporting troops to the embattled cavalry. In late afternoon on the thirty-first he ordered one of his brigades to march to the sound of guns off to the west, where he deduced, from the way the sound was receding, that Sheridan's troopers were being pushed back. It was the arrival of this brigade of Yankee infantry on his flank that determined Pickett to give up his offensive and, in the small hours of the morning, to pull back to Five Forks.[28]

The fact of the matter is that General Warren did about as well as anyone could have that night in moving the three divisions of the Fifth Corps to Sheridan's position. He had to act on contradictory orders. Unavoidable difficulties on the march were numerous, including the need to bridge flooding Gravelly Run. The head of the column reached Dinwiddie by daybreak on April 1. In the lead was Joshua Chamberlain's brigade, and Chamberlain went forward to Sheridan to report. Returning his salute, Sheridan asked, "Where is Warren?" in a tone that Chamberlain thought was more challenge than question. "He is at the rear of the column, Sir," he replied. "That is where I expected to find him," Sheridan muttered. "What is he doing there?" Chamberlain tried to explain that the general had to personally disengage his last division from yesterday's battlefield, and he felt relief when he was dismissed to attend to his brigade.[29]

Sheridan's tone accurately reflected his disposition that morning, which was sore-headed. He was still very much embarrassed by the sharp reverse his cavalry had suffered the day before. Now the enemy forces had slipped away from his front, and he would have to follow them to some new and probably fortified position at Five Forks. Although Grant had put a full infantry corps under his command, it was not the corps — and not the corps commander — that Sheridan had wanted. Under these circumstances, what General Warren did next was (in retrospect, at least) the worst possible thing he could have done. What he did next was nothing at all.

Warren reached Dinwiddie Court House with the last of his Fifth Corps divisions at 8 o'clock that morning. There he found a dispatch from Meade's headquarters telling him that as soon as he joined forces with Sheridan "you will be under his orders and will report to him." Warren would write, at a later date, that this order to serve under Phil Sheridan "gave me much satisfaction at the time of its receipt." That may be doubted. On that April 1 morning, with a battle clearly in the offing, it was three hours before Warren made any effort to see Sheridan, nor did he send a staff man to announce his arrival and the arrival of his corps. "Were Warren a mind-reader," remarked General Chamberlain, "he would have known it was a time to put on a warmer manner towards Sheridan." As it was, Warren's failure to report as ordered to his new chief in timely fashion bordered on insubordination; certainly it reflected a sulky resentment of his new, less exalted station.[30]

When finally Warren did report, at 11:00 A.M., he met a decidedly chilly welcome. "I made the remark to General Sheridan," Warren later testified, "that we had had rather a field day of it since yesterday morning. He said to me, 'Do you call that a field day?' I saw by the tone of his remark that he was not very well pleased with what I had said." Warren rather lamely explained that he meant only that General Lee "had given us about as lively a time as I had had in my experience." Sore-headed Sheridan obviously did not want to be reminded of that painful fact, and, said Warren, "we ceased conversation." The tardy, frosty encounter surely contributed to Sheridan's forming opinion of what he afterward described as his new subordinate's "manner" on this day of battle.[31]

Sheridan had spent most of the morning supervising the cavalry's follow-up of the enemy withdrawal toward Five Forks and pondering his course. At noon, in the midst of this study, he was visited by Lieutenant Colonel Orville Babcock, of Grant's headquarters. The message Babcock delivered to him was verbal and an eye opener: "General Grant directs me to say to you, that if in your judgment the Fifth Corps would do better under one of the division commanders, you are authorized to relieve General Warren, and order him to report to General Grant, at headquarters."[32]

This startling message, which, in the event, sealed Gouverneur Warren's fate, was the result of a sudden but nonetheless calculated decision on Grant's part — a decision triggered by a misunderstanding.

That morning, Grant's headquarters had sent Captain E. R. Warner to the Fifth Corps camp, rather than to Meade, to collect a status report. When during the night General Warren had left camp to shepherd the last of his divisions for delivery to Sheridan, he told his adjutant, Colonel Frederick Locke, that since Locke was not needed for the movement, he should stay behind and catch up on his sleep so as to be fresh for the day's duties. Reaching the Fifth Corps camp, Captain Warner woke up Locke to find out the exact whereabouts of the troops. When he had last seen them, said Locke, they were halted at the bridge being built over Gravelly Run. What the half-awake Locke neglected to explain, or perhaps what Warner failed to understand, was that this was very old news — 2:00 A.M. news, to be exact. When Captain Warner subsequently delivered his report at Grant's headquarters at 10 o'clock that morning, Warren had already been at Dinwiddie, along with all of his troops, for two hours.

Warner's false report acted on General Grant like the last straw. Here was what ought to be perhaps the final battle of the war, with the fighting seemingly in crisis, and (once again) corps commander Warren was lagging back and not getting his troops up to the front. Once before Grant had wanted to relieve Warren for this same offense and had allowed Meade to talk him out of it. Captain Warner heard Grant say that he "was sorry now that he had not done it — had not relieved him." U. S. Grant was not one to make the same mistake twice, nor was he one to think twice about the correction. He called over Colonel Babcock, just then preparing to leave for Five Forks, and told him to tell Sheridan to relieve Warren if he judged the Fifth Corps would "do better" under another commander.[33]

This supposed transgression was not by itself grounds enough for Grant to relieve Warren of his corps command. But to Grant it was more than enough for him to invite Phil Sheridan to find the grounds — or the excuse. "At all events," wrote a Fifth Corps staff man who witnessed these happenings, "General Grant knew that General Sheridan was not a person who could be intrusted with such a weapon and not use it."[34]

It might seem, at that noon hour on April 1, that events were conspiring against Gouverneur Warren. His checkered record as a corps commander had just been brought up in the general-in-chief's mind by a transgression he had not in fact committed. Already, perceiving himself demoted in the midst of the campaign, he had managed with his sulks to grate on the nerves of his new chief. And now that new chief had in his hands the means to sack him, and certainly the will to do so, if it should come to that. Still, to come to that was going to require a further fateful event or two.

At 1:00 P.M. Sheridan summoned Warren to bring up the Fifth Corps and to outline to him the plan of attack. The cavalry, Sheridan said, had sighted an east-west line of Confederate field fortifications along White Oak Road, centered on the Five Forks intersection. It was thickly manned by infantry and defended with artillery. Although hindsight would develop a detailed knowledge of this line on Sheridan's part, in truth he understood comparatively little about it when he presented Warren with his orders: The Rebels were in line of battle directly ahead; the cavalry would feint on the left; the Fifth Corps would attack on the right to turn the enemy's works; the assault was to be in full corps strength. "We talked that over until I understood it, I think," Warren recalled, "and he was convinced that I understood him."

One of Sheridan's staff directed Warren to mass his troops for the assault astride the Gravelly Run Church Road, which by report led directly to the enemy's targeted eastern flank. The staff man would later testify that he had made no actual reconnaissance of the enemy position; all he was told to do was to find a place to post the Fifth Corps for the attack which was concealed from the Rebels' sight. The three divisions were at rest some two and a half miles from the assembly point, and Warren sent a staff officer to bring them up. "He went off as fast as any man could go down that road," Warren remembered.[35]

While he waited for his troops, Warren the careful engineer sat down under a tree to make a little sketch of the planned attack. If the general scheme was Sheridan's, the specifics were left for him to work out. Warren seems to have assumed, in his newly subordinate role, that this planning function was the limit of his commander's discretion, and he did not reconnoiter the position he was to attack, nor did he order it done. His sketch showed the Confederate line, as he understood it, ending on the east in a slight bend at the junction of the White Oak and Gravelly Run Church roads. He placed Ayres's division on the left, to strike near the end of the works to fix the Rebels in place. On the right was Crawford's division, aimed squarely at the point where the line ended behind White Oak Road. Griffin was in rear of Crawford, to exploit the effect of his assault. Warren directed that when the battle line reached White Oak Road, "it will swing round to the left" to turn the position. As soon as the infantry engaged, Sheridan's cavalry would push forward against the rest of the Rebel works. Warren showed the sketch to Sheridan for his approval — "I understood that I was forming exactly as he wanted me," Warren recalled — then had copies made for his division and brigade commanders.[36]

It was an excellent plan, with but one failing — the Confederate battle line was not where it was thought to be. Instead of ending where the Gravelly Run Church Road intersected the White Oak Road, the line ended nearly a half mile short, or west, of that point. Furthermore, instead of terminating in a slight bend, the line actually turned sharply back at a right angle, forming a defensive "return" some 150 yards in length. As a consequence, when the Federal battle line emerged as planned into the open to reach the White Oak Road, it would be marching not toward the enemy's works but right past them and straight on into empty space. Responsibility for this planning blunder would never be admitted or even acknowledged. Certainly the fault was not Gouverneur Warren's, yet the effect of it would ruin him.

Had he been in hearty partnership with Sheridan that day, General Warren would likely have fed and rested his men upon arrival at Dinwiddie and then ordered them under arms, ready to march to the front on the instant. In the event, however, it took the usual time to call them together from their campfires and form them up and set them on the march. Their passage was over a single narrow muddy road, blocked by the cavalry's usual detritus, forage wagons and held horses. Warren matter-of-factly explained to an increasingly impatient Phil Sheridan that he could not be ready to attack before 4 o'clock that afternoon.

What seems to have bothered Sheridan the most during that tense Saturday afternoon was Warren's "manner." In his official report he hardly bothered to disguise his contempt: "General Warren did not exert himself to get up his corps as rapidly as he might have done, and his manner gave me the impression that he wished the sun to go down before dispositions for the attack could be completed." That could be read as a questioning of Warren's personal courage — and Warren would so read it.[37]

Joshua Chamberlain thought the trouble between the two men on April 1 was simply a clash of personalities. "General Warren's temperament is such that he, instead of showing excitement, generally shows an intense concentration in what I call important movements," Chamberlain said, "and those who do not know him might take it to be apathy when it is deep, concentrated thought and purpose." Sheridan of course did not know Warren. For his part, Warren took it as his primary duty in those hours to focus intently and coolly on the plan for battle, trusting his staff to bring up the troops with all due speed. As a Fifth Corps veteran put it, "He did not ride around swearing and cursing at a fearful rate." The three hours required to mobilize for the attack was a reflection of how the Army of the Potomac usually did these things. It was not Phil Sheridan's way, and he might better have set the whole operation in motion earlier in the day. In any case, by the time the fighting finally opened, his temper toward General Warren was perilously near the boiling point.[38]

George Pickett had five brigades of infantry and ten guns in his battle line, with cavalry guarding the flanks. He was outnumbered by perhaps two to one, but his greater problem was his open flanks, especially his left, four miles distant from the main Confederate entrenchments. Pickett himself and Fitz Lee, his cavalry commander, spent much of the day (and much of the battle) at a shad bake some distance behind their lines. They assumed that the Federals on their front that day were primarily cavalry, of which they had no great fear. Their absence generated a great deal of later criticism, but in the end it probably did not have much effect on the battle's outcome.

It was a few minutes after 4:00 P.M. when the Fifth Corps infantrymen stepped off to the attack. It was intended that Ayres's division on the left strike the enemy line first, near its eastern end, and Sheridan and Warren rode with it. Straight across White Oak Road strode the Yankee infantry — and found nothing to attack. Suddenly, from off to the left, Ayres's flank companies came under sharp fire from an enemy battle line. As was always the case with surprise flanking fire, there was some confusion and wavering in the ranks, but soon enough the veteran Romeyn Ayres took charge and changed front abruptly to the left and drove straight against their tormentors.

Meanwhile, on the right, Crawford's division, intended for the main assault against the end point of the Rebel line, kept on advancing straight ahead into empty space. An ever-widening gap opened between Ayres and Crawford. Warren reacted instinctively. One part of his assault was going awry; he would tend to it himself. Off he galloped after the errant Crawford, leaving the rest of his corps to shift for itself. This would be the final event, in the sequence of events, that sealed Warren's fate.

Samuel Crawford, it was said, was militarily narrow-minded,

"obeying orders in a certain literal fashion that saved him the censure of superiors." The attack might not be working out as it had been planned, but that was not for General Crawford to be concerned about. He would just keep going straight ahead until someone told him differently. In addition, Crawford had not forgotten the humiliation of Warren's public dressing-down the day before, and he was not going to do anything on his own initiative that might stir things up again.

Marching behind Crawford, Charles Griffin saw the flank fire open on Ayres, saw Ayres change front sharply to his left, saw the gap opening between the two lead divisions. His division was supposed to be in support of Crawford, but here was Ayres doing the only fighting to be seen — and Ayres looking as if he could use the support. Riding up to him, Griffin asked what had happened. "Nothing new," came Ayres's reply. "The same old story; Crawford has gone off and left me to fight alone." Griffin made a wheel left and went in to join the battle. One of Griffin's brigadiers, Joshua Chamberlain, came upon Phil Sheridan right on the battle line as he was putting his brigade into action. "By God, that's what I want to see!" Sheridan yelled to him over the din. "General officers at the front!"

As Ayres and Griffin got more of their commands into the fight, the pressure on the North Carolinians defending the line of the return that formed Pickett's left became overwhelming. The line began breaking apart, and then the Federals swept over it. Sheridan himself spurred his horse right over the breastworks to show the way. "We have a record to make, before that sun goes down, that will make hell tremble!" he called to the troops with him in the charge. "I want you there!"[39]

Meanwhile, off to the north and east, Warren could not immediately locate General Crawford to redirect his straying division. The first of Crawford's brigades that he came upon he dragged off toward the sound of the firing, told the brigadier to stay there to form the pivot for the division's change of direction, and rode off to corral the other two brigades. In his absence, one of Sheridan's staff found the waiting brigade and ordered it straight into the battle. This left the others of Crawford's command, as they came up, wondering what to do next. At last Warren managed to get all of Crawford's troops into action, at one point personally leading them over the barricades just as Sheridan had done, and in the act having his horse shot under him. The angle at which Crawford's belated troops struck the enemy turned out to be fortuitous — they drove right into the rear of the reeling defenders and accelerated the rout.

Warren sent his aide, Colonel Locke, to Sheridan to report the glad news — he was in the enemy's rear, cutting off his retreat, taking many prisoners. Sheridan, flushed with the victory at the return that he had just seen and helped lead, turned on the messenger. "By God, sir, tell General Warren he wasn't in the fight!" he raged at the thunderstruck Locke. "Must I tell General Warren that, sir?" Locke asked. "I would not like to take a verbal message like that to General Warren. May I take it down in writing?" Sheridan was unyielding: "Take it down, sir; tell him, by God, he was not at the front!" Soon thereafter, coming on Griffin, Sheridan told him he was now commander of the Fifth Corps.

A quickly scrawled order went off to Warren, relieving him and ordering him to report to Grant's headquarters. It was handed to Warren just as he was adding up the Fifth Corps' abundant spoils of victory. The fact of the victory, paradoxically, seemed only to stiffen Sheridan's resolve, and thus he would tell the stunned Warren, "I don't reconsider my decisions. Obey the order!"[40]

And the victory was as complete as any in the annals of the Army of the Potomac. The key junction of Five Forks was securely in Federal hands, Lee's western flank was turned, the way was opened to seize his South Side rail lifeline. Pickett's division was wrecked, with more than 500 dead and wounded and some 2,500 captured. Federal casualties came to 830, three-quarters of them infantry. The victory belonged to Warren's Fifth Corps. Grant responded promptly. "I have ordered an immediate assault along the lines," he announced to his staff. General Lee telegraphed President Davis, "I think it is absolutely necessary that we should abandon our position to-night."[41]

Sheridan's sacking of Gouverneur Warren was soon relegated to hardly more than a footnote in the overwhelming news of the subsequent race toward Appomattox and the ending of the war. Warren, as was his right under the Articles of War, applied for a court of inquiry, but Grant put him off with the excuse that assembling a court and witnesses was "impossible at this time." General Meade, concluding that an injustice had been done, reminded Grant a few days after Appomattox that a permanent head of the Fifth Corps was needed. "Should you be disposed to reassign General Warren I shall make no objection," Meade said diplomatically. Nothing came of this, for it surely would have required at least tacit acceptance by Sheridan. George Armstrong Custer, who had served some time under Sheridan, remarked of the Warren case that Phil Sheridan "was the kind of man to never take anything back," even if "ever so wrong."[42]

Grant remained determined to shut off any sort of inquiry into the matter, and so long as he was general-in-chief and then president he rebuffed all Warren's efforts for a hearing. It was only under President Hayes, Grant's successor, that a court of inquiry was finally convened, fourteen years after the fact, in 1879. Public interest in the case was whetted by the reversal, earlier that year, of the 1863 court-martial conviction of Fitz John Porter. Perhaps, thought Warren's supporters, the climate was right for visiting justice on onetime Army of the Potomac generals.[43]

The Warren court of inquiry — the military equivalent of a civilian grand jury — would drag on for almost two years, with the testimony and documents filling two large volumes. Its star witnesses included Warren (now reverted to lieutenant colonel in the regular army), Sheridan (now a lieutenant general), and Grant (now an ex-president), plus a number of prominent ex–Confederate officers. Sheridan's right to sack Warren was not at issue, but only his reasons for doing so.

As it happened, the Warren court of inquiry would never hear

Sheridan's true rationale for doing what he did on that April Saturday fourteen years before. Phil Sheridan did what he did, of course, because his superior, General-in-Chief Grant, had lost all confidence in Gouverneur Warren. Grant made sure Sheridan understood that fact, then invited him to replace Warren at the first sign of weakness. On April 1, after Warren's cool, aloof manner had served to prime him, Sheridan ignited in the heat of the battle and sacked Warren because he "wasn't in the fight" at his side in the one small segment of the battleground that he, Sheridan, witnessed.

The officers of the Warren court, tightly restricted to investigating only the events of March 31–April 1, examined four "imputations" derived from Sheridan's and Grant's official reports: (1) that Warren did not move properly or with his whole force to seize White Oak Road on March 31; (2) that he was slow, on the night of March 31, to bring his forces from White Oak Road to Dinwiddie to reinforce Sheridan; (3) that on April 1 he did not exert himself bringing up his troops and (said Sheridan) "gave me the impression that he wished the sun to go down before dispositions for the attack could be completed"; and (4) that at Five Forks he did not exert himself to inspire his troops when "portions of his line gave way."[44]

These were not reasons but only excuses that Sheridan cobbled together after the fact, and the court would devote week after week to debating minute-by-minute arcane detail. In the end it issued a narrow report derived from narrow issues. Warren was found not negligent in the White Oak Road fighting on March 31, although he ought to have moved faster and been at the front earlier. The court said it "was not practicable" for the Fifth Corps to have reached Dinwiddie by midnight on the thirty-first, although Warren ought to have reached there sooner than he did. He was not guilty of unnecessary delay in bringing his corps to the front on April 1, nor did he demonstrate that day any "such wish" for delay. Finally, no fault was found when Warren, acting in his role as corps commander on April 1, went off to redirect Crawford's division into the battle. While the court did not come right out and say so, it was obvious that there had been nothing in Warren's conduct at Five Forks to justify removing him from the command of the Fifth Corps.

The closest public statement of the real truth behind the Warren case came during Grant's testimony. Asked why he had given Sheridan leave to sack Warren, Grant answered, "I knew of his previous conduct. I was apprehensive that he might fail General Sheridan at the critical moment." Although not permitted by the court to bring up anything specific about that previous conduct, Grant went on to elaborate: "I wanted orders promptly obeyed . . . ; where officers undertook to think for themselves and consider that the officer who had issued the order did not understand the circumstances and had not considered the work to be done, it tended to failure and delay." And that he did not like, asked Warren's counsel. "And that I did not like," Grant agreed. "And that kind of conduct led to the removal of one officer." While this last would be stricken from the court-of-inquiry record, to the thoughtful listener it must have echoed loud and clear.[45]

The Warren court completed deliberations and forwarded its findings to the War Department on November 8, 1881. There the report remained, held in confidence by Secretary of War Robert T. Lincoln for more than a year. It appears that Lincoln was accommodating his father's two famous war-winning generals, sparing them any embarrassment over their wartime mistreatment of Warren. Then, on August 8, 1882, Gouverneur Warren died, from complications of diabetes. "I die a disgraced soldier" were his last words. Some three months later Secretary Lincoln directed that the record of the Warren court of inquiry be published.[46]

The sacking of Gouverneur Warren, on April 1, 1865, was beyond any doubt a grave injustice. However, perhaps had the same fate been visited upon one or two of the Army of the Potomac's less-than-stellar corps commanders back in 1862 or 1863, to serve as an indelible lesson to that army's high command, a kind of rough justice might have been the result. As it was, General Warren became a martyr to no cause at all.

NOTES

1. Joshua Lawrence Chamberlain, *The Passing of the Armies: An Account of the Final Campaign of the Army of the Potomac* (New York: Putnam's, 1915), 151; Horace Porter, *Campaigning with Grant* (New York: Century, 1897), 108.

2. Theodore Lyman, *Meade's Headquarters, 1863–1865: Letters of Colonel Theodore Lyman from the Wilderness to Appomattox*, ed. George R. Agassiz (Boston: Atlantic Monthly Press, 1922), 56–57.

3. Lyman, *Meade's Headquarters*, 26; Charles S. Wainwright, *A Diary of Battle: The Personal Journals of Colonel Charles S. Wainwright, 1861–1865*, ed. Allan Nevins (New York: Harcourt, Brace & World, 1962), 338–39.

4. William W. Swan, "Battle of the Wilderness," *Papers of the Military Historical Society of Massachusetts* (Boston, 1896), vol. 4, 129; Gordon C. Rhea, *The Battle of the Wilderness: May 5–6, 1864* (Baton Rouge: Louisiana State University Press, 1994), 141, 432–33; Gouverneur K. Warren to Horace Porter, Nov. 21, 1875, Warren Papers, New York State Library.

5. Paul Andrew Hutton, "Sheridan: Paladin of the Republic," *Military History Quarterly* (Spring 1992), 84; Horace Porter, *Campaigning with Grant*, 84; Lyman, *Meade's Headquarters*, 106.

6. Meade to Grant, Grant to Meade, May 12, 1864, *Official Records* 36:2, 654.

7. Meade to John A. Rawlins, June 21, 1864, Meade Papers, Historical Society of Pennsylvania; Lyman journal, May 8, 1864, in Gordon C. Rhea, *The Battles for Spotsylvania Court House and the Road to Yellow Tavern, May 7–12, 1864* (Baton Rouge: Louisiana State University Press, 1997), 68.

8. Bruce Catton, *Grant Takes Command* (Boston: Little, Brown, 1968), 261; Catton, *A Stillness at Appomattox* (New York: Doubleday, 1954), 211; Meade to Rawlins, June 21, 1864, Meade Papers; Charles A. Dana to Stanton, July 1, 1864, *OR* 40:1, 28.

9. Lyman, *Meade's Headquarters*, 147; Emerson Gifford Taylor, *Gouverneur Kemble Warren* (Boston: Houghton Mifflin, 1932), 186.

10. Warren to Meade, Grant to Meade, Aug. 21, 1864, *OR* 42:2, 368, 355.

11. U. S. Grant, *Personal Memoirs of U. S. Grant* (New York: Webster, 1885), vol. 2, 445; *New York Herald*, July 24, 1875, Warren Papers, New York State Library. Grant's comments on Warren in his *Memoirs*, even their phrasing, owe much to Meade's letter of June 21, 1864, that called for Warren's sacking.

12. Grant to Sheridan, Mar. 28, 29, 1865, *OR* 46:3, 234, 266.

13. La Salle Corbell Pickett, *Pickett and His Men* (Atlanta: Foote & Davies, 1900), 386.

14. Grant to Sheridan, Mar. 29, 30, 1865, *OR* 46:3, 266, 325.

15. Horace Porter, "Five Forks and the Pursuit of Lee," *Battles and Leaders of the Civil War* (New York: Century, 1887–88), vol. 4, 708; Catton, *Grant Takes Command*, 439.

16. Warren report, *OR* 46:1, 800; Alexander S. Webb to Warren, Mar. 29, 1865, *OR* 46:3, 256, 255; Wainwright, *Diary of Battle*, 508. Detailed accounts of the Five Forks operation are Chamberlain, *The Passing of the Armies;* William W. Swan,

"The Five Forks Campaign," *Papers of the Military Historical Society of Massachusetts* (Boston, 1907), vol. 6; Chris Calkins and Ed Bearss, *Battle of Five Forks* (Lynchburg, Va.: H. E. Howard, 1985); and Calkins, "The Battle of Five Forks," *Blue & Gray* (April 1992).

17. Lyman, *Meade's Headquarters,* 330; Horace Porter, "Five Forks," *Battles and Leaders,* vol. 4, 710; Philip H. Sheridan, *Personal Memoirs of P. H. Sheridan* (New York: Appleton, 1888), vol. 2, 144; Grant, *Memoirs,* vol. 2, 438–39. Newspaperman Sylvanus Cadwallader claimed that Sheridan told him some days later that at this conference Grant "conveyed" to Sheridan the notion of relieving Warren should it become necessary. Sylvanus Cadwallader, *Three Years with Grant,* ed. Benjamin P. Thomas (New York: Knopf, 1955), 301–2.

18. Warren to Webb, Webb to Warren, Mar. 30, 1865, *OR* 46:3, 304, 305.

19. Sheridan to Grant, Mar. 30, 31, Grant to Sheridan, Mar. 31, 1865, *OR* 46:3, 324, 380.

20. Grant to Meade, Webb to Warren, Mar. 30, 1865, *OR* 46:3, 324, 306; Andrew A. Humphreys, *The Virginia Campaign of '64 and '65* (New York: Scribner's, 1883), 330; Warren report, *OR* 46:1, 812.

21. Sam Paulette in Calkins, "Battle of Five Forks," *Blue & Gray,* 12; Charles H. Porter, "Operations of the Fifth Corps on the Left, March 29–31, 1865," *Papers of the Military Historical Society of Massachusetts,* vol. 6, 233, 228.

22. Cadwallader, *Three Years with Grant,* 299–301; Wainwright, *Diary of Battle,* 509. Although Cadwallader's memoirs are not always reliable, this eyewitness account appears credible. Wainwright's journal confirms such episodes of rage on Warren's part.

23. Warren report, *OR* 46:1, 816; Grant to Meade, Mar. 31, 1865, *OR* 46:3, 337; Lyman, *Meade's Headquarters,* 110.

24. Roger Hannaford in Stephen Z. Starr, *The Union Cavalry in the Civil War* (Baton Rouge: Louisiana State University Press, 1981), vol. 2, 440.

25. Horace Porter, "Five Forks," *Battles and Leaders,* vol. 4, 711; Sheridan to Grant, Mar. 31, 1865, *OR* 46:3, 381.

26. Grant to Meade, Webb to Warren, Meade to Warren, Grant to Meade, Grant to Sheridan, Mar. 31, 1865, *OR* 46:3, 340, 365–66, 367, 342, 381.

27. Sheridan to Warren, Apr. 1, 1865, *OR* 46:3, 419–20.

28. Warren to Webb, Mar. 31, 1865, *OR* 46:3, 364; Pickett report, *OR Supplement* 7, 781.

29. Chamberlain, *The Passing of the Armies,* 104.

30. Webb to Warren, Apr. 1, 1865, *OR* 46:3, 418; Warren report, *OR* 46:1, 829; Chamberlain, *The Passing of the Armies,* 116.

31. Warren testimony, "Proceedings of Court of Inquiry in the Case of Lieutenant-Colonel G. K. Warren," *OR Supplement* 8, 742; Sheridan report, *OR* 46:1, 1105; Charles H. Porter, "The Fifth Corps at the Battle of Five Forks," *Papers of the Military Historical Society of Massachusetts,* vol. 6, 247–48.

32. Horace Porter, "Five Forks," *Battles and Leaders,* vol. 4, 711; Babcock testimony, "Warren Court of Inquiry," *OR Supplement* 9, 901.

33. E. R. Warner testimony, "Warren Court of Inquiry," *OR Supplement* 8, 37–38.

34. Swan, "Five Forks Campaign," *Papers of the Military Historical Society of Massachusetts,* vol. 6, 408.

35. Warren testimony, "Warren Court of Inquiry," *OR Supplement* 8, 744.

36. Warren testimony, "Warren Court of Inquiry," *OR Supplement* 8, 747, 749.

37. Swan, "Five Forks Campaign," *Papers of the Military Historical Society of Massachusetts,* vol. 6, 374–75; Sheridan report, *OR* 46:1, 1105.

38. Chamberlain testimony, "Warren Court of Inquiry," *OR Supplement* 9, 236; Charles Porter, "Fifth Corps at Five Forks," *Papers of the Military Historical Society of Massachusetts,* vol. 6, 250.

39. Swan, "Five Forks Campaign," *Papers of the Military Historical Society of Massachusetts,* vol. 6, 396; Chamberlain, *The Passing of the Armies,* 130, 144.

40. Chamberlain, *The Passing of the Armies,* 142.

41. Calkins, "Battle of Five Forks," *Blue & Gray,* 51; Horace Porter, "Five Forks," *Battles and Leaders,* vol. 4, 715; Lee to Davis, *OR* 46:3, 1378.

42. Warren to Rawlins, Apr. 9, Grant to Warren, May 6, Meade to Grant, Apr. 18, 1865, *OR* 46:3, 679, 1103, 822; F. P. James to Warren, Apr. 1, 1866, Warren Papers, New York State Library.

43. See "The Court-Martial of Fitz John Porter" elsewhere in this collection.

44. "General Warren at Five Forks, and the Court of Inquiry," *Battles and Leaders of the Civil War,* vol. 4, 723–24.

45. Grant's testimony at the Warren court of inquiry, as recorded by a newspaper reporter, in Noah Andre Trudeau, *Out of the Storm: The End of the Civil War, April–June 1865* (Baton Rouge: Louisiana State University Press, 1994), 413–14.

46. Trudeau, *Out of the Storm,* 417; "Warren Court of Inquiry," *OR Supplement* 9, 1561.

Index